The Message for the Last Days

THE MESSAGE FOR THE LAST DAYS

Biblical and Historical Understanding of End Times

K.J. SOZE

The Message for the Last Days Copyright © 2019 by K.J. Soze. All Rights Reserved.

CONTENTS

	References and Copyrights	vii
	Introduction	1
1.	Bible Interpretation Principles	7
2.	The Land Covenant	28
3.	The Promised Land and the Kingdom of Heaven	43
4.	The New Covenant	63
5.	Christ's Inheritance	79
6.	The Second Coming of Christ	93
7.	The Resurrection of the Righteous	120
8.	Resting and Waiting	143
9.	Cultural Myths of Life After Death	167
10.	Human Nature	184
11.	Baptism and Rebirth	213
12.	Dueling Natures	242

13.	The Way to God	262
14.	Judgment of the Righteous	294
15.	Recompense for Faithful Labor	314
16.	End-Time Unity	332

Appendix 1 - Outline of Interpretive Methodology	347
Appendix 2 - Salvation Passages' Meaning Derived from Verb Tenses	350
Appendix 3 - Groupings of Key Passages	353
Bibliography	358

REFERENCES AND COPYRIGHTS

All Scripture quoted in this book is from the ESV®, except where noted.

Scripture quotations are from the ESV® Bible (The Holy Bible, English Standard Version®), copyright © 2001 by Crossway, a publishing ministry of Good News Publishers. Used by permission. All rights reserved.

Scripture quotations taken from the New American Standard Bible® (NASB), Copyright © 1960, 1962, 1963, 1968, 1971, 1972, 1973, 1975, 1977, 1995 by The Lockman Foundation. Used by permission. www.Lockman.org

Scripture quotations marked (NIV) are taken from the Holy Bible, New International Version®, NIV®. Copyright © 1973, 1978, 1984, 2011 by Biblica, Inc.™ Used by permission of Zondervan. All rights reserved worldwide. www.zondervan.com The "NIV" and "New International Version" are trademarks registered in the United States Patent and Trademark Office by Biblica, Inc.™

Scripture quoted by permission. Quotations designated

(NET) are from the NET Bible® copyright ©1996–2017 by Biblical Studies Press, L.L.C. All rights reserved.

Scripture quotations marked (YLT) are taken from Young's Literal Translation. Public Domain.

Scripture quotations marked (KJV) are taken from the King James Version. Public Domain.

All bold-face type within Scripture quotations has been added by the author for emphasis.

Copyright © 2018 – K.J. Soze

www.kjsoze.com

INTRODUCTION

Readers of any long, difficult book will know the temptation to skip to the last pages to find out what happens in the end. But there is no satisfaction in taking such a shortcut. The sum of the narrative ebbs and flows provide the conclusion its power and meaning. For readers of the Bible, the book of Revelation has a similar allure: *How does it all end anyway?* But the same principle applies: Revelation is the last book of the Bible we should study. Without a foundational understanding of the gospel message, we won't be able to understand the Apocalyptic prophecies.

Prior to a deep study of Revelation, it is best to read other related end-time passages from Genesis to Jude and study the series of covenants God made with his people. The covenants provide crucial background information for events yet to occur. We also need to understand this key biblical concept: the physical realm we observe on earth and the heavenly realm are on separate planes, bridged only by the spiritual realm. Good biblical scholarship therefore requires us to discern whether a given passage refers to the physical (visible, earthly) realm, the heavenly (unseen) realm, or the spiritual realm (the link between the seen and unseen).

Given the modern appetite for this topic, I expect you have already encountered many of the competing schools of thought on end-time prophecies and events. You may be familiar with terms such as *premillennial* and *amillennial,* or understand the differences between *pre-tribulation, post-tribulation,* or *pre-wrath rapture.* If not, I will provide definitions as appropriate, but this book is not meant to be an exhaustive primer on competing viewpoints. Certainly there are plenty of good books and websites that dig into each of these perspectives. I do assume that you share a belief that God created the world (focusing here on *intelligent design* rather than method) and that God continues to be active in our lives. Other readers are welcome, but be warned that if you disagree here, you'll likely be at odds with the rest of my conclusions.

I aim to show in these pages how the gospel is integral within end-time events. Some Christians shrug off the Bible's prophetic passages altogether, figuring that if we're saved, why bother thinking about these complexities? But the strongest gospel message we can help deliver is the complete gospel that culminates with the last days.

This book compares literal interpretations of the Bible to figurative interpretations to show how each affects our belief system—and how preconceived belief systems affect our interpretations.

Our goal should be to set aside our preconceptions and objectively interpret Bible passages related to end times—even if the passage uses figurative language. Figurative language, after all, can be used to describe an event that literally occurred. Christ's first advent, for instance, was the literal fulfillment of prophecies that included figurative language. The prophetic metaphors and visions ultimately corresponded to physical outcomes on earth that humans could observe.

Shouldn't it follow that Jesus' second coming would also be a literal event foretold by figurative end-time prophecies?

Not according to many popular end-time beliefs. Although such adherents believe that prophecies about the first advent were literally fulfilled, they do not believe in the literal fulfillment of the remaining second-advent prophecies. I suspect that many people who hold such beliefs are not consciously aware of the inconsistency. So I urge you as you read this book to deliberately examine the basis for your own end-time beliefs. See what holds up under scrutiny.

The gospel in the Bible is a message of redemption and resurrection—not merely a path to spiritual enlightenment. If you don't believe Jesus lived, died, and was physically resurrected, you probably won't like the literal treatment of biblical prophecies presented in this book. However, if you believe Jesus walked the earth, died, and was bodily resurrected, and if you believe the Bible contains prophecies that correspond to end-time events, then you should read on.

This book was written for you whether you are a dispensationalist, a preterist, an amillennialist, a post- or pre-millennialist, whether you're into replacement theology or covenant theology. I don't ask you to approach this book from one specific *ist* or *ism*—only that you open yourself to the possibility that there is a common, objective ground of interpretation for the gospel in relation to end-times. You may encounter challenges in these pages to long-held beliefs. Should this happen, ask the Holy Spirit to reveal the truth about his Word. Whether he leads you out of old misconceptions or into renewed conviction, praise God and rejoice in his truth.

This book focuses on the continual unveiling of God's unified plan to redeem mankind. According to God's plan, he saves all people the same way, no matter what period of history they live in. A common thread weaves throughout the old covenants and into the new covenant, whereby we see how God's Word ties everything together into the same gospel message for all people throughout history.

There is no fundamental difference in how someone gets "saved" in the Old Testament versus the New Testament: the Holy Spirit produces faith within a person who in turn believes in God for eternal life. We in our modern lives rely on the same faith that saved those who lived thousands of years before Christ. The timing of Christ's first advent did not change how God implements salvation for everyone. As God says in Malachi 3:6, *"For I the Lord do not change."*[1]

Both the Old and New Testaments repeatedly use language that says God "pours out his Spirit." The same God that poured his Spirit upon the Old Testament saints now reveals himself to us:

---

1. See also Hebrews 6:17 and James 1:17.

*"If you turn at my reproof, behold, **I will pour out my spirit** to you; I will make my words known to you."*

—Proverbs 1:23

*"God's love has been **poured out into our hearts through the Holy Spirit**, who has been given to us."*

—Romans 5:5

*"[God] has also put his seal on us and **put his Spirit in our hearts** as a guarantee."*

—2 Corinthians 1:22

The passage in Joel 2:28 is repeated in Acts 2:17: *"And in the last days it shall be, God declares, that **I will pour out my Spirit on all flesh**."*

God used the same plan for salvation then as He does today. Whether a person lived on earth before or after the death and resurrection of Christ makes no difference. All people throughout history are saved through faith in the grace of the promises made all the way back in Genesis 3:15 and onward throughout Scripture.

*"Israel who pursued a law that would lead to righteousness did not succeed in reaching that law. Why? Because **they did not pursue it by faith**, but as if it were based on works. They have stumbled over the stumbling stone, as it is written,*

'Behold, I am laying in Zion a stone of stumbling, and a rock of offense;
and whoever believes in him will not be put to shame.'"

—Romans 9:31–33[2]

What is faith? It is a bridge in one sense of the term. It connects the grace given to us by the Spirit with our reliance upon this gift. Faith begins to form when we receive God's grace, then is completed when we act in obedience to God. Faith is a bridge from grace given to living by this gift. And in faith we await God's final installment of his promise to us—the second coming of his Son to our world.

The author takes no credit at all for anything found to be correct in this book. Any truth in this book is rooted in the biblical passages alone. This author takes full responsibility for any error of interpretation or commentary.

Please leave a review for this book at the store where you received it from, or on Goodreads – www.goodreads.com/KJSoze

---

2. What about people who have never heard this gospel based upon faith in the promises of God? Read Romans 1, 2, and 10 for a further exploration of that topic.

CHAPTER 1.

BIBLE INTERPRETATION PRINCIPLES

A key to understanding the Bible is learning how to properly interpret it through the guidance of the Holy Spirit. Sounds simple. However, cultural traditions and personal biases complicate our efforts. Another barrier arises from the biblical concept that there are three realms of existence: our physical world, God's heavenly realm, and a spiritual realm that bridges the other two. This multi-realm structure can create paradoxes where something is true in one realm but may seem contradictory in another realm. Passages that seem contradictory are possible to harmonize by identifying their relationship to these separate realms. But we will be frustrated and confused if we try to force all passages into merged realm context. The kingdom of heaven's interaction on earth is a good example that will be thoroughly explored.

As discussed in the Introduction and Appendix 1, biblical prophecies can utilize literal or figurative language while referring to the physical, heavenly, or spiritual realm.[1]

---

1. This creates six possible combinations: Literal/Physical, Literal/Heavenly, Literal/Spiritual, Figurative/Physical, Figurative/Heavenly, and Figurative/Spiritual.

Knowing the point of reference in a given passage will untangle many complex paradoxes found in Scripture. The big picture and complete context of the Bible will start to come together as you sort the paradoxical puzzle pieces according to their categories. With proper perspective comes correct insight.

If this sounds like a lot of work, don't blame God for making it difficult for us to understand the Bible in its original context—the fault belongs to our own culture and traditions. Our experiences and biases obstruct our efforts to interpret passages objectively. Depending on tradition or preconceived notions, a person generally falls into one school of interpretation and follows along with others in that grouping:

1. A belief that the Bible is primarily focused on the spiritual realm and our mystical enlightenment;
2. A belief that the Bible is concerned with our welfare in both the physical and spiritual realms;
3. A belief that the Bible is primarily concerned with the physical realm and our bodily welfare.

People within the first camp do not necessarily give every passage a spiritual interpretation. They acknowledge that there are actual historical events mentioned in the Bible. But they predominantly view the language of the Bible as metaphorical, analogical, symbolic, or allegorical. This approach allows us to make Bible passages mean whatever we want to believe. Interpretation becomes a subjective matter—but this book is about objective approaches to the Bible. If you yourself tend to read the Bible through a purely spiritual lens, this book will present some interpretations you perhaps have not considered before. I challenge you to read with an open mind.

Likewise, people in the third camp do not necessarily interpret every passage literally. There are obvious metaphors (figurative language) in the Bible, but for the most part, this person believes in the history of the Bible, the miracle accounts, the existence of Satan, and the fulfillment of prophecies. People in this camp believe that prophesied events that have not yet occurred will be fulfilled on earth; they are not focused on spiritual fulfillment.

A 2016 Barna study found that about 7 percent of Americans fall into this third camp. Most proclaimed Christians fall into Camp 2.[2]

Camp 2 is the hardest perspective to nail down because there is room for numerous belief systems between the extremes of the physically focused and spiritually focused camps.

At the dawn of Christianity, believers mostly fell into either a Hebrew way of thinking (an eastern perspective) or a Greek (western-centric) mindset. Within 100 years after the time of the apostles, each viewpoint had its

---

2. "The State of the Church 2016." Barna Group, 2016. Accessed on April 30, 2019, at www.barna.com/research/state-church-2016/ - Note: this link may be broken. Other trends are found in the 2019 survey here - https://www.barna.com/research/state-of-the-bible-2019/.

champions—such as Irenaeus (eastern)[3] and Clement of Alexandria (western).[4]

At the turn of the 5th Century, Augustine of Hippo arrived on the scene. In his book *City of God*, he argued for the amillennialist view that the thousand-year reign of Jesus on earth as described in Revelation 20[5] should not be interpreted literally.[6] His argument, using a Camp-2 hybrid approach, was predominantly accepted for most of western Church history up through the Reformation and Protestant periods. Since the post-Reformation period, several Protestant groups have shifted to more literal

---

3. Irenaeus believed the revelation received by the Hebrew apostles was sufficient for modern instruction: *"But Polycarp also was not only instructed by apostles, and conversed with many who had seen Christ, but was also, by apostles in Asia...always taught the things which he had learned from the apostles, and which the Church has handed down, and which alone are true. To these things all the Asiatic Churches testify, as do also those men who have succeeded Polycarp down to the present time"* (Against Heresies, III.3.4, III.4.3).

4. Clement believed the Greek cultural mindset could lead a person to righteousness: *"Accordingly, before the advent of the Lord, philosophy was necessary to the Greeks for righteousness. And now it becomes conducive to piety; being a kind of preparatory training to those who attain to faith through demonstration"* (Stromateis 1.5).

5. The passage reads as follows: "Then I saw an angel coming down from heaven, holding in his hand the key to the bottomless pit and a great chain. And he seized the dragon, that ancient serpent, who is the devil and Satan, and bound him for a thousand years, and threw him into the pit, and shut it and sealed it over him, so that he might not deceive the nations any longer, until the thousand years were ended. After that he must be released for a little while. Then I saw thrones, and seated on them were those to whom the authority to judge was committed. Also I saw the souls of those who had been beheaded for the testimony of Jesus and for the word of God, and those who had not worshiped the beast or its image and had not received its mark on their foreheads or their hands. They came to life and reigned with Christ for a thousand years. The rest of the dead did not come to life until the thousand years were ended. This is the first resurrection. Blessed and holy is the one who shares in the first resurrection! Over such the second death has no power, but they will be priests of God and of Christ, and they will reign with him for a thousand years" (Revelation 20:1–6).

6. St. Augustine. *City of God*, Book XX, Chapter 7. Accessed on April 30, 2019, at www.newadvent.org/fathers/120120.htm

interpretations within the modern premillennial movement (which argues that the millennial kingdom described in Revelation 20 will literally come to pass).

Let's try to group the primary perspectives on Revelation 20 according to whether they interpret the passage literally or figuratively, and whether they look for fulfillment in the physical, heavenly, or spiritual realm.

1. New Age/Gnostic[7]—this camp expects a figurative fulfillment in the spiritual realm, focused on the mystical implications.
2. Amillennial/postmillennial[8]—these viewpoints differ on whether the language of the passage is literal or figurative.
3. Premillennial[9]—this camp expects a literal fulfillment in the physical realm.

If you don't feel like your own view is represented by one of these labels, don't worry; we're merely looking to simplify discussion for now. I myself do not intend to rigidly argue for one of these labels over another—except to recommend against the extreme represented by the Gnostics and the mystics. I appreciate the premillennial's insistence on looking for literal fulfillment of prophecy, but some

---

7. Gnostics believe the physical world is an evil, inferior realm. The soul is trapped within the body and must be set free through "gnosis," or spiritual knowledge. Gnostics see no value in any sort of earthly millennial kingdom.
8. Amillennialists do not believe the passage refers to a literal thousand-year reign. Postmillennialists believe this refers to a victorious reign of the church on earth before Christ's second coming.
9. Premillennialists interpret this passage literally, expecting Christ to reign for a thousand years on earth upon his second coming.

adherents can be too rigid in their focus on the physical realm

In the Introduction, I shared my perspective that God has a single plan of redemption, and if I were to adopt a single label, it would represent that belief. I believe that God has been using the same plan from Genesis 3 onward to redeem all mankind. He rolls it out in stages, but there is only one plan.

Because God does not change His nature over time, we can study the interwoven biblical passages to discover an objective interpretation of God's progressing plan. From Old Testament to New Testament, every passage of Scripture unfolds. We can easily follow the progression of the covenants God made with Abraham, with the nation of Israel, and with David—and finally the new covenant.

The main point of Scripture in this view is that there is only one plan of redemption for all people throughout all history. As we look at various passages throughout this book, this is the lens I will be using. To illustrate the book's perspective by way of contrast, let's look at one of the labels of interpretations—preterism.

One of the primary beliefs of preterism is that Christ's kingdom has already begun in full revelation. Preterism holds that Christ came in AD 70 to establish his current kingdom—which is spiritual, not a physical reign over any earthly territory. Preterists are unable to claim any physical observation of the second coming, but point to the destruction of the Temple in that same period as evidence. The cessation of Temple worship finalized God's judgment on Israel, and the Spirit now resides in the souls or "temples" of all true believers.

Full preterism depends on a figurative interpretation of Acts 1:11, which quotes an angel as saying, *"Men of Galilee, why do you stand looking into heaven? This Jesus, who was taken up from you into heaven, will come in the same way as you saw him go into heaven."* Had Christ returned to earth physically in AD 70 on any scale, it would have been reported by the early Church and historians. But since preterism looks to a spiritual kingdom and not an earthly one, isn't it reasonable to argue for an already fulfilled spirit-only return of Christ to fulfill second advent prophecies?

Unfortunately for the preterists, a majestic, physical return of Christ is very clearly spelled out in many passages that heavily convey if not demand a literal interpretation. Acts 1:11 speaks to the logistics that of Christ's return, comparing it to the ascension the disciples had just witnessed. Other passages state that all people on earth will see his physical return.[10]

So preterism's hyper-focus on the spiritual realm holds up under a stubborn insistence on viewing passages through a figurative lens. While preterists do not go to the extremes of the Gnostics in this regard, the method of biblical interpretation is similarly flawed. I won't be discussing any purely spiritual interpretations of the Bible. This cannot help us in our goal to pursue objective interpretations of prophetic passages that refer to events within the physical realm. Of course, some prophetic passages do indeed relate to events in the heavenly or spiritual realms, so we will

10. See Matthew 24:30; Revelation 1:7.

need to apply discernment. Clearly understood passages like Acts 1:11 help us narrow down possible meanings of more difficult texts after we realize Christ is coming back to earth physically. Once a big picture starts to develop, our interpretive work becomes much easier.

In other words, we will be using a literal interpretive method that takes literal or figurative language and places it into a realm. Even figurative language in the Bible often speaks to an event that will certainly happen in the heavenly realm or spiritual realm, so it ends up "literally" occurring. This approach allows objective meanings to be derived in any realm.

Throughout this book we will be exploring various amillennial and premillennial viewpoints and how they relate to the gospel. I'm narrowing the focus to these two perspectives as they are by far the most popular schools of end-time thought in Christianity.

When the Bible mentions the kingdom of God, the language often makes particular reference to our earthly realm; other passages specifically refer to a heavenly kingdom ("the kingdom of heaven"). It is important that we recognize these two different types of kingdom passages, noting which realm is relevant to each specific verse.

In the majority of end-time views of interpretation, a physical realm (where we reside) and a heavenly realm (where Christ is ruling from right now) are acknowledged. They both work "in parallel" with each other—in other words, the dual realms interact. Without an understanding of dual-realm interaction in spiritual language, we are bound to come up with confusing interpretations or private interpretations, subjectively selecting which passages speak literally of the physical realm on earth and which speak figuratively of another realm.

Many passages in the Bible mention events going on in heaven and on earth at the same time, describing how spiritual warfare quietly affects earthly events. This dual interaction concept explains many end-time events.

We tend to focus on our preconceived beliefs when interpreting difficult verses, either leaning toward a physical or spiritual implication. But the Bible states both realms work in parallel, the seen and the unseen together.[11] This will help us to understand end-time prophecies.

Galatians 4:6 shows all three realms interacting: *"God sent forth the Spirit of his Son into our hearts."* This is a merger of spiritual activity sent from the heavenly realm into our physical body.[12] Two realms interact in the Holy Spirit.

This verse in Galatians demonstrates the spiritual realm meeting our physical body in our inner being. There are numerous passages like this (see also the examples from the Introduction about God pouring out his Spirit). Does the verse describe an actual event taking place, or are we supposed to derive some mystical meaning? If we take the multi-realm approach and a literal interpretation, we know

---

11. For examples of multiple realms interacting, see Job 1:6–12; Daniel 10:10–14; Luke 22:31–32; 2 Corinthians 10:3–4; Galatians 5:17; Ephesians 6:12; Colossians 1:16; and Hebrews 9:19–26.
12. Note that "heart" is a clearly understood metaphor found in the Bible; it refers to our mind, conscience, or inner being, not a pumping organ.

the verse refers to something that God does in the physical realm.

The idea of one realm touching another can be difficult to grasp. We may find it hard to fully understand how our inner being meets the Holy Spirit. But God can simply send forth "the Spirit of his Son" in the form of a Bible verse entering our consciousness.

As confusing as they may be to us, the spiritual aspects of the Holy Spirit living in us and the battles between the physical and heavenly realms are far easier for us to understand than the prophecies of future events. This is because we do not always know if a prophecy passage is speaking to a vision of the heavenly realm or the future physical realm; after all, the event hasn't happened yet.

We tend to declare a Bible passage as figurative or spiritually oriented when a literal meaning within our physical realm would be difficult to comprehend or believe. This is a reasonable impulse. It would be a very difficult task to arrange literal interpretations of end-time prophecies into a coherent sequence of events. The imagery of Revelation doesn't fit neatly into a timeline. But that doesn't totally let us off the hook, as many end-time prophecies do refer to physical events. How do we practically discern and interpret all these passages? In our case herein, we first need an understanding of God's master plan that is to be continually carried out until the last day—the end of this age as we know it.

The difficult passages become clearer if we keep in mind the common thread throughout the Old and New

Testaments. We can compare passages for coherency with the rest of Scripture. Self-evident passages of Scripture interpret difficult passages of Scripture.

Many people read difficult passages, then utilize a preconceived notion to achieve an interpretation that "makes sense." This is wrong. We should instead put our opinions on hold, go read other passages that provide more clarity, then return to the difficult passage to make sure it fits with the rest of Scripture.

Let's start with an easy comparison. Here are two examples of spiritual resurrections using figurative language:

*"If then you have been **raised** with Christ, seek the things that are above, where Christ is, seated at the right hand of God. Set your minds on things that are above, not on things that are on earth. For you have died, and your life is hidden with Christ in God. When Christ who is your life appears, then you also **will appear** with him in glory."*

—Colossians 3:1–4

*"But God, being rich in mercy, because of the great love with which he loved us, even when we were dead in our trespasses, made us alive together with Christ—by grace you have been saved—and **raised** us up with him and seated us with him in the heavenly places in Christ Jesus, so that in the **coming ages** he might show the immeasurable riches of his grace in kindness toward us in Christ Jesus."*

—Ephesians 2:4–7

Notice both passages speak to being "raised" in the past

tense, referring to a spiritual type of resurrection. Later, in both passages, there is a switch to a future tense ("will appear" and the "coming ages").

The word "raised" in these passages comes from a Greek root word that means "lifted" or "wakened." This root differentiates from other resurrection passages that use a "standing up" root-word meaning. Passages that denote a physical or bodily resurrection to show the action of a dead body rising use the "standing up" root. In contrast, both passages above are easily recognizable as spiritually "raised" language, not physical "lifting" to heaven language. "Raised" is a metaphor, but it refers to an event that actually took place: a believer was born again, becoming baptized by the Spirit.

It would be nice if we could always spot the difference between physical and spiritual prophecies so easily. The same interpretive principles always apply—first look at root-word usage and its usage in other passages—however, prophecy is a more complicated endeavor for the reason previously stated: we don't always know what realm the writer is referencing. If a given passage doesn't clearly indicate a specific realm, then we can only go to other passages to see if there are already established meanings of similar words, phrases, or concepts.

To begin examining end-time prophecies, we should first read literally, then make an initial attempt to place these passages within a realm. This placement should be informed by our knowledge of the context of identical terms used in similar passages. If literal fulfillment proves impossible within the physical realm or heavenly realm, then we are left to treat the language figuratively in an attempt to obtain spiritual meaning. In any case, all interpretations found in this book will fit into this key idea: God doesn't change. He has one single continuing plan for redemption, and prophecies of the second advent will realize the same literal fulfillment on earth that first-advent prophecies enjoyed.

Old Testament passages that were literally fulfilled at the first advent sometimes contain additional prophecies about the second advent. We should evaluate these passages first, establishing whether figurative or literal language is used. Logic maintains that if a first-advent prophecy realized literal fulfillment, then the second half of the passage should not switch to a mystical meaning regarding the second advent.

If we are going to offer opinions about our own spiritual interpretations of non-essential topics, just make sure that they do not undermine unity in the Body of Christ per Romans 14. We are offered many freedoms in Christ relating to many topics. These are nonessential issues. However, we are expected to have Christian unity in the gospel as only one gospel message is correct. If our end-time opinions begin to contradict the gospel, we need to promptly reevaluate our beliefs.

Is the gospel based on physical salvation, spiritual salvation, or both? We often fixate on spiritual salvation, but the gospel also promises a future bodily resurrection upon the merger of the earthly and heavenly realms.

We need to be aware that some end-time labels of

interpretation present contrary gospel messages. You may find this hard to believe, presuming that the gospel is incredibly simple, but there are certainly different gospel messages being promoted today. Before we tackle this topic, let's look at how some people fall into misinterpretations.

Pre-conceived notions and private interpretive methods have led to the development of numerous dubious end-time interpretations. For example, Matthew 24:36 says that no person can know "the day and the hour" of Christ's second advent. Many inflate the concept of imminence to mean that Christ's return will be a total surprise to believers. This inflated concept then adjusts all other passages about timing, insisting that the entire timetable is unknowable. The entire concept of a pre-tribulational rapture is built upon this imminence foundation. Private interpretation of this one verse has built a whole industry of end-time beliefs.

Instead of looking up the source of "the day and the hour" from a Hebrew perspective, some people just assume this to mean that Christ could come back at any moment. The element of complete surprise seems necessary. But the expression may come from a Hebrew idiom that refers to spotting the new moon; the general timing is known but not the exact timing until it is actually witnessed. More specifically to end times, the phrase refers to a bridegroom coming for his bride at the end of the betrothal. The father of the groom sets the exact time for when the couple's dwelling place will be ready. This means the bride knows the general timing (or season) but not the details. The bride and her family only know the groom is coming in about one year, so they can prepare themselves generally for the arrival. This idiom should not dictate any theology or lead us to make assumptions about Christ's advent timing.

Another view based on a more correct English translation is that no one "perceives" the day and the hour; in the perfect-tense use of the word, nothing has happened yet. Knowledge comes by perception (of the signs). The signs are to come first, and then we can know or perceive. The angels don't know when the signs will start either.[13]

Other views based upon Matthew 24 and Mark 13 state that while unbelievers will be unaware of Christ's return, believers should look for signs, such as the fig tree example, to be aware of the general season of the second coming. Nobody knows when the signs will appear and thus initiate the end of the age. The start of the end could come as a surprise at any moment under this view, but then become obvious to believers only.

Noah knew judgment was coming prior to the moment when wrath was poured out on earth. The flood was a surprise to unbelievers but not Noah. The Father gave the timing of the first advent of Christ to prophets, priests, magi, and shepherds. And so we may infer that the elect will know the general timing of the second advent. We should look to other clearer passages to understand more.

There are many interpretations of this one short statement from Christ, but the reality is that only one of them is correct (or another view is correct that is not popular or well known). Instead of forcing our opinion on the passage or making this statement fit our beliefs, we can simply put

---

13. See Matthew 24:36; Mark 13:32.

it on hold, go to other passages to see what can be learned, then return to find meaning in "the day and the hour."

A similar concept is found in 1 Thessalonians 5:2, which says *"the day of Lord will come like a thief in the night."* At first glance, we may assume this supports the imminence interpretation of the "day and the hour" passage regarding the timing of Christ's second advent. However, a couple of lines later in verse 4, Paul states that believers will not be surprised (unprepared) that day. As shown in numerous passages, we the bride must be prepared; this is a key concept.

An entire belief system about end times tries to justify itself based on isolated verses like Matthew 24:36 or 1 Thessalonians 5:2. Another verse used as support is Revelation 22:20 where Jesus says, *"Surely I am coming soon."* Preterists point to this verse, and a possible pre-AD 70 publication date, as evidence for a quiet second coming. But "soon" could also be translated "quickly," thus referring to the manner of his return and not its imminence. In other words, it will be a fast process when he does come, not a long, drawn-out process of arrival, with judgment and salvation swift on his heels.[14]

Ezekiel 12:23–28 demonstrates that the ancient world did not share our modern concept of terms like "delay," "quickly," or the general timing of future events. The ancient concepts seem confusing to us. See for instance Ezekiel 12:27; God speaks about distant events, but in the following verse states that there will be no delay in these future events occurring. When we take these and all related

---

14. See Hebrews 10:37 and Romans 9:27–28.

passages together, we can safely infer that Christ will assuredly come again, and it will be a fast process. If we try to infer more than that, we're on shaky ground.

The apostles and Christ himself stated that he would certainly come back, and meanwhile we are to be patient as referenced in the Old Testament prophecy of Habakkuk 2:3.[15] The main point from all these related passages is to provide confidence and patience that Christ will surely come again and that he will act swiftly when he does.

Matthew 24:34 states that this "generation" will not pass until statements (prophecies) made by Christ in that chapter are realized. If one is biased toward an interpretation that he would come back to earth in a 30 to 40-year generational period—that the people standing next to him listening to the prophecy firsthand would see the second coming—in this case, he certainly must have returned by AD 70. Other people interpret "generation" to mean "people" or "Israelites," while still others believe that Jesus' audience would live to see signs pointing to Christ's return (but not the return itself).

If we use Matthew to interpret Matthew, we notice that the word "generation" appears several times. Matthew 23:36 is a good example: "Truly, I say to you, all these things will come upon this generation."

The verses directly preceding Matthew 23:36 speak to fathers and sons over a very long time period, not just the people listening to Christ at that moment. In this case,

---

15. "For still the vision awaits its appointed time; it hastens to the end—it will not lie. If it seems slow, wait for it; it will surely come; it will not delay."

"generation" refers to those who killed the prophets throughout the nation's history. So we see that "generation" in the book of Matthew does not have to mean a 30 to 40-year cluster of people, but refers to a group of people over a vast period. Matthew 24:34 should not be used to calculate timing; a likelier interpretation is that the people of Israel will continue to exist until the end times. To confirm our supposition, we need to move on to clearer passages.

Almost any meaning can be manufactured if one spiritualizes a passage subjectively. Let's take care not to do so intentionally. The Bible never promotes private interpretation. We rely on the work of the Holy Spirit to form one collective Body. One faith, one baptism, one Church, one God (Ephesians 4:4–6). Although we are individually gifted to share the gospel in distinct ways, we are not free to subjectively interpret what the gospel message is. If there is one Spirit, there can only be one core message. Prophets were not even allowed to opine on what they were given. Does God invite us to develop different gospels or different end-time interpretations? No. Yet we find many gospels today.

*"For we did not follow cleverly devised myths when we made known to you the power and **coming** of our Lord Jesus Christ, but we were eyewitnesses of his majesty. For when he received honor and glory from God the Father, and the voice was borne to him by the Majestic Glory, 'This is my beloved Son, with whom I am well pleased,' we ourselves heard this very voice borne from Heaven, for we were with him on the holy mountain. And **we have the prophetic word more fully confirmed**, to which you will do well to pay attention as to a lamp shining in a dark place, until the day*

dawns and the morning star rises in your hearts, knowing this first of all, that **no prophecy of Scripture comes from someone's own interpretation.** *For no prophecy was ever produced by the will of man, but men spoke from God as they were carried along by the Holy Spirit."*

—2 Peter 1:16–21[16]

In the above passage, Peter describes the Transfiguration event in which he had a vision of the second "coming" (*parousia* in the N.T. Greek). The full account in Matthew 17 shows how he became confused; thinking it was a real-time event, he urged his fellow disciples to help him make physical shelters for Moses and Elijah. Peter also had trouble with a supernatural event in prison (Acts 12:6–9), and he did not know if it was really happening or if it was a vision. Peter was confused both times. However, he was sure that true revelation and prophecy comes from the Holy Spirit. The prophet cannot muster up his own inspired words.

Also take note of the line about a "prophetic word more fully confirmed." Peter had read passages from the prophets about the second coming, but his vision provided extra confirmation that these passages were true. He not only read about the glory of Christ, but he saw it in a vision. It felt so real that he thought it was coming to pass at that very moment. When he saw the vision of the future, he knew with absolute certainty Christ would come back to earth in great glory, as described by the prophets. The description of bright robes and a radiant face is what was written in the

---

16. See Matthew 17 for the full account of the Transfiguration vision of the second advent.

Old Testament and matches the Transfiguration vision that Peter saw.

There are many additional difficult passages we could explore, but I don't want to look at these for now.[17] Instead, let's proceed by examining clear passages that can speak for themselves and provide for a general understanding of what God has in store.

As we assemble the crystal-clear passages, a big picture will develop, allowing other prophecies to fill in the gaps. This is similar to how most people assemble a jigsaw puzzle: start with the border pieces to set the parameters, and save the most difficult pieces for last.

When considering complex passages with unknown meanings, the key is that they must not conflict with known interpretations of other clear passages. They cannot conflict with each other since there is one Spirit who has inspired the totality of God's Word. All Scripture must be in unison. The Holy Spirit weaves only one core message throughout the Bible, as is revealed within the literal interpretive method.

Understanding what the kingdom of God or kingdom of heaven means is crucial to understanding end-time events

---

17. If you're curious, there are numerous books and papers that explore opposing viewpoints of controversial end-time passages. Here are a few links to get you started.Pre-wrath rapture: Chris White. "The Pre-Wrath Rapture Explained." November 23. 2011. bibleprophecytalk.com/bpt-keeping-a-consistent-hermeneutic-with-the-rapture. Accessed June 3, 2019.Pre-tribulation rapture: "What is the End-Times Timeline?" Got Questions. www.gotquestions.org/end-times-timeline.html. Accessed June 3, 2019.Post-tribulation rapture: "Post Tribulation Rapture Belife." Post Tribulation People. www.posttribpeople.com/Post-Tribulation-Belief.html. Accessed June 3, 2019.

yet to be fulfilled. All other passages fall into line once we understand the differences between the coming kingdom and the current kingdom that has already been established. The kingdom is a case of "now and not yet." The kingdom is established now, but it is not yet fully established; a paradox to us.

Before a future kingdom can be established, there is a piece of land to consider, as any kingdom must be built upon some foundation. But is this foundation made of earth, spiritual bedrock, or both?

CHAPTER 2.

THE LAND COVENANT

To gain an understanding of end-time events, the best place to start is in the book of Genesis. We'll examine Adam's fall into sin in Genesis 3, then move on to the covenant God formed with Abraham.

Let's look at verse 15 as God curses the serpent that led Adam and Eve into sin:

"I will put enmity between you and the woman,

and between her offspring and your offspring;

he shall bruise your head,

and you shall bruise his heel."

—Genesis 3:15

Most scholars agree that Christ is the seed of Eve prophesied here to "crush" or "bruise" the devil's head. According to one view, Christ already defeated death and the devil. Another view looks forward to the day when death and the devil are cast into the lake of fire. A further dual view offers a longer process in which Christ himself first gains a personal victory over death and the devil, then later wins a full victory over his enemies—a victory in which we too can partake. Under this progressive timetable scenario, Christ's resurrection is the first fruits of victory over death, but we must wait to join him in victorious resurrection.

Whether Christ has already fulfilled Genesis 3:15 or portions of this prophecy have yet to be fulfilled, the main theme of this prophecy is clear: Christ is our ultimate hope for salvation. The timing of when Christ fully destroys the devil depends on the resolution of other timeline-related questions. We'll come back to this verse once we've developed more information.

As we move on from Adam past Noah to the Abrahamic covenant, we begin to enter an arena of controversy. Commentators offer vastly different interpretations of God's covenant with Abraham, which has critical implications regarding the new covenant that we live under today. We must gain an accurate understanding of the Abrahamic covenant in order to understand the nature of our own salvation and the impending end of the age.

Injudicious readers often lump all Old Testament covenants together as one overarching contract between God and his people. But the Bible describes other covenants made to Noah, Moses, and David. Each covenant legally needs to stand on its own as a separate agreement, oath, or testament. The Old Testament covenants do not combine neatly into one contract, nor does that covenant simply get superseded by the new covenant when Jesus arrives on the scene. Each separate covenant has its own repercussions. Our preconceived notion of a two-covenant system (a single old covenant rendered void by a new covenant) blinds us to other possibilities. Our understanding of end-time events—and Christianity itself—suffers as a result.

There are two basic types of covenants: unilateral and bilateral. Both types are binding, with a breach of contract carrying a penalty for the offending party.

The specific penalties for breaking a covenant depend on the gravity of the covenant itself, whether a casual agreement, a blood oath, or something in between. But the covenants that God made with his people were of the strongest possible bond. Blood was shed to seal the agreements. In some of these biblical examples, this entailed an animal sacrifice. The implication was that violation of the terms of the covenant would result in new bloodshed—a penalty of death.

In a bilateral covenant, both parties agree to fulfill certain conditions. If either party fails to meet their responsibilities, the covenant is broken and the other party is not required to fulfill any remaining expectations. The breaching party is obligated to pay penalties for breaking the covenant.

A unilateral covenant is a strong promise or oath from one party to another party. Only the party that makes the oath needs to follow the specified terms. Nothing is required of the other party except to accept or reject that which is promised. If the party making the oath is in breach, then that party must pay a penalty. The threat of the penalty motivates the party making the unilateral covenant to fulfill the obligation and assures the recipient that the promise will be kept.

God's offer of salvation is an example of such an unconditional covenant; an individual must receive God's offer in faith and thus become a recipient of his blessings, or else reject God completely. We'll take a closer look at the striking similarities between the Abrahamic covenant and the new covenant gospel message later in this book.

Abrahamic vs Mosaic

The Abrahamic covenant contains several distinct promises; however, the land aspect of the covenant is the most controversial and creates the most confusion.[1]

Abraham was given three main promises in the covenant God made with him.

1. He was to be the father of many nations—a great nation of nations.
2. All nations would be blessed through Abraham. Now, the focus of this promise is not Abraham himself, but one of his descendants. This promise points to the Messiah, the descendant of Abraham who would bless all nations. We see this promise gain clarity with the establishment of the 12 tribes of Israel, and God further affirms his promise in a covenant with David. In reading the New Testament, the Gospels leave no doubt that Jesus Christ was the

---

1. For a full biblical description of the Abrahamic covenant, see Genesis 12:1–3; 13:14–17; 15:5–18; 17:1–10; and 22:16–18.

Messiah, the fulfillment of this promise to Abraham.

3. Abraham and his descendants would forever have a land of their own. But did this everlasting land promise refer to literal soil, spiritual dust, or both?

As promised, a multitude of nations arose from Abraham's descendants. And the second part of the promise was also fulfilled: the tribe of Judah carried the seed of Abraham that ultimately bloomed in the son of Mary through whom the whole world would be blessed. But what came of the promise of a homeland? We learn that the main blessing of land went via birthright to Joseph's children (Ephraim first, then Manasseh).[2] Unfortunately, within a few generations, the tribes of Ephraim and Manasseh—and the entire nation of Israel—were living as slaves in Egypt. So God called out to Moses.

Here are the key passages for the Mosaic covenant: Exodus 19:4–6; 24:7; Deuteronomy 6:1–6; 7:11–14; 8:17–20; 9:4–7; and chapter 28.

"Now if you obey me fully and keep my covenant, out of all nations you will be my treasured possession. Although the whole earth is mine, you will be for me a kingdom of priests and a holy nation."

—Exodus 19:5–6

Notice the difference in language from the Abrahamic covenant to the Mosaic covenant. God's promises to Abraham demonstrate a one-way, unilateral covenant (unconditional upon the receiver), but God's promises to

---

2. See Genesis 48.

Moses were part of a two-way, bilateral covenant—dependent on Israel's obedience.

The apostle Paul explains that God's promises to Abraham are irrevocable (Romans 11:28–29). Not even the creation of a new covenant could undo these underlying promises to Abraham. Paul also compares the Abrahamic and Mosaic covenants:

"To give a human example, brothers: even with a man-made covenant, no one annuls it or adds to it once it has been ratified. Now the promises were made to Abraham and to his offspring. It does not say, "And to offsprings," referring to many, but referring to one, "And to your offspring," who is Christ. This is what I mean: **the law***, which came 430 years afterward,* **does not annul a covenant previously ratified by God***, so as to make the promise void. For if the* **inheritance** *comes by the law, it no longer comes by promise; but* **God gave it to Abraham by a promise***."*

—Galatians 3:15–18

So the Abrahamic covenant was an irrevocable promise (or oath) from God, where the blessings of the Mosaic law covenant were conditional upon the recipients of the nation of Israel keeping their side of the agreement. God would bless them in the land **if** they kept his laws.

It is inaccurate to merge the Old Testament covenants between God and his people, according to Paul. We should make note of the differences between the Abrahamic covenant, the Mosaic covenant, and the new covenant. Each of these covenants has consequences for us today. The differences distinguishing the covenants are crucial and relate to the meaning of salvation, while providing insight into the most important end-time events. We can't underestimate or look past the promises made to Abraham and simply jump to the new covenant.

So let's take a closer look. Here the Lord reiterates his promises to Abraham:

"And he said to him, 'I am the Lord who brought you out from Ur of the Chaldeans to give you this land to possess.' But he said, 'O Lord God, how am I to know that I shall possess it?'"

—Genesis 15:7–8

The promises God made to Abraham were unconditional gifts. Abraham's only task was to make a series of animal sacrifices through which God would certify his covenant (Genesis 15:9–20). Abraham went into a sleep-like state while God gave him the land promise; Abraham didn't need to agree to anything. He only needed to believe God.[3]

"When the sun had gone down and it was dark, behold, a smoking fire pot and a flaming torch passed between these pieces. On that day the Lord made a covenant with Abram, saying, 'To your offspring I give this land, from the river of Egypt to the great river, the river Euphrates.'"

—Genesis 15:17–18

"For when God made a promise to Abraham, since he had no one greater by whom to swear, he swore by himself."

—Hebrews 6:13

---

3. God did institute the law of circumcision as a sign of the covenant—but not at this time.

Many today don't understand the significance of Genesis 15:17–18, but this passage may help explain the basis of why Christ went to the cross. The use of a blood sacrifice to seal the covenant conveyed a clear meaning within that culture.

"The one who passes between the divided halves of the slain animals invokes death upon himself should he break the word by which he has bound himself in the oath."

—Claus Westermann, *Genesis 12–36: A Commentary*[4]

By sealing the covenant through a blood sacrifice, God swore that he would give up his life if he did not honor his agreement to give Abraham the land promised. Unbelievable? Let's carry this further.

Abraham had asked God, *"How am I to know?"*—or, how was he to know he would receive the land? After this blood sacrifice, Abraham knew God's promise was profoundly serious. Belief in God's gift of the promises formed Abraham's faith in God. Sound familiar? The same faith-by-grace concept is still used today. Remember, "God does not change" (Malachi 3:6).[5]

Now that we have some background, we can get back to Paul's comparison of the Abrahamic and Mosaic covenants in Galatians 3. Keep in mind the word "inheritance," as God uses it in his promises to Abraham. We will revisit this term later. Inheritance language in the New Testament invokes

---

4. Claus Westermann. *Genesis 12-36: A Commentary.* Augsburg Publishing House, 1981, p. 225.

5. Also see Hebrews 6:17 and James 1:17.

these promises from Genesis—specifically the promise of eternal life in a homeland.

Seed: Singular or Plural?

When it comes to understanding God's redemption plan for all people, this Galatians passage is one of the most interesting in the Bible. It links salvation back to the first plan laid out in Genesis, then threads it all the way through to end-time events. We generally think of John 3:16 as the quintessential salvation verse, but this passage from Paul explains how to tie a nice bow around the entire Bible. Of course, if you insist on treating all Old Testament covenants as a single evolving contract, Paul's teaching won't make much sense at all. In that way, Galatians 3 provides a helpful litmus test for your beliefs about the gospel—and by extension the end times.

First, this passage shoots down many dispensational beliefs completely.[6] God doesn't offer a gospel message of law to Old Testament saints and a gospel message of grace to New Testament saints. Indeed, the promises given to Abraham are the very basis for the salvation message. (The word Paul uses to describe the promise to Abraham—inheritance—is the same word he uses to describe New Testament salvation.[7]) Christ came to fulfill God's promises to Abraham. This will become clear when we look at the new covenant, which is connected to the Abrahamic covenant.

Notice how Paul differentiates between "offspring" and

---

6. Dispensationalism is the belief that God reveals himself in stages throughout history, also changing or evolving how he extends salvation to the world.
7. See Ephesians 1:11–14.

"offsprings" in Galatians 3 when trying to clarify the Abrahamic covenant. "Seed" or "offspring" are singular nouns but can refer to many people within a single group of people. But Paul wants to latch on to a solitary sense of the word.

This seems like a crazy argument at first glance, talking about one descendant of Abraham when the original context of the Genesis passage points to a plural group. This begs the question of whether the contradiction comes down to a mistranslation of the Genesis passage. Should English translators have presented Abraham's offspring as a singular descendant?

We must go back to the Abrahamic covenant passages in Genesis to see if Paul is speaking literally or if he is using figurative language. There are numerous covenant passages, so we need to determine which one(s) Paul is referring to.

In the original Hebrew text and LXX Greek version of the Old Testament, close attention should be paid to the root word for seed (or offspring) in Genesis 13:15 compared to verse 16. Verse 16 clearly refers to a larger group of Abraham's descendants. But in verse 15, the root is singular and may indeed point to an individual. As this is the verse in which the promise is delivered, verse 15 has profound implications for end times and the coming age. Let's look at a few different translations of this key verse:

ESV: *"All the land that you see I will give to you and your **offspring** forever."*

THE MESSAGE FOR THE LAST DAYS 37

YLT: *"For the whole of the land which thou are seeing, to thee I give it, and to thy **seed**—to the age."*

NIV (including verse 16): *"I will give all the land that you see to you and your **descendants** forever. And I will make your descendants like the dust of the earth, so that if anyone is able to count the dust of the earth, then your descendants also can be counted."*

See how from a root word meaning "seed" the translator can choose a word like "descendant"—or "descendants" as in the NIV example. This translation choice makes a huge difference. By decentralizing the focus from one anointed individual, it becomes possible to adopt many mistaken beliefs about the nation of Israel, salvation, and end times.

"Descendants" is not a good English translation of the root word because it forces a plural meaning where there should be ambiguity. The translator should not decide whether the writer of Genesis meant to point to one person or a group of people. The decision to remove ambiguity suggests a desire to shade the meaning of the text to fit an existing bias or preconceived notion.

Genesis 22:17–18 offers an even more egregious example of translator bias in a covenantal context. By needlessly using a plural form of the root, the translator threatens to create a tremendous amount of confusion.

ESV (22:17–18): *"I will surely bless you, and I will surely multiply your **offspring** as the stars of heaven and as the sand that is on the seashore. And your **offspring** shall possess the gate of **his** enemies, and in your offspring shall all the nations of the earth be blessed, because you have obeyed my voice."*

NIV (22:17): *"I will surely bless you and make your **descendants** as numerous as the stars in the sky and as the sand on the seashore. Your **descendants** will take possession of the cities of **their** enemies..."*

KJV (22:17): *"That in blessing I will bless thee, and in multiplying I will multiply thy **seed** as the stars of the Heaven, and as the sand which is upon the sea shore; and thy **seed** shall possess the gate of **his** enemies..."*

Notice how the translator gets to choose whether "seed," "offspring," or "descendant(s)" is used. Many English translations use the plural when the root word of the second "seed" of verse 17 is associated to the singular masculine.[8]

For argument's sake, it doesn't matter if the singular seed refers to Isaac, Abraham's son, or Christ, his distant progeny. The main point is that the recipient of God's promise is not supposed to be a nation or large group of people. By choosing "descendants" instead of "descendant," the translator must further use the phrase "their enemies" to enforce the plural—and not "his enemies," which appears in the original Hebrew and LXX Greek.

And so this case of translator bias or error results in a flawed notion that the entire nation of Israel was meant to inherit this promise within the covenant. Dispensationalists may point first to the NIV's translation of Genesis, then to Paul's contrary interpretation and call it evidence of God's shifting plans. But Christ didn't replace

---

8. See Hebrew example at https://biblehub.com/text/genesis/22-17.htm. Accessed June 7, 2019.

the nation of Israel as the primary inheritor of God's promise to Abraham—he was the prophesied seed all along. We will examine many more similar passages.

Let's consider another aspect of Genesis 22:18. This verse states that through Abraham's offspring all nations would be blessed. A singular offspring—Christ—fits this description much better than a plural multitude of descendants. The Promised Land was ultimately Christ's inheritance; he succeeded in blessing the nations through his work on the cross.

If God already had plans to fulfill his promises to Abraham through Christ, unilaterally blessing Abraham and his descendants without any conditions, why then did he give the law to Israel? Why did God give Abraham the law of circumcision? Hold on to these questions as we continue on.

Christians universally agree that Christ is the promised Savior of Abraham's seed. The land covenant is the main source of debate. We need to understand how the land covenant relates to the kingdom of heaven.

Unfortunately, the land covenant aspect often gets lumped in with the Mosaic covenant and the nation of Israel. But as we've already noted, the Mosaic covenant is different from the Abrahamic covenant in many fundamental ways.

The new covenant does not replace the Abrahamic covenant—but it follows the same template. Just as Abraham received a promise of an inheritance—a homeland—we inherit in Christ a new heavenly home. Here's the kicker: Abraham's promised inheritance isn't *like* the inheritance we receive in Christ; it's the same inheritance.[9]

*"In him you also, when you heard the word of truth, the gospel of your salvation, and believed in him, were sealed with the promised Holy Spirit, who is the guarantee of our **inheritance** until we acquire possession of it, to the praise of his glory."*

—Ephesians 1:13–14

The inheritance concept appears in numerous salvation passages. What do we inherit? The answer is the unconditional promise of eternal life in the land given to Abraham that Christ came to confirm and fulfill.

Peter states a similar future concept about receiving our inheritance:

*"According to his great mercy, he has caused us to be born again to a living hope through the resurrection of Jesus Christ from the dead, to an **inheritance** that is imperishable, undefiled, and unfading, kept in heaven for you, who by God's power are being guarded through faith for a **salvation** ready to be revealed in the last time."*

—1 Peter 1:3b–5

We will later revisit the concept of inheritance in conjunction with the land and eternal life. The key thing to remember for now is that it links back to a blood oath God swore to Abraham in which he pledged an eternal gift of land. This oath is "irrevocable" and "cannot be annulled," as

---

9. See Romans 15:8 and Hebrews 4:2.

stated in the New Testament. The inheritance is still valid today.

CHAPTER 3.

THE PROMISED LAND AND THE KINGDOM OF HEAVEN

What is the big deal with the land covenant? How does it relate to the new covenant or eternal life in heaven? Is there any lingering spiritual significance to a certain small piece of land in the Middle East? Would building a temple in the heart of Jerusalem actually usher in a new age? Let's go back to the Scriptures and see what we can learn.

As we've noted earlier, Jerusalem was destroyed in AD 70, and the Jewish people were scattered. There are myriad passages about a return to the land, and about as many opinions about what that might signify. Some people think God is finished with the old covenants; if we are under the new covenant now, the old coordinates of the Promised Land shouldn't matter. Others think that there was poetic grace in the modern reestablishment of Israel, but the connection to the land is sentimental. Still others think of a trek to Israel as an opportunity to commune richly with God at a mystical location.

There are several factors to consider here. Are we supposed to focus on physical or spiritual descendants of Abraham?

On an earthly or heavenly homeland? Our answers will help us determine whether the land covenant promises are already fulfilled or pending.

As we read the next few passages, consider the possible combinations of factors. To what do these land covenant prophecies refer?

1. A return to a physical piece of land?
2. A figurative return to a state of mind?
3. The return of physical bloodline descendants of Abraham to a Jewish state in the old borders of Israel?
4. The return of spiritual descendants of Abraham to the physical boundaries of the Promised Land?

"I will strengthen the house of Judah,

and I will save the house of Joseph.

I will bring them back *because I have compassion on them,*
and they shall be as though I had not rejected them,
for I am the Lord their God and I will answer them....

I will whistle for them and gather them in,
for I have redeemed them,
and they shall be as many as they were before.

Though I scattered them among the nations,
yet in far countries they shall remember me,
*and with their children **they shall live and return**."*

—Zechariah 10:6, 8–9

"**In that day** the root of Jesse, who shall stand as a signal for the peoples—of him shall the nations inquire, and his resting place shall be glorious. In that day the Lord will extend his hand yet **a second time to recover the remnant** that remains of his people, from Assyria, from Egypt, from Pathros, from Cush, from Elam, from Shinar, from Hamath, and from the coastlands of the sea.

He will raise a signal for the nations
and **will assemble** the banished of Israel,

and **gather the dispersed** of Judah
from the four corners of the earth."

—Isaiah 11:10–12

"For the children of Israel shall dwell many days without king or prince, without sacrifice or pillar, without ephod or household gods. Afterward the children of Israel shall **return and seek** the Lord their God, and David their king, and they shall come in fear to the Lord and to his goodness **in the latter days**."

—Hosea 3:4–5

Take a closer look at the last of these passages. Notice that "return" may be literal. Hosea states, "return and seek." "Seek and find" would probably be better wording if a spiritual return to God were the intended meaning. Why is "return" mentioned first, then "seek"? In a literal interpretation, it looks as if there is something calling them back as the first step (perhaps the "whistle" call mentioned in Zechariah 10:8); then they are to seek God's goodness after they return. We may be tempted to rule out the idea that these passages refer to Gentiles, that a spiritual return is implied, or that the prophecies have already been fulfilled. But let's continue on for now.

"Return" may indicate a physical action and "seek" a spiritual one. Perhaps this passage has dual meanings. After all, the book of Hosea concerns the northern tribes of Israel who had been dispersed into other lands as divine punishment for their unfaithfulness. They were lost physically and spiritually.

As for Hosea's mention of David, is he talking about David's resurrection in a future kingdom, or Christ, who is the heir of David's throne? David had been dead for hundreds of years when Hosea wrote this passage, so it is most likely one of these options. This detail is not yet clear. We need to look further.

Let's take a stance right now and presume that these passages are pointing toward a physical return to an earthly location, not just a spiritual return in the heart, nor a "return" to a substitutionary heavenly realm. If this literal interpretation is contradicted by other passages, we can start over again and consider other meanings.

If Hosea was indeed writing about a physical return, has such a return happened already, or is it yet to occur? Is God done with the blood descendants of the nation of Israel as many seem to think? Does the Church fulfill aspects of these prophecies by being grafted into the nation of Israel? To answer these questions, we need to look again at Abraham and the promises he received from God.

Abraham did not receive his inheritance of land while he was alive. How do we reconcile this fact to God's unconditional promise that a new homeland would belong to him forever?[1] The only way Abraham could receive this promise physically from God is to be resurrected and enter the Promised Land. A mystical interpretation of the land promise is lacking; the founders of the Church considered it obvious that God had promised physical land.

"Then [Abraham] went out from the land of the Chaldeans and lived in Haran. And after his father died, God removed him from there into this land in which you are now living. **Yet he gave him no inheritance in it, not even a foot's length**, *but promised to give it to him as a possession and to his offspring after him, though he had no child."*

—Acts 7:4–5

Here in Stephen's testimony, we see that although God promised the land to Abraham and his offspring, Abraham never inherited it during his lifetime. Perhaps Abraham received a spiritual inheritance or a heavenly reward, but how can he possibly take physical possession of the land now that he is dead on this earthly realm? How can he receive and enjoy what God promised to give him? Can God somehow yet keep his promise, or did he let himself off the hook by changing terms via the new covenant?

The easiest way to resolve these questions is to assume that the land of God's promise was a metaphor for a spiritual or heavenly inheritance. Abraham will not physically come back from the dead to live in the land, will he? Let's look at a few more passages to try to resolve this question.

---

1. Or "to the ages" according to a literal translation.

"Simeon has related how God first visited the Gentiles, to take from them a people for his name. And with this the words of the prophets agree, *just as it is written,*

'After this I will return,

and I will rebuild the tent of David that has fallen;

I will rebuild its ruins,

and I will restore it,

that the remnant of mankind may seek the Lord,

and all the Gentiles who are called by my name,

says the Lord, who makes these things known from of old.'"

—Acts 15:14–18

This passage draws from Amos 9 (from the LXX). Let's read a portion of Amos 9 not included in the Acts quotation.

"'Behold, the days are coming,' declares the Lord,

'when the plowman shall overtake the reaper

and the treader of grapes him who sows the seed;

the mountains shall drip sweet wine,

and all the hills shall flow with it.

I will restore the fortunes of my people Israel,

and they shall rebuild the ruined cities and inhabit them;

they shall plant vineyards and drink their wine,

and they shall make gardens and eat their fruit.

I will plant them on their land,

and ***they shall never again be uprooted***

out of the land *that I have given them,'*

says the Lord your God.'"

—Amos 9:13–15

Some people believe that God will ensure that the nation of Israel will permanently reside within the Promised Land, reading the above passage literally; others believe that God is no longer personally invested in Israel as a geopolitical entity, and assume the promise here has been superseded—if it was ever meant as a literal promise in the first place. Regardless of our contemporary perspective, it is crystal clear from the Old and New Testaments that Israel was expecting a physical restoration based on the land promise given to Abraham. Israel expected a Messiah who would bring a physical fulfillment of this promise, not a spiritual one. And the early leaders of the Church did not put their hope in a spiritual return of Christ, but rather a literal, physical return.

In Acts 7, Stephen provides a historical summary of the nation of Israel. He describes how Abraham and his offspring (including the singular anointed) were given an earthly land promise that not even Joshua or David would fully realize. For a time, Israel occupied the land as tenants.

But they did not possess it for "eons," "to the ages," or "forever" as God had promised. What happened here? Some scholars say Israel forfeited their inheritance when they failed to keep the terms of the Mosaic covenant. The dispensational view says that once the Mosaic covenant was broken, God started a new age and a new plan of salvation, establishing the Church and discarding all aspects of the old covenants.

As we've already seen in Galatians 3, dispensationalism is contradicted by a careful reading of Scripture—we'll look at other rebutting passages later. Even if Christ's death legally fulfilled a blood sacrifice, this did not annul the promises to Abraham; according to many New Testament passages, the promises remain open. Abraham's inheritance is here explicitly linked to the kingdom of heaven.

Christ simplifies the whole situation for us in the Sermon on the Mount, where he draws from Psalm 37.

"But the meek shall inherit the land and delight themselves in abundant peace."

—Psalm 37:11

"The righteous shall inherit the land and dwell upon it forever."

—Psalm 37:29

"Blessed are the meek, for they shall inherit the earth."

—Matthew 5:5

It would seem that Christ means to assure his audience that his heavenly kingdom is a fulfillment of the Abrahamic covenant: the meek will indeed inherit the earth and dwell upon it forever. But was Christ speaking figuratively or literally?

Let's assume Christ made a literal statement about physical land. For this assumption to be valid, Christ's blessing needs to comply with the other characteristics of the land covenant we know to be true. Here are four points of comparison:

1. Like the Abrahamic covenant, the blessing is everlasting--continuing minimally until the end of an age, or else eternal.
2. Like the Abrahamic covenant, Christ sets no conditions for the meek to receive the blessing.
3. The blessing is extended to any who possess meekness—not merely physical descendants of Abraham.
4. Christ equates the inheritance of the Promised Land to inheritance of the kingdom of heaven on earth.[2]

One immediate problem with the first point is that there is no clear word for "eternity" or "infinity" in the Hebrew language. The root often means "age," so Hebrew speakers would use the phrase "forever and ever" to describe the concept of eternity. Let's look at one passage describing time and purpose within the Abrahamic covenant.

"He provides food for those who fear him;

he remembers his covenant forever.

---

2. Within the New Testament, the concept of land is clarified and developed. We'll take a closer look later in this book.

He has shown his people the power of his works,

*in giving them the **inheritance** of the nations.*
The works of his hands are faithful and just;

all his precepts are trustworthy;

*they are **established forever and ever,***

to be performed with faithfulness and uprightness.

***He sent redemption** to his people;*

*he has commanded **his covenant forever.***
Holy and awesome is his name!"

—Psalm 111:5–9

The most important concept in this passage from Psalm 111 is "redemption." God has a redemptive plan to save his people and honor his promise to Abraham. God is doing the redeeming work tied into the inheritance.

Certain Psalms can sound a lot like allegories, but let's agree with Paul that the covenant to Abraham was not made void and still has an everlasting concept intact. Also, remember that Israel at the time of Psalm 111 was not an everlasting empire (even though they experienced some high points under David and Solomon and received favorable treatment from the Phoenicians regarding trade and travel).

As for the second point regarding the unilateral nature of Christ's blessing, let's look back at the original promises made by God to Abraham. The word "if" is never used—though it does appear in the Mosaic covenant that was broken by Israel. Remember, Paul clearly differentiated between the two main Old Testament covenants and stated the Abrahamic could not be nullified as it was ratified by God himself, whereas the Mosaic law covenants depended on Israel's compliance, which was lacking.

In our third point of comparison, we note that Christ's blessing seems to be available to a larger pool of people than only blood descendants of Abraham. This change is based upon the merger of Hebrews and Gentiles to form a single congregation of God's people. New Testament writers tend to refer to God's people not only as Israel but as the Church, the body of Christ, or the brethren. This shift is demonstrated by the writings of Paul, especially in Romans 9–11. Old Testament language used specific phrases such as "chosen people," but the promises to Abraham also opened up to a broader group of nations that included Gentiles. Romans 15:8–12 offers a summary of Old Testament promises to the Gentiles and states the dual purpose for Christ coming in the first advent: to confirm the promises to the patriarchs, and to bring the Gentiles into these promises.

The book of Acts starts with the broad deployment of the Holy Spirit, which creates a single congregation: the Church of all believers. The Gentiles were officially "grafted" into the nation of Israel, adopted as Abraham's descendants.

According to our fourth point of comparison, Christ meant to equate the Promised Land with the earthly arrival of the kingdom of heaven. There is a strong correlation of land with kingdom language in the New Testament. Old

Testament believers had faith in the land covenant being fulfilled someday (specifically that they would be raised from the dead to live in the land forever). This concept carried over into the New Testament, but the word "kingdom" also shows up frequently in N.T. writings. So let's compare New Testament "land" passages to those translated as "kingdom."

The Promised Land and the Kingdom of Heaven

First, it is very clear that Christ created and inherits the whole earth.[3] We are now called joint heirs or fellow heirs (Romans 8:17) in salvation. All enemies (mainly death and the devil) need to be conquered for co-heirs to claim their inheritance of the land and eternal life.

*"Then comes **the end, when he delivers the kingdom** to God the Father after destroying every rule and every authority and power. For **he must reign until he has put all his enemies under his feet**. The last enemy to be destroyed is death."*

—1 Corinthians 15:24–26[4]

*"And every priest stands daily at his service, offering repeatedly the same sacrifices, which can never take away sins. But when Christ had offered for all time a single sacrifice for sins, he sat down at the right hand of God, **waiting from that time until his enemies should be made a footstool for his feet.**"*

---

3. See Psalm 2:8; Romans 4:13; Colossians 1:16; Hebrews 1:2; 2:10.
4. Note that Christ must reign for a while before ultimately destroying death in the **end**. Then the kingdom is finally delivered.

*has spoken to us by his Son, whom **he appointed the heir of all things**"* (1:2).

The author keeps building upon the inheritance theme in reference to the promises God made in the past to Abraham.

*"Are they not all ministering spirits sent out to serve for the sake of those who are to **inherit salvation?**"*

—Hebrews 1:14

Hebrews 4 speaks of rest—but is this physical rest in the land or spiritual?

*"Therefore, while the **promise** of entering his rest still stands, let us fear lest any of you should seem to have failed to reach it. For **good news came to us just as to them**, but the message they heard did not benefit them, because they were not united by faith with those who listened."*

—Hebrews 4:1–2

In 4:2 we see that the nation of Israel lost the conditional promise (contained in the Mosaic covenant) because they lacked faith. The gospel presented under Moses contained good news as it was not just about the conditions of the law. The Mosaic covenant was tied to the Abrahamic as we shall see further. This is extremely important: the core gospel message has never and will never change. Christ built upon it, but the underlying message is constant.

*"For if Joshua had given them rest, God would not have spoken of **another day later on**. So then, **there remains a Sabbath rest***

for the people of God, for whoever has entered God's rest has also rested from his works as God did from his."

—Hebrews 4:8–10

This reference to Joshua shows that Israel did not receive the total promise of the land when they entered Canaan. According to 4:1, the promised rest still stands. If the land itself couldn't bestow rest, there must be another, more profound rest to come. This rest only became possible after Christ finished his work on the cross and fulfilled the law. A key question is whether we receive this "rest" now or following this earthly life. We'll explore this question in detail later. The short answer is that we can have rest now with a permanent rest to come.

*"For when God made a promise to Abraham, since he had no one greater by whom to swear, he swore by himself, saying, 'Surely I will bless you and multiply you.' And thus Abraham, having patiently waited, obtained the promise. For people swear by something greater than themselves, and in all their disputes an oath is final for confirmation. So when God desired to show more convincingly to the **heirs of the promise the unchangeable character of his purpose, he guaranteed it with an oath**, so that by two unchangeable things, in which it is impossible for God to lie, we who have fled for refuge might have strong encouragement to hold fast to the **hope set before us.**"*

—Hebrews 6:13–18

Does this "heirs of the promise" concept refer to Abraham's children or all nations? The promise to Abraham makes clear that all nations will blessed; salvation is offered to all whether through blood or adoption.

And so the author of Hebrews links God's promise to salvation. Inheritance is associated with both a spiritual salvation and the earthly land of promise. How do we tie this together? First remember that Christ is the Heir of the earth and the recipient of the land promise.[7] When reading these passages, we get the sense that there is something about the promise not yet fulfilled.

"I tell you, many will come from east and west and recline at table with Abraham, Isaac, and Jacob **in the kingdom of heaven***, while the sons of the kingdom will be thrown into the outer darkness. In that place there will be weeping and gnashing of teeth."*

—Matthew 8:11–12

Again, whether we read this as literal or figurative, what is the meaning? This passage describes Gentiles hanging out with the patriarchs in the kingdom while certain blood descendants of the patriarchs are banished. Also, see interesting statements about drinking in the kingdom (Matthew 26:29).

Following the time of the patriarchs, God began to reveal more of his master plan through the prophets. At the pinnacle of the nation of Israel's history, David prophesied future days of glory. And generations later, even as the nation descended into idolatry and ruin, prophets declared the end of sickness and disease, the taming of wild animals, the end of all catastrophes, of everything bad. These prophecies will be described in relation to other future events in Volume II. They seem to describe a perfect version

---

7. See Psalm 2:8; Romans 4:13; Galatians 3:16; Hebrews 1:2; 2:10.

of life on earth, not a bodiless existence in some celestial realm.

These promises and prophecies sound like heaven on earth. Is it truly God's intent to restore all earthly things back to an immaculate Edenic state? We believe God promises resurrection from the dead for the saints, but will he restore creation itself?

Peter said that Jesus is the one *"whom heaven must receive* **until the time for restoring all the things** *about which God spoke by the mouth of his holy prophets long ago"* (Acts 3:21).

And in Romans, Paul offers similar teaching:

"The Spirit himself bears witness with our spirit that we are children of God, and if children, then heirs—heirs of God and **fellow heirs with Christ,** *provided we suffer with him* **in order that we may also be glorified** *with him.*

For I consider that the sufferings of this present time are not worth comparing with the glory that is to be revealed to us. For the creation waits with eager **longing for the revealing** *of the sons of God. For the creation was subjected to futility, not willingly, but because of him who subjected it, in hope that the* **creation itself will be set free from its bondage** *to corruption and obtain the freedom of the glory of the children of God. For we know that the whole creation has been groaning together in the pains of childbirth until now. And* **not only the creation, but we ourselves,** *who have the firstfruits of the Spirit, groan inwardly as we* **wait eagerly for adoption as sons, the redemption of our bodies."*

—Romans 8:16–23

When God delivered the territory of the Promised Land to Joshua and the Israelites, he fulfilled the promise he had made to Moses—but his promise to Abraham was not yet fulfilled. Even with the Canaanites routed, sin remained. No earthly kingdom can subdue a sin-infested land; only a heavenly kingdom can drive out the infection. Without a truly righteous King, Priest, and Judge, the land will remain mired in a sinful state.

The Mosaic law showed Israel how to have a relationship with God and with others by living righteously. They agreed to keep the laws of this covenant, to turn away from sin. But instead they rebelled over and over again.

"See, I [Moses] have taught you statutes and rules, as the Lord my God commanded me, that you should do them in the land that you are entering to take possession of it. Keep them and do them, for that will be your wisdom and your understanding **in the sight of the peoples***, who, when they hear all these statutes, will say, 'Surely this great nation is a wise and understanding people.'* **For what great nation is there that has a god so near to it as the Lord our God is to us, whenever we call upon him?** *And what great nation is there, that has statutes and rules so righteous as all this law that I set before you today?"*

—Deuteronomy 4:4–8

Here we see a very important use of the law. It is the gospel. God's word is his message to his people—and to the rest of the world. Just as Israel was called to shine a light to the neighboring nations, we reveal God to the people around us. So while the law is useful to curb selfish behavior, to please God, and to maintain civil order, we also reflect God's nature through our behavior.

The Israelites as a whole did not reflect God's nature and were not able to possess the land under the conditional old covenant. Only God can cleanse the land and offer true rest. He uses a new, unconditional covenant for redemption; this new covenant is a continuation of the promises to Abraham.

Through the Mosaic covenant, God provided his people with a set of laws based upon grace; by following these instructions, Israel would experience God's blessing and protection in the land. Through the Abrahamic covenant, God swore an oath of unconditional grace; he established laws governing his actions toward Abraham and Abraham's offspring. This interplay of law and grace creates a lot of confusion with Christians, but there is a simple explanation that reflects the light of the gospel.

Both the Abrahamic and Mosaic covenants are connected in that they each contain a land promise. When the conditions of the Mosaic covenant were violated and the contract broken, God decided to make a new covenant. But instead of reasserting the previous conditions, God's new covenant reaches further back and takes on the unilateral format of the Abrahamic covenant. Once again he offers an unconditional promise of eternal life in the Promised Land. And this time he directly extends the offer to the entire world.

CHAPTER 4.

THE NEW COVENANT

What do biblical writers mean when they talk about a generic "covenant" or an "old covenant" in contrast to the new or final covenant?

The very name of the Old Testament creates some confusion. "Testament" and "covenant" have the same meaning. This prompts us to err by lumping the Abrahamic covenant and the Mosaic covenant into one. By extension, we might then assume that the New Testament or new covenant replaces the Abrahamic covenant. But the New Testament writers themselves continued to wait for God to fulfill the promises contained in the Abrahamic covenant, treating these promises as prophecies of end-time events.

So if biblical writers don't have all Old Testament covenants in mind when they use the phrase "the (old) covenant," how can we be sure which covenant is being spoken of? Here are some clues to help us discern their intent:

When you encounter the term "covenant" within a declaration, expect that the writer had the Mosaic covenant in mind if there are mentions of conditions and bidirectional responsibilities. Look for references to a "promise," "inheritance," or other unconditional language when in relation to the Abrahamic covenant.

The term "blood covenant," however, invokes a link from the Mosaic back to the Abrahamic covenant. Exodus 24:7-8 provides us with an example of the sprinkled blood of the covenant that God made with Israel as confirmation of the promises and requirements described in Exodus 19-24. We find God's grace referenced prior to the law being given and covenants made. God stated "my" covenant in Exodus 19:5.[1] Notice he didn't state "our" covenant. Both of these passages seem to connect God giving his promises to Israel as the first step before they can agree to keep any laws or conditions.

Exodus 19-24 is where a large portion of the law was given to Israel so we have these bookend passages referenced above to understand the relationship of law to grace. Grace was stated prior to the law being handed out and confirmed after.

We see a connection between all covenants, whether conditional or unconditional. They trace back to Abraham and the land promise as we see all throughout the books of Moses. Grace and law interrelate.

"I also established my covenant with them to give them the land of Canaan, the land in which they lived as sojourners."

— Exodus 6:4

---

[1]. We see the term "my" covenant in Zechariah 9:11. Christ also used the same term at the Last Supper.

"then I will remember my covenant with Jacob, and I will remember my covenant with Isaac and my covenant with Abraham, and I will remember the land."

— Leviticus 26:42

Law and Grace

Has the "law" that Israel received through the Mosaic covenant been fulfilled by Christ? Did Christ make the law void? Or does the law remain in place, awaiting further action from Christ? Notice what Jesus said regarding his intentions:

"Do not think that I have come to abolish the Law or the Prophets; I have not come to abolish them but to fulfill them."

—Matthew 5:17

Law and grace are critical biblical concepts. We often think of them as contradictory, but the truth is that they work in concert. The law is not obsolete, as the New Testament makes clear, and has not been abandoned; God still upholds the law today. But the law does not smother grace; we do not receive inheritance of the land or eternal life through good works or our adherence to the law. So if the law endures, yet cannot deliver our inheritance, what is its end-time relevance?

The following three points about the law are important to consider:

1. Israel continually broke the covenant they made through Moses.

2. God's law reveals his nature. Since God doesn't change, his law remains intact.
3. Like Israel before us, we fall short of God's perfect standard. Christ alone fulfilled the Father's law.

Just as we need to distinguish between the Abrahamic and Mosaic covenants, we need to separate God's natural law (the general truths that define who God is and how he chooses to relate to his creation) from Mosaic law (the specific behaviors that demonstrated Israel's devotion to God). The laws delivered to Israel at Mount Sinai were based on underlying laws that already existed. By clarifying these separate terms, we can understand why Christ came to earth and identify what he fulfilled. We will then know if any laws await an end-time fulfillment.

"It is because the Lord was not able to bring this people into the land that he swore to give to them that he has killed them in the wilderness."

—Numbers 14:16

According to this passage in Numbers, God had sworn to give the land to those who left Egypt. But except for Caleb, Joshua, and the younger generation, those who left Egypt did not enter the promised land. Did God break his oath? No, only the people who broke the covenant were exempted from the promise. God kept his side of the Mosaic covenant.

Here are other passages that describe Israel in relation to the Mosaic covenant –

*"Then men will say, 'Because **they forsook the covenant** of the*

—2 Kings 17:15

"[T]hey did not obey the voice of the Lord their God, but **transgressed his covenant**, even all that Moses the servant of the Lord commanded; they would neither listen nor do it."

—2 Kings 18:12

"They **did not keep God's covenant**

but refused to walk according to his law....

Their heart was not steadfast toward him;

they **were not faithful to his covenant**."

—Psalm 78:10, 37

"They have turned back to the iniquities of their ancestors who refused to hear my words, and they have gone after other gods to serve them; the house of Israel and the house of Judah **have broken my covenant** which I made with their fathers."

—Jeremiah 11:10

"For thus says the Lord God, 'I will also do with you as you have done, you who have **despised the oath by breaking the covenant.**'"

—Ezekiel 16:59

"[Y]ou brought in foreigners, uncircumcised in heart and uncircumcised in flesh, to be in my sanctuary to profane it, even my house, when you offered my food, the fat and the blood; for **they made my covenant void**—this in addition to all your abominations."

—Ezekiel 44:7

*"Set the trumpet to your lips! One like a vulture is over the house of the Lord, because **they have transgressed my covenant** and rebelled against my law."*

—Hosea 8:1

There are many other verses about how Israel failed to keep the law and therefore broke God's covenant with them. Stephen sums up the situation for us:

*"You stiff-necked people, uncircumcised in heart and ears, **you always resist the Holy Spirit. As your fathers did**, so do you. Which of the prophets did your fathers not persecute? And they killed those who announced beforehand the coming of the Righteous One, whom you have now betrayed and murdered, you who **received the law** as delivered by angels **and did not keep it."***

—Acts 7:51–53

Stephen declares that the Holy Spirit was active in Old Testament times. Pentecost was therefore an outpouring of the same Spirit already at work in the world, not a different dispensational Spirit sent for New Testament believers only.[2]

*"The apostles and the elders were gathered together to consider this matter. And after there had been much debate, Peter stood up and said to them, 'Brothers, you know that in the early days God made a choice among you, that by my mouth the Gentiles should hear the word of the gospel and believe. And God, who knows the heart, bore witness to them, **by giving them the Holy Spirit just***

---

2. Compare to Hebrews 4:2, which we examined in the previous chapter.

as he did to us, and he made no distinction between us and them, having cleansed their hearts by faith. Now, therefore, why are you putting God to the test by placing a yoke on the neck of the disciples that neither our fathers nor we have been able to bear? But **we believe that we will be saved through the grace of the Lord Jesus, just as they will.**"

—Acts 15:6–11

Stephen, Peter, and the writer(s) of Hebrews declare that the New Testament gospel message was given to their Old Testament ancestors and that the same Holy Spirit had been present with them. Then, as now, the path to righteousness was to follow Abraham's example of faith.[3] We cannot achieve right standing with God through the law. Our key priority is to believe in God's promises of grace, to receive the gift of faith. Yes, faith is a gift from God, not simply a belief. We will discuss this in more detail in chapters 8 and 10.

Nowhere in Scripture is the Abrahamic land covenant shown to be broken. This promise of grace remains. But the terms of the Mosaic covenant have been broken again and again as we have just seen. This poses a problem. Though we cannot keep the law, God cannot discard it. He cannot offer us a lawless gospel. Righteous living does not save us—only grace can do that—but law still features in God's new covenant with his people.

Paul offers us some inspired words about law and grace in relation to Jews and Gentiles. He demonstrates how the same gospel is given to all people.

---

3. See Romans 4:16.

"But now the righteousness of God has been manifested apart from the law, although the Law and the Prophets bear witness to it—the righteousness of God through faith in Jesus Christ for all who believe. For there is no distinction: for all have sinned and fall short of the glory of God, and are justified by his grace as a gift, through the redemption that is in Christ Jesus, whom God put forward as a propitiation by his blood, to be received by faith. This was to show God's righteousness, because in his divine forbearance he had passed over former sins. It was to show his righteousness at the present time, so that he might be just and the justifier of the one who has faith in Jesus.

"Then what becomes of our boasting? It is excluded. By what kind of law? By a law of works? No, but by **the law of faith**. For we hold that one is justified by faith apart from works of the law. Or is God the God of Jews only? Is he not the God of Gentiles also? Yes, of Gentiles also, since God is one—who **will justify the circumcised by faith and the uncircumcised through faith**. Do we then overthrow the law by this faith? By no means! On the contrary, **we uphold the law**."

—Romans 3:21–31

"Is the law then contrary to the promises of God? Certainly not! For if a law had been given that could give life, then righteousness would indeed be by the law....

"There is neither Jew nor Greek, there is neither slave nor free, there is no male and female, for you are all one in Christ Jesus. And if you are Christ's, then you are Abraham's offspring, heirs according to promise."

—Galatians 3:21, 28–29

The phrase "heirs according to promise" means that salvation is tied to God's oath to Abraham. God offers us grace even before we learn his standards of law or justice. (Note that God's law still exists despite our ignorance. Though he may reveal his grace without initially revealing his law as in his interactions with Abraham, his grace and law are intertwined.) Through grace we receive salvation—both the spiritual sense of being brought into God's righteousness and the physical promise of an inheritance: an eternal resurrected life in the Promised Land. God's promises to Abraham are the basis of the salvation he makes available to Abraham's physical and spiritual descendants—all of whom can only receive that gift through faith.

These passages from Peter and Paul in Acts 15, Romans 3, and Galatians 3 all explain that there is only one way to be saved: by grace, through faith. This same message echoes throughout the Old Testament. Jews and Greeks, Hebrews and Gentiles, all are heirs to the promise of grace by faith, as described more fully in Romans 9–11.[4]

The law without faith is futile, but that doesn't mean the law is disposable. God cannot offer us salvation apart from the law.

What about the unconditional nature of grace? If the fulfillment of the promise of eternal life depends upon perfect righteousness, why didn't God give the law to Abraham? Because God understood that Abraham's righteousness would never be sufficient. It wasn't up to Abraham to satisfy the requirements of the law. That would

---

4. Also see Romans 8:16–17.

fall to Christ; he kept God's law because we could not. Now, by grace, we are brought into Christ's perfect righteousness ourselves. So, in essence, the law does save us—but we must solely rely upon grace and Christ's righteousness on our behalf.[5]

Christ shares with us in the inheritance granted to him as the Descendant of Abraham. He is the Grantor and Grantee (similarly, Christ is David's Lord and Son as shown in Luke 20:41-44). Abraham demonstrated belief that God, by grace, would deliver on his promises and give Abraham an eternal land inheritance. The same faith that Abraham exemplified is given to us as well; in faith, we believe that Abraham's Descendant blessed the earth according to the promise and invites us to live with him forever as co-heirs of the earth.

The inheritance theme is a common thread coursing throughout Scripture:

- Genesis 15:7; 17:5–8
- 1 Chronicles 29:14–18
- Psalm 2:8; 37:29; 105:6–11;115:16
- Isaiah 45:18
- Ezekiel 47:13–23; 48:29
- Matthew 5:5; 19:27–29
- Romans 4:13–18; 8:16–17; 15:8–9
- Galatians 3:13–29
- Ephesians 2:11–22; 3:6

5. See Romans 8:3–4.

- Colossians 1:12–16
- Hebrews 1:2

These passages provide a foundational understanding of the significance of the first and second advents of Christ.

We know God created the earth for this purpose:[6] not merely to keep it for himself in the person of Christ, but to share in it with us and dwell with us. This is the reason for creation. God shares the inheritance due his Son, making us co-heirs (Romans 8:16–17); we will be counted as Abraham's offspring (Galatians 3:29) as long as we share Abraham's faith (mentioned in Romans 4:16).

This new testament builds upon the blood covenant of Genesis 15; the inheritance we receive does not change or replace the Abrahamic promises.

The inheritance plan brings "all Israel" (all Old and New Testament saints) back to an Edenic world. Throughout Scripture, this process of redemption is described using terms like restoration, renewal, and regeneration.[7] Land and saints alike will be transformed. Descriptions of this future Paradise do not include the devil or death; these are counted among the enemies that will be defeated forever.

"All Israel" is to share in the inheritance that God promised to Abraham long ago; this category includes any Gentiles who through the gift of faith accept this timeless gospel of salvation. Christ fulfilled the law once and for all on

---

6. See Isaiah 45:18; Colossians 1:16; Hebrews 2:10.
7. See Romans 8:16–25.

the cross, while God's offer of grace has remained since Genesis 3:15.

Here are some of the passages that speak of Gentiles becoming adopted into Israel:

- John 4:20–22; 10:16
- Romans 9:4–8, 24–26; 10:8–13, 17-20; 11:11–32; 15:8–12
- Galatians 3
- Ephesians 2:11–22; 3:6

"...so that in Christ Jesus **the blessing of Abraham** *might come to the Gentiles, so that we might receive the promised Spirit through faith."*

—Galatians 3:14

"This means that it is not the children of the flesh who are the children of God, but the **children of the promise are counted as offspring***."*

—Romans 9:8

All people who receive faith by grace in "the blessing of Abraham" are united in one gospel. The blessing goes back to the promise that all nations will be blessed by the Descendant of Abraham.

A very important supporting passage is found in Romans 15. Paul explains a dual purpose of Christ's first coming: he came to confirm God's promises to Abraham (and the other patriarchs) and to invite the Gentiles to respond to this message of grace. The promises to Abraham formed the gospel that we still have today.

*"For I tell you that Christ became a servant to the circumcised to show God's truthfulness, in order to **confirm the promises** given to the patriarchs, **and** in order **that the Gentiles might glorify God** for his mercy."*

—Romans 15:8–9a

Paul writes extensively about this in Romans 9-11. It is very clear that the Church has become the umbrella of "all Israel," as salvation is based on the promise that the Savior would come through Abraham's seed to bless all nations.[8]

All Israel, Old and New Testament saints alike, will be saved under the same gospel message.

"Lest you be wise in your own sight, I do not want you to be unaware of this mystery, brothers: a partial hardening has come upon Israel, until the fullness of the Gentiles has come in. And in this way all Israel will be saved, as it is written,

'The Deliverer will come from Zion,

he will banish ungodliness from Jacob';

'and this will be my covenant with them,

when I take away their sins.'"

—Romans 11:25–27

---

8. "All Israel" includes Jews and the Gentile believers, including those from the "lost" northern tribes.

Here Paul addresses the mystery that "all Israel will be saved." He includes all 12 tribes and the Gentiles, whom he describes as the wild branches grafted into the natural branch—all will receive the promise.[9] Only a remnant of Israel's blood descendants will be saved according to Romans 9:27, so Paul's statement here regarding "all Israel" does not refer to all Jewish individuals, but rather Israel's wider spiritual family. "All" means all types of people on earth.

Christ alluded to an adoptive "all Israel" in John 10:16, building off of a common Old Testament metaphor comparing Israel to sheep. *"And I have other sheep that are not of this fold. I must bring them also, and they will listen to my voice. So there will be one flock, one shepherd."* Along with the Jewish people of the southern kingdom, Christ includes Gentiles and people from the lost northern tribes; together they comprise "all" Israel.

---

9. See Ephesians 3:1–10.

CHAPTER 5.

CHRIST'S INHERITANCE

We must remember that the conditional covenant God made with Moses and the nation of Israel did not supersede or nullify the Abrahamic promise.[1] So while Christ fulfilled the terms of the law to redeem us, he wasn't necessarily focused on the Mosaic law in particular, but on the promise to Abraham that had yet to be fulfilled along with the Father's natural law. To fulfill the promise to Abraham, Christ declared his right to receive the inheritance. This explains the preponderance of joint-heir or co-heir language.[2]

Christ deserves the inheritance through the law; as the rightful heir, he nullifies any claims of the accuser (Satan). And so Christ, Abraham's Seed, is set to receive the inheritance promised to Abraham.

As the Heir mentioned in the unconditional Abrahamic promise, Christ fulfills the law of the Father, then inherits all the earth. Although the earth belongs to God, Christ's intervention demonstrates that God did not simply create

---

1. See Galatians 3 and Romans 11:28–29.
2. See Romans 8:16–17.

the earth for himself, but he desired to dwell with us and share in humanity's conditions.[3]

In the end-times, Christ will return to the earth to receive the land portion promised to Abraham as his inheritance (called the heavenly country or kingdom of heaven)—thus literally fulfilling the promise. And then Christ in turn will share his inheritance with his co-heirs.

Abraham received God's promise that he, Abraham, would inherit land in which to dwell forever. The only way God can literally keep this promise is to resurrect Abraham and allow him to enter the earthly land. The land promise would not amount to much if it was only meant to cover a few generations of descendants from Joshua to the diaspora. Paul clarifies this further:

"For the promise to Abraham and his **offspring** that **he** would be **heir of the world** did not come through the law but through the righteousness of faith. For if it is the **adherents** of the law who are to be the heirs, faith is null and the promise is void. For the law brings wrath, but where there is no law there is no transgression.

"That is why it depends on faith, in order that **the promise may rest on grace and be guaranteed to all his offspring**—not only to the **adherent** of the law but also **to the one who shares the faith of Abraham**, who is the father of us all, as it is written, 'I have made you the father of many nations'—in the presence of the God in whom he believed, **who gives life to the dead** and calls into existence the things that do not exist. In hope he believed against hope, that he should become the father of many nations, as he had been told, 'So shall your offspring be.'"

---

3. See Hebrews 2:10–18; 4:15; 5:7–9.

—Romans 4:13–18

Again, Paul uses the singular when he could have used a different plural noun for "offspring" being the heir of the world. There is only one "he" in Romans 4:13, so it either must be Abraham or Christ that inherits the world according to the text. Hebrews 1:2, 2:10, and Colossians 1:16 state that Christ has the claim to the earth, so even if it is not crystal clear in Romans, "he" must mean Christ in light of all Scripture. Abraham is promised a portion of the earth, so he is a co-inheritor, as we are.

Another point Paul makes is that the plural offspring group of "adherents" do not inherit the earth based upon the Mosaic law; co-heirs receive their promise as a gift, not by their works.

One "Adherent" did, in fact, keep the law, but that is not the main point of this passage. We don't share with Christ in keeping the law—we share in Abraham's faith, becoming co-heirs by grace. Also, we need to keep in mind that Abraham believed in the resurrection of the dead.[4] He believed that God could raise his son Isaac from the dead (Genesis 22) and that he himself would be raised from the dead someday to enter the Promised Land (Hebrews 11:10–16).

We are declared righteous not through our own works but through Christ's perfection under the law:

"Therefore, as one trespass led to condemnation for all men, so one act of righteousness leads to justification and life for all men. For

---

4. See Hebrews 11:19.

as by the one man's disobedience the many were made sinners, so by the one man's obedience the many will be made righteous."

—Romans 5:18–19

We are saved by faith under the promise, which is grace, but we are made righteous under the law. Read the entirety of Romans 4–5 for a great summary of what we have looked at so far.

The interplay between law and grace can be difficult to understand because of how the Mosaic covenant seems to overlap with the land promise of the Abrahamic covenant. But we can distinguish them accordingly:

- The land portion of the Mosaic covenant to Israel was conditional.
- The Abrahamic land promise always remained unconditional.
- Israel failed to obtain the fulfillment of the land promise.
- Christ fulfilled the conditions of the law that predates Mosaic law.
- Christ is the main Heir of the land promise to Abraham.
- **Christ received both claims: the promise to the land and fulfillment of the law to obtain the land.**
- Christ is the fulfillment of Abraham's promised blessing to all nations.[5]

---

5. This promise to bless all nations is further developed in Judah's blessing and the Davidic covenant.

- Abraham obtained faith by believing in God's promises and obeying God's instructions. All nations are blessed because of Abraham's great faith—but this faith was a gift, not something he mustered up within himself through pure determination. And we can follow his example to obtain faith today.

- We are co-heirs with Christ in the redemption of the earth and the resurrection of our bodies (Romans 8:16–23); co-heirs with Christ, we receive an inheritance according to the promises God made to Abraham (Galatians 3:29).

The New Covenant

The new covenant is related to the Abrahamic covenant and supersedes the Mosaic covenant. There are many prophecies in the Old Testament that speak to a new covenant that God pledged to make with his people.

*"'And a Redeemer will come to Zion, to those in Jacob who turn from transgression,' declares the Lord. 'And as for me, **this is my covenant** with them,' says the Lord: 'My Spirit that is upon you, and my words that I have put in your mouth, shall not depart out of your mouth, or out of the mouth of your offspring, or out of the mouth of your children's offspring,' says the Lord, 'from this time forth and forevermore.'"*

—Isaiah 59:20–21

This prophesies how Christ would bring the new covenant to redeem Israel.

Another passage shows that God's new covenant would

again include his law—but this time his people would be fully equipped to walk in righteousness.

*"And **I will give you a new heart**, and **a new spirit I will put within you**. And I will remove the heart of stone from your flesh and give you a heart of flesh. And **I will put my Spirit within you, and cause you** to walk in my statutes and be careful **to obey my rules."***

—Ezekiel 36:26–27

Jeremiah 31:31–40 is often hailed as the official prophecy for the new covenant, so let's look. It offers a clear reference to the enslavement in Egypt and the covenant that followed, so we can be sure that God is talking about the Mosaic covenant, not the Abrahamic promises.

*"Behold, the days are coming, declares the Lord, when **I will make a new covenant** with the house of Israel and the house of Judah, **not like the covenant that I made with their fathers** on the day when I took them by the hand to bring them out of the land of Egypt, **my covenant that they broke**, though I was their husband, declares the Lord. For this is the covenant that I will make with the house of Israel after those days, declares the Lord: **I will put my law within them**, and **I will write it on their hearts**. And I will be their God, and they shall be my people."*

—Jeremiah 31:31–33

As can be imagined, Christians disagree over how to interpret this passage. Has God already fulfilled this prophecy by grafting the Church into the nation of Israel, or is there a literal fulfillment for actual blood descendants yet to come? Thankfully, this is not the only passage to consider.

Let's now look at Hebrews 8. This is where we find a direct quote of Jeremiah 31. Here are several key verses about what parts of the Jeremiah 31 prophecy have been fulfilled or not, canceled or kept open:

*"They serve a copy and shadow of the heavenly things. For when Moses was about to erect the tent, he was instructed by God, saying, 'See that you make everything according to the pattern that was shown you on the mountain.' But as it is, **Christ has obtained a ministry** that is as much **more excellent than the old** as the covenant **he mediates** is better, since it is enacted on **better promises**. For if that first covenant had been faultless, there would have been no occasion to look for a second....*

"In speaking of a new covenant, he makes the first one obsolete. And what is becoming obsolete and growing old is ready to vanish away."

—Hebrews 8:5–7, 13

The "first" covenant indicated here must be the Mosaic covenant because the writer of Hebrews uses different words for the Abrahamic covenant: the "promise" or the "inheritance." Paul also differentiated between the two in this way in Galatians 3. Combining the two into a single covenant is our own modern mistake.

The author of Hebrews says the new covenant described in Jeremiah 31 is currently at work. Christ is "mediating" the new covenant in the present tense (Hebrews 8:8–12).

God only has one plan for redemption, one gospel, and one Spirit. He does not have a separate plan for the salvation and spiritual regathering of scattered Israel. Jeremiah prophesied of the day when the people of Israel would return to God after receiving his Spirit in their hearts—a salvation method that is identical to how Gentiles receive the gift of the Holy Spirit and turn to God. Same God; same salvation plan; same work of the Holy Spirit to save us all.

*"Therefore [Christ] is the **mediator of a new covenant**, so that those who are called may receive **the promised eternal inheritance**, since a death has occurred that redeems them from the transgressions committed under the first covenant."*

—Hebrews 9:15

This verse ties the new covenant to the Abrahamic land promise and eternal life; Hebrews 9:15 is of utmost importance in terms of understanding salvation. Christ himself instituted the new covenant and is the sole mediator for redemption. Christ announced the new covenant during the Lord's Supper in the upper room.

*"For I received from the Lord what I also delivered to you, that the Lord Jesus on the night when he was betrayed took bread, and when he had given thanks, he broke it, and said, 'This is my body, which is for you. Do this in remembrance of me.' In the same way also he took the cup, after supper, saying, 'This cup is the new covenant in my blood. Do this, as often as you drink it, in remembrance of me' For as often as you eat this bread and drink the cup, you proclaim the Lord's death **until he comes**.*

Whoever, therefore, eats the bread or drinks the cup of the Lord in an unworthy manner will be guilty concerning the body and blood of the Lord. Let a person examine himself, then, and so eat of the bread and drink of the cup."

—1 Corinthians 11:23–28

This passage makes clear that the new covenant will continue until Christ returns to the earth.[6]

By partaking in the Lord's Supper, we remind each other that Christ is coming back again to complete all that has been promised and to grant us our share in the inheritance, which includes land and eternal life. The new covenant promise of unity in Christ was fulfilled at Pentecost, where the Holy Spirit was poured out to all, Hebrews and Gentiles alike; everyone is grafted into the same promised inheritance.[7]

According to Ezekiel 36:16–23, God withdrew the blessings of the Mosaic covenant from Israel because of their sin. God's reputation needed to be upheld. Therefore, a new covenant was needed, as described in Ezekiel 37.

"Then he said to me, 'Prophesy to the breath; prophesy, son of man, and say to the breath, Thus says the Lord God: Come from the four winds, O breath, and **breathe on these slain, that they may live**.*' So I prophesied as he commanded me, and the breath came into them, and* **they lived and stood on their feet**, *an exceedingly great army.*

"Then he said to me, Son of man, these bones are the whole house of Israel. Behold, they say, 'Our bones are dried up, and our hope is lost; we are indeed cut off.' Therefore prophesy, and say to them,

---

6. Also see Matthew 26:29, Mark 14:25, and Luke 22:18.
7. See Romans 11:11–24.

*Thus says the Lord God: Behold, **I will open your graves and raise you from your graves**, O my people. And **I will bring you into the land of Israel**. And you shall know that I am the Lord, when I open your graves, and raise you from your graves, O my people. And **I will put my Spirit within you**, and you shall live, and I will place you in your own land. Then you shall know that I am the Lord; I have spoken, and I will do it, declares the Lord....*

*"Then say to them, Thus says the Lord God: Behold, I will take the people of Israel from the nations among which they have gone, and will **gather them from all around**, and bring them to their own land. And I will make them one nation in the land, on the mountains of Israel. And one king shall be king over them all, and they shall be no longer two nations, and no longer divided into two kingdoms. They shall not defile themselves anymore with their idols and their detestable things, or with any of their transgressions. But **I will save them** from all the backslidings in which they have sinned, and **will cleanse them**; and they shall be my people, and I will be their God.*

*"My servant David shall be king over them, and they shall all have one shepherd. They shall walk in my rules and be careful to obey my statutes. **They shall dwell in the land** that I gave to my servant Jacob, where your fathers lived. They and their children and their children's children **shall dwell there forever**, and David my servant shall be their prince forever. I will make a covenant of peace with them. It shall be **an everlasting covenant** with them. And I will set them in their land and multiply them, and will set my sanctuary in their midst forevermore. **My dwelling place shall be with them**, and I will be their God, and they shall be my people. Then the nations will know that I am the Lord who sanctifies Israel, **when my sanctuary is in their midst forevermore**."*

—Ezekiel 37:9–14, 21–28

If we don't believe the heavenly kingdom will arrive physically on earth in the future, then this passage will not make much sense. We are left with figurative interpretations that speak to a spiritual return, or Israel's rebirth as a geopolitical nation in 1948—or we fall into the mystic void altogether.

It is difficult to take this passage literally, with its description of physical resurrection; however, the book of Revelation sheds a lot of light on Ezekiel. We can read, for example, how God will dwell with his people (Revelation 21–22). Do Revelation and Ezekiel point to a heaven where God and his people will be together forever in another realm? Or do these books state that God will come to earth to reside with his people, thereby literally fulfilling all promises? Why did Christ inherit the earth? Certainly not to blow it up and shuttle us off to a different realm.[8] (Later we'll explore this topic further.)

The Outpouring of the Spirit

Previously, we observed the bridge prophecy that links Joel 2:28 to Acts 2:17: *"And in the last days it shall be, God declares, that **I will pour out my Spirit on all flesh.**"* How does the new covenant separate national Israel from spiritual Israel? There is no distinction for salvation purposes. All people are saved the same way.

The Spirit's key role is to enable eternal life, which is a different act than granting physical life. We must be filled

---

8. See Isaiah 45:18.

with the Spirit to be born again by faith, as is mentioned all throughout Scripture. In future chapters, which deal with the resurrection of the righteous, we will discuss the Spirit's role in more detail.

In the Old Testament, we meet the Spirit as he dwells in the Holy of Holies, a single, fixed location. As the concept of the Holy Spirit expands in Scripture, the Spirit is poured out on all flesh and comes to dwell in human temples. Through the new covenant, God's glory spreads throughout the earth to achieve redemption for all peoples at their location. Christ fulfilled the law through atonement at the one-time event of the cross; from that point onward, the single location of a tabernacle or temple was not needed for mediation between God and his people. Christ is now the mediator throughout all the earth.

The new covenant confirms God's promise to Abraham that all people throughout the world who share in the same faith will receive the same gift: bodily resurrection into the land inheritance. The gift of salvation and entrance into the Promised Land of heaven is offered freely to physical descendants of Abraham; they do not need to keep the Mosaic law as the law has been fulfilled for all people.

The new covenant also ties in the spiritual descendants of Abraham under the same gift of salvation. Whether Jeremiah 31 has been fulfilled through the inclusion of Gentiles or points to a future fulfillment for the Jewish people, the same salvation is available to all people. The new covenant was confirmed by Christ, who fulfilled the law. Christ came to fulfill the law (Matthew 5:17) and confirm God's promises (Romans 15:8).

People debate whether our salvation inheritance entails physical or spiritual resurrection. But it is clear that Israel is saved under the new covenant, not through the Mosaic covenant. God divorced Israel (Jeremiah 3:6–18), but Revelation tells us of a new marriage contract that will be celebrated in the future.

We cannot save ourselves by keeping the law; only God's gift of faith will save us by adopting us into his original promise to Abraham. This promise has been carried over and tied into the new covenant.[9]

Christ came to fulfill God's promises to the patriarchs. God does not ever abandon Abraham's physical descendants.[10]

"Who is a God like you, pardoning iniquity

and passing over transgression

*for **the remnant of his inheritance?***

He does not retain his anger forever,

because he delights in steadfast love.

He will again have compassion on us;

he will tread our iniquities underfoot.

You will cast all our sins

into the depths of the sea.

---

9. See Hebrews 9:15.
10. Volume II will explore this point in greater detail.

You will show faithfulness to Jacob

and steadfast love to Abraham,

as you have sworn to our fathers

from the days of old."

—Micah 7:18–20

CHAPTER 6.

THE SECOND COMING OF CHRIST

In many algebra textbooks, the solutions appear in the back of the book. But students quickly discover that copying these answers down will not help them understand how to solve algebraic equations. What a student must do is apply what he has learned to a problem, then see if his solution lines up with the answer sheet. If not, he'll know to reexamine his methodology.

Likewise, we won't be able to make much sense of end-time prophecies by flipping straight to the apocalyptic verses. To understand what the time of tribulation or "time of Jacob's trouble" (Jeremiah 30:7) entails, we first need to establish a framework to guide our interpretive efforts. Faced with many confusing variables, we need to identify the constant in the equation, then define the variable according to what is known. In other words, all our end-time interpretations and assumptions should be measured against the context of what God has been accomplishing throughout human history.

So we need to start at the beginning, learning the basics of how God revealed himself to his people and established a relationship with them. Then we need to look forward, learning what we can about the inheritance God has promised through his covenants, old and new.

Having done this foundational work in the previous chapters, we're ready to look at some specific end-time prophecies. But some end-time passages are clearer than others, so let's start with these and improve our interpretive framework in preparation for the more complex passages to come.

The End of the Age

"Concerning the coming of our Lord Jesus Christ and our being gathered to him, we ask you, brothers, not to become easily unsettled or alarmed by some prophecy, report or letter supposed to have come from us, saying that the day of the Lord has already come."

—2 Thessalonians 2:1–2

A similar concept is found in 2 Timothy 2:18, stating the fact that the resurrection has not yet occurred. Paul differentiates physical resurrection from spiritual "raising" in many passages.

Why did people in Paul's day wonder if the day of the Lord had already happened? Surely Christ's return would not be easy to miss. The earliest Church fathers would have recorded a physical reappearance of Christ, no matter how brief. Yet the rumors spread. Then, in AD 70, the Temple was destroyed and the Jewish people were scattered. This felt to many early Christians like the prophesied end of the age. But though the destruction of the Temple was a seismic event Christ himself predicted, in no specific prophecy does the destruction of the Temple portend the physical return of Christ. As traumatic as the event was to the Jewish people, it did not mark the end of human history or the arrival of God's final judgment for all the earth. Nor did it fundamentally change what God was already doing through his Spirit in the world.

A few hundred years later, Eusebius and Augustine seized upon the idea that the Temple destruction had marked some kind of profound spiritual turning point, treating it as a climactic age ending event in human history. The historian Josephus adopted a similar perspective, which is understandable given his Jewish-Roman heritage. And even today, many preterists and amillennialists point to Christ's prophecy in Matthew 24:1–2 as evidence that the new covenant caused the Church to usurp Israel's place. According to this view, the destruction of the Temple was God's judgment marking the end of the Old Testament age and ushering in the Church age through the spiritual return of Christ.

But as we've seen, Christ will physically come back to earth. How have so many believers across history overlooked this clear biblical teaching?

Matthew 24 and the book of Revelation are difficult to understand at first. They are more easily placed into timing sequences based upon other passages. We need to study the whole Bible—not just passages like Matthew 24 in isolation. And while ancient voices like Eusebius and Augustine can provide us with good insights, we should critically examine each teaching before accepting it as truth. Their replacement theology as described above does not hold up to biblical vetting.

The second coming of Christ is sure to be the most important historical event since creation itself; according to prophecy, upon Christ's return he will bring about the restoration of all things.[1] Christ enabled redemption when he came to earth the first time, but this second advent will mark the climax of redemption. We can see that the theme of restoration is central to the Jewish mindset in Luke 2:38; later, following Christ's resurrection, his apostles are certain the final restoration is at hand:

"So when they had come together, they asked him, 'Lord, will you at this time restore the kingdom to Israel?'"

—Acts 1:6

Christ was about to ascend to heaven, but the apostles were fixated on their earthly realm. They didn't question Christ about heaven, didn't understand that He had to return to the Father, and didn't understand how heaven would come to earth to bring about the restoration they longed for.

If the apostles believed a spiritual or heavenly kingdom reign was the final fulfillment of the Old Testament covenants, they would have been jumping up and down in the Acts 1 account. But the apostles never demonstrate such sentiment at any point in the New Testament. They knew an everlasting kingdom was to be physically established on the earth. Going to heaven in a different realm was not the salvation they hoped for. It is very important that we

---

1. See Acts 3:21.

understand this mindset that linked the land promise to the kingdom to come.

The Big Three

The apostles' focus, without question, is on the "Big Three" end-time events. Listed below, these should serve as guideposts to help us chart out the sequence of events in Matthew 24 and Revelation.[2]

1. **Second Advent**: the physical return of Christ to earth (Acts 1:9–11; Hebrews 9:28)

2. **Resurrection**: a bodily resurrection like Christ's (Philippians 3:21) for the saints (Daniel 12:1-3)

3. **Judgment:** God's assessment of our faith, to take place following the second advent (Matthew 16:27; John 5:24–29; 1 Corinthians 4:5)

First Christ will come again to earth, then the just will receive bodily resurrection, and finally God will judge each resurrected person. (These judgments are evaluative, for rewards given or taken away).

All other events before and after the second coming need to be viewed in light of the return of Christ. Christ's return is the primary focus as it is the inciting incident for our resurrection and God's judgment. Together, these Big Three end-time events inform our perspective on all other prophesied occurrences. As we seek to determine the location, timing, and significance of each end-time event,

---

[2]. Remember that we must start with clear passages to help us interpret the unclear. Some of the passages below include descriptions of multiple related concurrent events. These cluster passages are particularly illuminating.

the Big Three gives us our moorings. We will see how the return, resurrection, and judgment relate to the new covenant and land promise later.

Christ is coming back to earth again. This will be a physical return, not a spiritual return. This has not happened yet. Acts 1:11 shows that his next coming will mirror his ascension into heaven (where he resides in a risen body today).

"And if I go and prepare a place for you, I will come again and will take [receive] you to myself, that where I am you may be also."

—John 14:3

Christ stated he is returning to earth so we can be together with him. God and his people dwelling together is a common theme throughout Scripture. This dwelling will occur when the earthly and heavenly realms meet (Ephesians 1:10), culminating at the end of time (Revelation 21:3–6).

"Then will appear in heaven the sign of the Son of Man, and then all the tribes of the earth will mourn, and they will see the Son of Man coming on the clouds of heaven with power and great glory. And he will send out his angels with a loud trumpet call, and they will gather his elect from the four winds, from one end of heaven to the other."

—Matthew 24:30–31

Peter, James, and John saw a glimpse of this "great glory" described in Matthew 24:30 previously in the vision at the

Transfiguration event.[3] They saw white clothing, brightness, and a radiant face. Such elements also feature in the visions of the Old Testament prophets (including Daniel 10:2–14) and in John's apocalyptic visions (Revelation 1:12–16).

Many other passages describe the physical return of Christ. He will come with angels, the righteous dead will be raised, and there will be a gathering of all the saints in one place so we can finally dwell with him forever—these same themes are repeated over and over.

Many passages correlate to Matthew 24:30–31 and its description of angels, a trumpet, a voice, and clouds at the second coming/resurrection event. These include the following:

- Matthew 13:24–43; 16:27
- Mark 8:38
- Luke 21:27
- John 5:28
- 1 Corinthians 15:52
- Philippians 3:14
- 2 Thessalonians 1:7
- Jude 1:14–15
- Revelation 1:7.

These passages describe God's people meeting Christ in the air—but what happens next? Will we all head off to heaven

---

3. See Matthew 17:1-9.

or back to a newly restored earth? This is where many people get confused.

Gathered or Taken?

There is a very interesting passage in 1 Thessalonians that includes the same familiar elements of the second advent (trumpet, angels, etc.). As you read, see whether a figurative or literal interpretation makes more sense. Even if some of the language is figurative, is Paul trying to describe physical aspects of Christ's return?

*"For **since we believe that Jesus died and rose again**, even so, through Jesus, God will bring with him those who have fallen asleep. For this we declare to you by a word from the Lord, that we who are alive, who are left until the coming of the Lord, will not precede those who have fallen asleep. For the Lord himself will descend from heaven with a cry of command, with the voice of an archangel, and with the sound of the trumpet of God. And the dead in Christ will rise first. Then we who are alive, who are left, will be **caught up** together with them in the clouds **to meet** the Lord in the air, and so we will always be with the Lord."*

—1 Thessalonians 4:14–17

Paul does not specify whether we will go to some celestial realm or back to earth to be with Christ in this passage, but there are some other important details here that we can later compare with other passages.

First, notice how Paul immediately sets the tone by stating a sincere belief. Based on his firm understanding that Christ physically rose from the dead, he also has confidence that all believers who fell asleep (died) will likewise be physically raised.[4]

Also notice the words "to meet" in verse 17. The root word for "to meet" is found three times in the New Testament. Here are its two other appearances:

*"But at midnight there was a cry, 'Here is the bridegroom! Come out **to meet** him.'"*

—Matthew 25:6

*"And the brothers there, when they heard about us, came as far as the Forum of Appius and Three Taverns **to meet** us. On seeing them, Paul thanked God and took courage."*

—Acts 28:15

The Greek root translated "to meet" fits our normal English usage of the phrase. To meet someone at the door is generally to welcome them into a building. To meet someone for dinner may involve going to a restaurant that is halfway between the parties involved.

So is Christ coming to meet us halfway on our trip from earth to heaven? Or are the living believers rising to meet Christ on his way from heaven to earth? In the Matthew and Acts "meeting" passages, there is a return to the starting point after the meeting. And in the 1 Thessalonians passage, the point of reference is Paul's position, not Christ's position. Christ will come to raise and transform saints on earth. Why would Christ bring the spirits of dead saints

---

4. Paul speaks of the resurrection of the dead more than anyone else, as we shall see in chapter 7.

to earth if they are all going back to heaven? We will get more clues later as to why we would meet Christ in the air and not on the ground, and why God would not simply transport us to some heavenly realm.

Another root word to focus on in the 1 Thessalonians 4 passage is translated "caught up." This is the rapture event. There are many disagreements about where precisely the rapture will fall in relation to the tribulation, but we do not need to worry about timing at this point. For now we simply want to understand the root word itself. "Caught up" means to seize, catch, snatch, or grab on to.

*"And have mercy on those who doubt; save others by **snatching** them out of the fire; to others show mercy with fear, hating even the garment stained by the flesh."*

—Jude 22–23

This passage in Jude is a metaphor using the same root word that is translated "caught up" in 1 Thessalonians 4. Jude used the Greek word in figurative language, instructing believers to assist in salvation by keeping someone from damnation. (Again, let's overlook the various physical and spiritual interpretations of hell for now).

Jude used "caught up" figuratively, while Paul used the same root word in a literal fashion. However, the basic concept is the same: Christ and believers can each perform works of salvation by "snatching." Christ literally saves people from death while believers can help save people from death as well (likely by spreading the gospel, given Jude's New Testament context). The wicked are destroyed, or taken away—a different root than what is used to describe the just being saved (snatched) from destruction.

Proponents of a pre-tribulation rapture often point to Luke 17:33–37 as an illustration of what it might look like when God spirits away his people. But this passage is actually describing an opposite event. The Biblical texts show that the saved (raptured) are the ones left behind to be with Christ in his earthly kingdom. Christ's parable of wheat and tares (Matthew 13:24–43) reveals the same concept. The rapture event is not believers being "taken" to heaven. "Taken" has a negative connotation here. Instead, we are grabbed (snatched) out of harm's way, while the ones "taken" in Luke 17 are discarded or disposed like trash.

Old Testament prophecies, Christ's statements in the Olivet Discourse and on the Temple grounds, and John's vision in Revelation 19:11-18 all mention the destruction of many people upon the Messiah's second coming. So when we read about believers being caught up in the air, this is salvation from the judgment upon the earth. These passages describe how avian scavengers like vultures and eagles will arrive to clean up the mess after the destruction. We are spared, kept safe, delivered—not taken or thrown away.

When correlating Luke 17 to other passages, the case for a pre-tribulational rapture appears thin. The doctrine depends on an equivalent meaning of believers being "taken" with "caught up." To be taken is to fall under judgment and destruction; to be caught up is to be delivered.

"There will be two women grinding together. One will be taken

and the other left.' And they said to him, 'Where, Lord?' He said to them, 'Where the corpse is, there the vultures will gather.'"

—Luke 17:35–37

The passage in Luke 17:22-37 is clearly describing Christ's return, which is very different from the pre-trib rapture understanding. The evil are taken and the good are left to be with Christ. The people being taken in this passage are being destroyed; they are described as a corpse or a dead body.

"Taken" recalls the tares of Matthew 13:38–42, which are thrown outside the kingdom in an illustration of damnation.

"Left" recalls the wheat of Matthew 13:30, or those who are "left" in 1 Thessalonians 4:17; these are the raptured, the recipients of salvation.

End-Time Timing

Matthew 24 cannot be understood without reading other statements Christ made in Luke 17 and 21. His prophecy in Matthew 24 is not meant to be a continual chronological narrative. Note how the destruction of the Temple is prophesied first, followed by a description of the end of the age in response to the disciples' questions; Christ does not explicitly say that the destruction of the Temple will incite the end of the age or happen concurrently. So our focus here will be on the multiple other prophecies featured in Matthew 24.

The wicked will be destroyed and judgment will occur

following the visible return of Christ. Acts 1:11 states with certainty that Christ is coming back physically. Matthew 24:30–31 and related passages reveal that there will be loud noises and visual effects that will capture the attention of the entire world—then we will be gathered together "in the clouds" (the Old Testament concept of where God dwells in glory). Under Christ's protection, we will be spared from the wrath coming upon the earth. When the danger is past, then we will return to earth alongside our savior.

The 1 Thessalonians 4 passage does not offer any specific timing that places Christ's return and the resurrection of dead believers (saints) before or after a tribulation period. But this is vital information if we are indeed called to be prepared for the arrival of the bridegroom. So we must look to other passages for clarity about the resurrection of the dead or other end-time events to further understand how they fit together in a timeline.

Timing is everything. Instead of looking at more difficult passages, let's look at some short, basic passages about timing.

*"Martha said to him, 'I know that he will rise again in the resurrection on **the last day.**'"*

—John 11:24

*"There is a judge for the one who rejects me and does not accept my words; the very words I have spoken will condemn them at **the last day.**"*

—John 12:48

Here we have the resurrection and judgment at the last day. What is "the last day"? We won't find the full answer in these short verses, but we do start to get a sense that the end of the age is tied to the return of Christ.

Passages regarding the advent of Christ often feature the Greek word *parousia*, sometimes translated as his "coming." This word specifically connotes a royal arrival, as seen in 1 John 2:28. So according to a literal translation, Christ doesn't merely pop into view—he presents himself with pomp and authority. Christ's second advent is a royal event that all eyes will see.

A visually related term describes the appearances of Christ following his resurrection.[5] Taken out of context, some may think Christ's coming speaks of spiritual, symbolic, or metaphorical appearances and means something besides a physical return. However, the use of related "optic" and "epiphany" root words conveys the idea that physical eyes will see him. Passages such as Matthew 24:30, Luke 17:24; 17:30 and Revelation 1:7 convey a physical arrival of Christ.

This is why Acts 1:11 is so crucial to our understanding of end-time events; it discourages us from over-spiritualizing the second coming (even though there are some metaphors to understand). These advent passages below often relate to the timing of the return, resurrection, and judgment.

Acts 1:11 describes the way Christ will return to earth—the same single event featured in the following passages:

- Job 19:25

---

5. See Luke 24:34 and Acts 1:3.

- Isaiah 26:21; 35:4; 40:10; 59:17–20; 62:11
- Daniel 7:22
- Matthew 16:27; 24:30–31; 25:31
- Luke 17:24–30; 21:25–28
- 1 Corinthians 4:5; 15:23
- Philippians 3:20
- Colossians 3:4
- 1 Thessalonians 2:19; 3:13; 4:16–17; 5:1-4, 23
- 2 Thessalonians 1:7, 10; 2:8
- 1 Timothy 6:13–16
- 2 Timothy 4:1, 8
- Titus 2:13
- Hebrews 9:27–28
- 1 Peter 1:7; 5:4
- 1 John 2:28; 3:2
- Jude 14.

To discern the timing of end-time events, an extremely helpful tactic is to find verses that mention two or three of the Big Three events in the same short passage and see how they relate together. This establishes the major end-time events that will occur on the last day of this age.

There are only a few short passages in the New Testament that speak to all three key events in the same cluster.[6] More

---

6. See John 5:24–29; Philippians 3:10–21; 1 Peter 1:3–9.

commonly found are groupings of two of the Big Three events within short passages.

- Resurrection at the second coming: Job 19:25–27; Isaiah 26:19–21; 1 Corinthians 15; Colossians 3:4; 1 Thessalonians 4:13–17

- Judgment at the second coming: Matthew 16:27; 25:31–34; 1 Corinthians 4:5; 2 Timothy 4:1–8; Hebrews 9:27–28; 1 Peter 5:1–4; 2 Peter 3:1–13

- Resurrection and judgment: Daniel 12:1-3; Luke 14:13–14 (parable example); Acts 17:31–32; 24:14–15)

The associations between these three events suggest a timing with very short intervals. The author of a cluster passage may be focused on one event but often associates it with another one of the Big Three which either just happened or will swiftly follow.

If only one obscure passage referenced all three events, or if we could only find a couple of ambiguous passages referencing two of the events, we could be skeptical regarding their proximity. However, as shown in the references above, the evidence is overwhelming that all three events will happen in quick succession.

Scholars in the school of literal interpretation know there is a second coming, physical resurrection, and divine judgment. How do we know the sequence of these events? Because the events are so frequently clustered together in the same passage.

"Truly, truly, I say to you, whoever hears my word and believes

him who sent me has eternal life. He does not come into judgment, but has passed from death to life.

"Truly, truly, I say to you, **an hour is coming, and is now here**, when the dead will hear the voice of the Son of God, and those who hear will live. For as the Father has life in himself, so he has granted the Son also to have life in himself. And he has given him authority to execute judgment, because he is the Son of Man. Do not marvel at this, for **an hour is coming** when **all who are in the tombs will hear his voice and come out**, those who have done **good to the resurrection of life**, and those who have done evil to the resurrection of judgment."

—John 5:24–29

Jesus states that the sound of his voice at the second advent precedes the resurrection of the just (which is the gift of eternal life). His voice calls people out of the grave (like Lazarus; see John 14:43–44).[7] It should be noted that the righteous receive the salvation gift of life as a reward. Christ returns, the dead hear his voice, and the resurrection is underway.

While resurrection must wait for the second coming of Christ, notice that spiritual salvation is described in the present tense: "The hour is coming **and** is now here." In this present moment, the spiritually dead may hear the voice of Christ and be saved. Yet the main thrust of the rest of the passage is more focused on physical resurrection. Those

---

7. John 11:17 tells us that Lazarus had been in the tomb for four days. This is relevant to Christ's resurrection power because according to the Talmud, "corruption sets in the third day after death" (Tholuck after Wetstein). All other biblical accounts of resuscitation (including Christ's own resurrection) took place within three days. Lazarus would have been considered beyond reach, his soul perished. But Lazarus was raised anyway, providing hope to all.

who hear his voice now and those who hear his voice upon being resurrected will be saved. (We'll spend more time in chapter 7 comparing spiritual salvation to physical salvation.)

It would be very easy to spiritualize this whole passage with nonliteral tombs or metaphorical meanings of Jesus' voice, but Christ obviously believed in a physical resurrection. He famously debated the Sadducees, who did not believe in physical resurrection because it was not clearly described in the first five books of the Bible (the Pentateuch was the only Scripture the Sadducees read). But Christ pointed out that Moses described God as the God of living patriarchs:

"There came to him some Sadducees, those who deny that there is a resurrection, and they asked him a question, saying, 'Teacher, Moses wrote for us that if a man's brother dies, having a wife but no children, the man must take the widow and raise up offspring for his brother. Now there were seven brothers..., and likewise all seven left no children and died. Afterward the woman also died. In the resurrection, therefore, whose wife will the woman be? For the seven had her as wife.'

And Jesus said to them, 'The sons of this age marry and are given in marriage, but those who are considered worthy to attain to that age and to the resurrection from the dead neither marry nor are given in marriage, for **they cannot die anymore**, *because* **they are equal to angels** *and are sons of God,* **being sons of the resurrection**. *But that* **the dead are raised**, *even Moses showed, in the passage about the bush, where he calls the Lord the God of Abraham and the God of Isaac and the God of Jacob. Now he is not God of the dead, but of the living, for all live to him.'"*

—Luke 20:27–38

Here is another passage that includes all the Big Three events:

"Blessed be the God and Father of our Lord Jesus Christ! According to his great mercy, he has caused us to be born again to a living hope through **the resurrection of Jesus Christ from the dead**, **to an inheritance** *that is imperishable, undefiled, and unfading,* **kept in heaven** *for you, who by God's power are being guarded through faith* **for a salvation ready to be revealed in the last time.** *In this you rejoice, though now for a little while, if necessary, you have been grieved by various trials, so that* **the tested genuineness of your faith**—*more precious than gold that perishes though it is tested by fire—may be found to result in praise and glory and honor* **at the revelation of Jesus Christ.** *Though you have not seen him, you love him. Though you do not now see him, you believe in him and rejoice with joy that is inexpressible and filled with glory, obtaining the outcome of your faith, the salvation of your souls."*

—1 Peter 1:3–9

This passage may strike you as somewhat confusing. It does not present its featured events in a specific order, and the code words might not yet be apparent for a reader unfamiliar with this passage. However, when reading this passage closely, we can see that the "revelation of Jesus Christ" at the "last time" are key statements that dictate the timing of other related events.

We have all elements of the Big Three in this passage from Peter:

- The Epistle of 1 Peter starts by stating that Jesus' resurrection from the dead is the cornerstone to the reader's inheritance. This declaration is then carried through the rest of the passage.
- Immortality, translated here as something "imperishable," is the inheritance that is kept in heaven for our future salvation upon the revelation (appearance) of Christ.
- We will pass the judgment test if our faith is genuine.
- The "revelation of Jesus Christ" is the second coming.
- Once Christ comes, he grants immortality; the two are tightly associated in their timing. Once a person's faith is judged true, he or she is granted the inheritance—but this judgment is predetermined, not a throne-room judgment of deeds (see chapters 14 and 15).

Here are some simpler passages with references of two of the Big Three events.

*"For the Son of Man is **going to come** with his angels in the glory of his Father, and **then he will repay** each person according to what he has done."*

—Matthew 16:27[8]

*"[Y]ou will be blessed, because they cannot repay you. For you will be **repaid at the resurrection of the just**."*

—Luke 14:14

---

8. This is similar to Revelation 22:12 and several passages in Isaiah.

Here the just are resurrected and rewarded (a good type of judgment) in the same moment. This teaching comes from a parable, but is true to the way Christ generally described the timing of end-time events.

*"Therefore judge nothing before the appointed time; **wait until the Lord comes.** He will bring to light what is hidden in darkness and will expose the motives of the heart. **At that time each will receive their praise from God.**"*

—1 Corinthians 4:5

*"I charge you in the presence of God and of **Christ Jesus**, who is **to judge the living and the dead**, and **by his appearing and his kingdom**..."*

—2 Timothy 4:1

*"I have competed well; I have finished the race; I have kept the faith! Finally **the crown** of righteousness **is reserved** for me. The Lord, the righteous Judge, **will award** it **to me in that day**—and not to me only, but also to all who have set their affection **on his appearing.**"*

—2 Timothy 4:7–8

*"Just as people are destined to die once, and after that to face judgment, so Christ was sacrificed once to take away the sins of many; and **he will appear a second time**, not to bear sin, but **to bring salvation to those who are waiting for him.**"*

—Hebrews 9:27–28

Salvation can be used as a term for resurrection and eternal life in the land, but it is not clearly defined in the passage above. Yet it includes very clear language about the second coming and judgment. This passage combines salvation and judgment and presents them as events precipitated by the second coming.

Since the ascension, Christ has not yet appeared in body. Physical salvation happens at the resurrection when we see Christ; we will become like his resurrected, glorified body, as we see in Philippians 3:20–21.

We can see through association that the second coming, the resurrection, and judgment for the inheritance of eternal life will happen in immediate succession. The second coming is the key event, instigating the other two. Some of the passages above state these things plainly, and sometimes implied language is used, yet there are no conflicts or contradictions in these passages.

Everything related to the end times hinge on these Big Three events, either leading to or resulting from the second advent and the bodily resurrection of the just.

Second Advent in the Old Testament

Old Testament end-time passages about the second advent are tough to understand for Greek thinkers. And so modern Christians are tempted to bypass the confusion and adopt one of these viewpoints:

1. **Dispensationalism or Replacement Theology:** proponents of these viewpoints simply state that the new covenant replaces the old covenant. Abraham's promises are canceled, already fulfilled, or replaced. Problem solved.

2. **Poetry:** instead of drawing literal conclusions about the events described within prophetic passages, proponents argue that Old Testament prophecy should be read as poetry, interpreting these passages through the lens of metaphor and symbolism. Problem solved.

When we have been blinded by preconceived notions, we'll find ourselves forcing awkward interpretations onto clear passages. Sometimes we develop these notions through our Church traditions—a few of which may not hold up to scrutiny. It takes a lot of bravery and determination to test the answers we have been handed. Remember to compare your interpretations to what is clearly true about the Big Three end-time events.

Yet some verses are difficult to understand no matter how carefully you read them. Are you supposed to give the words literal or figurative meaning? In Zechariah 14:4, the Lord's feet stand on the Mount of Olives. We know that Christ physically left earth from the Mount of Olives and will return in a manner opposite his ascension.[9] So is Zechariah 14:4 a literal prophecy of a physical second coming?

If we take this verse literally, it describes the future establishment of Christ's heavenly kingdom on earth. If we take it figuratively, it could refer to Christ's continued reign in the heavenlies, a realm featuring a mystical Mount of Olives. Or it could refer to the Church age; depending on our creativity, we could make it mean just about anything we want to believe. However, as we read the following

---

9. See Acts 1:11

verses of Zechariah 14:16-21, we encounter references to specific feasts and the participation of nations formerly at war with Israel. These details are hard to understand as references to the Church age or as metaphors for previously fulfilled prophecies. There are other options as well: perhaps this passage has already been literally fulfilled, or perhaps this passage has been made void by the new covenant, and thus irrelevant. Interpretation is the key.

The two advents of Christ are both part of God's continuing plan of salvation. Some passages in the Old Testament describe these appearances of Christ in such similar terms that they almost seem to be happening at the same time. In Zechariah 9, for instance, verse 9 describes the triumphal entry, while verse 10 speaks to Christ's physical reign over the earth.

"Rejoice greatly, O Daughter of Zion! Shout, Daughter of Jerusalem! See, your king comes to you, righteous and having salvation, gentle and riding on a donkey, on a colt, the foal of a donkey."

—Zechariah 9:9

"I will take away the chariots from Ephraim and the war-horses from Jerusalem, and the battle bow will be broken. He will proclaim peace to the nations. His rule will extend from sea to sea and from the River to the ends of the earth."

—Zechariah 9:10

Verse 9 was fulfilled in the physical realm during Christ's life on earth following his first advent (Matthew 21:1–11). Verse 10 describes the nature of his reign to follow the second coming. It seems impossible to state that though verse 9 happened on earth, verse 10 relates to a heavenly realm or a spiritual reign of peace.

Luke states that Christ quoted this Isaiah passage below concerning Himself. He didn't quote the entire passage, as he knew exactly what parts related to His first coming, and what parts related to his second.

"The Spirit of the Lord God is upon me,

because the Lord has anointed me

to bring good news to the poor;

he has sent me to bind up the brokenhearted,

to proclaim liberty to the captives,

and the opening of the prison to those who are bound;

to proclaim the year of the Lord's favor,

and the day of vengeance of our God..."

—Isaiah 61:1–2a

We read in Luke 4:18–21 that he read from the scroll, but stopped mid-sentence after saying that he was proclaiming "the year of the Lord's favor," then he *"rolled up the scroll, gave it back to the attendant and sat down. The eyes of everyone in the synagogue were fastened on him, and he began by saying to them, 'Today this scripture is fulfilled in your hearing.'"*

The "year of the Lord's favor" related to Jesus' first coming. Jesus didn't read the last part of the verse in Isaiah

61:2 because the "day of vengeance of our God" relates to his second coming. He only fulfilled the first part of the passage in his audience's hearing.

Examples provided by Isaiah and Zechariah clearly show the differences between the first and second advents. The humble Messiah proclaims and brings salvation at the first advents, while the King brings vengeance and reigns over the earth at the second.

The book of Revelation is adept at organizing the Old Testament prophecies, as it correlates much of its body in synchronicity with the Old Testament. There are hundreds of Old Testament references in Revelation, including many about the second advent.[10]

Sometimes it is easy to spot figurative language in the New Testament, and sometimes it is not. First Corinthians 15 is almost impossible to read with a figurative interpretation (aside from simple metaphors such as "feet"). The physical resurrection is paramount and can't be missed in this passage.

*"**But in fact Christ has been raised from the dead**, the firstfruits of those who have fallen asleep. For as by a man came death, by a man has come also the resurrection of the dead. For as in Adam all die, **so also in Christ shall all be made alive**. But each in his own order: Christ the firstfruits, **then at his coming those who belong to Christ**. **Then comes the end**, when he delivers the kingdom to God the Father after destroying every rule and every authority and power. For he must reign until he has put all his enemies under his feet. **The last enemy to be destroyed is death.**"*

---

10. Volume II will take a closer look at Revelation's Old Testament references.

—1 Corinthians 15:20–26

There is no commentary needed if we believe this passage will be literally fulfilled (with exceptions made for "feet" and other clear metaphors). Verse 20 sets the tone as the basis of a physical resurrection. We will be resurrected or transformed to receive immortality at the second coming. There is no reference here to a tribulation period, so we can't assume any timing to the tribulation period.

A purely figurative read of this chapter just doesn't make any sense. There can only be one correct interpretation of this passage. Acts 1:11, this passage from 1 Corinthians 15, and other literal Big Three passages make no room for a figurative culmination of our age.

There will always be plenty of opportunities to debate controversial topics such as the tribulation period, but let's not debate cornerstones of the foundation of faith.

We can obtain some spiritual meaning from 1 Corinthians 15 and similar passages. However, when literal interpretations put the focus on the physical realm and heavenly realm working in parallel towards a merger on earth, all end-time passages start to align and make sense as a whole. We are spiritually saved now and will be physically saved on earth in the future. As soon as we understand this paradox concept of the resurrection, more pieces of the puzzle will fall into place. A physical return of Christ and a bodily resurrection of the justified go hand in hand.

CHAPTER 7.

THE RESURRECTION OF THE RIGHTEOUS

The resurrection of the righteous (also known as the saints or the just) is part of a judgment process; the relationship between resurrection and judgment will be discussed further in chapters 14 and 15. For now we will focus on resurrection.

God's gift of salvation entails the receipt of an immortal body. Depending on whether the recipient is still alive upon the return of Christ, God will either raise the person from the dead or transform the individual's mortal body to an immortal version.

This sounds like foolish talk to our modern ears. Most people speak of the spirit or soul when describing the afterlife, but the Bible describes transformed, glorified physical matter. If this sounds strange to you, you're not alone; two thousand years ago, King Agrippa was just as incredulous at Paul's testimony.

"And now I stand here on trial because of my hope in **the promise made by God to our fathers**, *to which our twelve tribes hope to attain, as they earnestly worship night and day. And for this hope*

*I am accused by Jews, O king! Why is it thought incredible by any of you **that God raises the dead**?"*

—Acts 26:6–8

Here Paul associates the promise to Abraham and the other Patriarchs with the resurrection, without directly mentioning the land promise. Yet the inheritance contains a promise of both land and eternal life according to other passages.

The physical aspect of salvation is all about obtaining immortality. We will not receive this gift until the second advent during the physical return of Christ when the resurrection of the righteous takes place. There are several predictions in the Old Testament of the resurrection, but they do not always associate the timing with the Messiah's second coming since the first advent had yet to occur. Daniel 7 and 12 discuss and correlate the Big Three end-time events—Christ's return, the saints' resurrection, and divine judgment. Job 19 depicts the resurrection at the coming of the Redeemer.

Key resurrection passages include the following:

- Job 19:26
- Psalm 16:10; 17:15; 49:15
- Isaiah 26:19
- Ezekiel 37:7–14
- Daniel 12:2–3
- Luke 14:14; 20:36

- John 5:28–29; 6:40; 11:24
- Acts 24:15
- 1 Corinthians 15:23, 52
- Philippians 3:21
- Colossians 3:4
- 1 Thessalonians 4:16
- 1 Peter 1:3–9; 5:4
- 1 John 3:2.

Christ came the first time to atone for our sins and conquer death for himself so he could defeat death for us later on.[1] He will come a second time to establish his heavenly reign on the restored earth. Notice the Master's plan to unite heaven and earth in Ephesians 1.

*"In him we have redemption through his blood, the forgiveness of our trespasses, according to the riches of his grace, which he lavished upon us, in all wisdom and insight making known to us the mystery of **his will**, according to **his purpose**, which he set forth in Christ as **a plan for the fullness of time, to unite all things in him, things in heaven and things on earth**. In him we have obtained an **inheritance**, having been predestined according to the purpose of him who works all things according to the counsel of his will, so that we who were the first to hope in Christ might be to the praise of his glory. In him you also, when you heard the word of truth, the **gospel of your salvation**, and believed in him, were sealed with the promised Holy Spirit, who is the guarantee of **our inheritance until we acquire possession of it**, to the praise of his glory."*

---

1. See Romans 6:5–9.

—Ephesians 1:7–14

Throughout the Bible, from the Old Testament to the New, the only hope offered to humanity rests on the resurrection event and the invitation to enter the kingdom of heaven on earth. There is no other complete gospel message found in the Bible; every passage of hope shares this ultimate meaning. You could call this the total unveiling because it climaxes with the fulfillment of all promises made to Adam and Eve on down. Nobody is left hanging with unfulfilled promises.

Resurrection: Physical or Spiritual?

Salvation is mentioned in the past, present, and future tense so we need to consider the timing of salvation, but we also need to differentiate spiritual salvation from physical salvation. Physical salvation is always depicted at the future resurrection event of all believers—which is the full realization of salvation. We will discuss this topic more within this chapter.

The resurrection event is the second of the Big Three cluster. This is presented as an actual event in the truest physical sense. There are certainly places in Scripture where the word "salvation" is used figuratively; however, the main message of the Bible is a description of God's redemption plan. He provides the means for eternal life, allowing us to dwell together with him forever. This is the restoration of all things: God and his people together again in a physical sense, not as spirit or consciousness or anything mystical. Our redemption is primarily focused on the physical resurrection of our bodies.

Several passages do focus on spiritual salvation, as we have seen earlier. These passages are intended to provide great comfort for believers in their current state. We are blessed in the assurance that our salvation is kept in heaven. This knowledge will instill hope in us until we are ultimately saved on the day of the redemption.[2] We wouldn't need hope at all if we were completely saved today.

The word "resurrection" in the New Testament comes from *anastasis*, a Greek root word meaning "to stand up" (John 11:23–24). Passages describing a spiritual salvation or resurrection do not use this particular root.

In 2 Timothy 2:18 Paul clarifies that bodily resurrection is a single future event. It had not yet occurred at the time of the letter's composition, and it was not a mystical resurrection, as some in Paul's day were preaching.

First John 3:2 also states that Christ's appearing is in the future, and we will be transformed at that time. Earlier in the letter, 1 John 2:28 correlates Christ's physical appearing with his coming (*parousia*). The second coming and physical "appearing" are synonymous in the advent passages mentioned herein. So the resurrection will happen when Christ physically comes again as the Royal King.

*"...that I may know him and the power of his resurrection, and may share his sufferings, becoming like him in his death, that by any means possible I may attain **the resurrection from the dead**. Not that I have already obtained this or am already perfect, but I press on to make it my own, because Christ Jesus has made me his own. Brothers, I do not consider that I have made it my own. But*

---

2. See Romans 8:23–25.

*one thing I do: forgetting what lies behind and **straining forward** to what lies ahead, I press on toward the goal for the prize of the **upward call** of God in Christ Jesus."*³

—Philippians 3:10–14a

Bodily resurrection happens in the future at the "upward call" (second coming). Paul states that he hasn't obtained a "standing up" resurrection, so he is not talking about spiritual salvation in this passage; he is predominantly focused on the bodily resurrection in Philippians 3 and all his related salvation passages. The one exception is 2 Corinthians 6:1–2. Here Paul discusses spiritual salvation alone, in a context of being kept by the Spirit in present tense.

Spiritual resurrections use different Greek roots such as those meaning "lifted" or as "raised" in ESV translations of Ephesians 2:4–7 and Colossians 3:1–4 (which we'll examine shortly).

The "Now and Not Yet" Paradox

We are saved, and we are not yet saved. We need to understand this "now and not yet" concept if we are to understand end times. Salvation is a paradox that God uses throughout Scripture. There are many passages that speak of physical salvation through bodily resurrection, others speak of spiritual salvation, and thankfully, some speak of both types to help differentiate the two.

*"For the grace of God has appeared, **bringing salvation** for all people, training us to renounce ungodliness and worldly passions,*

---

3. "Perfect" refers to the glorified body.

and to live self-controlled, upright, and godly lives in the present age, **waiting for** *our blessed hope,* **the appearing** *of the glory of our great God and Savior Jesus Christ."*

—Titus 2:11–13

Now we have received spiritual salvation based on the first advent, as verse 11 implies.

We are not yet ultimately saved; we must wait for the blessed hope mentioned in verse 13, which comes at the second advent. The blessed hope is Christ's "appearing," which is his physical return stated in the future tense.

Christ's appearing will let us see him with our eyes; this is the *parousia*, the moment when physical salvation comes.

The main point to consider in this Titus passage is that God has brought salvation to us today while we wait for ultimate salvation: the future physical appearing of Christ (see Romans 8:11, 23 for the redemption of our body).

"Beloved, we are God's children now, and **what we will be has not yet appeared**; *but we know that* **when he appears** *we shall be like him, because* **we shall see him** *as he is."*

—1 John 3:2

Salvation came at Christ's first appearing and will come again in its ultimate form at the second. We are now God's children because of the first advent, but we won't mature until we experience transformation at the second advent—when we shall receive a glorified body.

"But God, being rich in mercy, because of the great love with

which he loved us, even when we were dead in our trespasses, made us alive together with Christ—by grace you **have been saved**—*and* **raised** *us up with him and seated us with him in the heavenly places in Christ Jesus, so that in the* **coming ages**[4] *he might show the immeasurable riches of his grace in kindness toward us in Christ Jesus."*

—Ephesians 2:4–7

Notice the Ephesians 2 passage speaks to being "raised" in the past tense, referring to a spiritual resurrection. Later in the passage, there is a switch to the future tense of the "coming ages." Future timing is based on Ephesians 1:7–14, which refers to the merger of heaven and earth taking place in "the fullness of time." This is the event at which God will grant us our share in the inheritance of the kingdom of heaven.

The word "raised" in Colossians 3:1–4 (see below) and Ephesians 2:4–7 comes in both instances from a root literally translated as "lifted." As noted earlier, bodily resurrection is based on a different Greek root, *anastasis* (to stand up).

It is not hard to differentiate between literal and figurative language when it comes to the resurrection. We receive the gifts of spiritual and physical salvation at different times—now and not yet—but here in the same earthly realm until the merger of heaven and earth. Passages that speak of being raised or lifted to heaven in a spiritual sense are written in the past or present tense. These state that the Holy Spirit is a seal or guarantee until the second coming;

---

4. See Ephesians 1:7–14.

your spirit is kept with Christ in heaven until he comes back to earth at the merger.[5]

In passages that describe Christ's physical, visible return to earth (Matthew 24:30), we often find references to our own bodily resurrection (for example, see Job 19:25–27). "Appearing" is used in the future tense in second advent passages mentioned in 2 Thessalonians 2:8, 2 Timothy 4:8, Titus 2:13, Hebrews 9:28, 1 Peter 5:4, and 1 John 3:2. See also Colossians 3 for a description of what will happen when Christ appears.

*"If then you have been **raised** with Christ, seek the things that are above, where Christ is, seated at the right hand of God. Set your minds on things that are above, not on things that are on earth. For you have died, and your life is hidden with Christ in God. **When Christ** who is your life **appears, then you also will appear with him in glory.**"*[6]

—Colossians 3:1–4

This passage in Colossians clearly uses figurative language in the opening verse, using the term "raised" in the past tense. But an actual event took place when the reader was baptized and born again. Paul is referencing a spiritual "lifting" event, and then speaks to the appearing (second coming) in a future tense based upon the many passages that speak of "appearing" in the physical sense such as after Christ's bodily resurrection from the grave when he visited the disciples.

---

5. See Ephesians 1:13–14.

6. Colossians 3:6 refers to God's wrath to associate with the second coming.

The term "in glory" refers to how we will dwell together in God's presence. We will receive his full glory. The "poured out" glory of the Spirit has been dwelling in God's people since Pentecost; Paul described this as a seal for what is to come. Prior to Pentecost, God's glory on earth was confined to the Holy of Holies. But this, too, was but a partial display of God's glory.

John 17:5 describes the glory found in the presence of God. Titus 2:13 describes the glory to accompany Christ's future return. 1 John 3:2 does not use the term "glory" but states we will be like him in his presence.

*"When the Son of Man **comes in his glory**, and all the angels with him, then he will sit on his glorious throne."*

—Matthew 25:31

*"And now, Father, glorify me in your own presence with the **glory** that I had with you before the world existed."*

—John 17:5

*"When Christ who is your life appears, then you also **will appear** with him **in glory**."*

—Colossians 3:4

*"So I exhort the elders among you, as a fellow elder and a witness of the sufferings of Christ, as well as a partaker in the **glory that is going to be revealed**."*[7]

—1 Peter 5:1

---

7. Peter saw a glimpse of glory firsthand during the first advent but will see full glory with us at the "revealing," or second coming.

*"For we did not follow cleverly devised myths when we made known to you the power and coming [parousia] of our Lord Jesus Christ, but we were eyewitnesses of his majesty. For when he received honor and **glory** from God the Father, and the voice was borne to him by the Majestic Glory, "This is my beloved Son, with whom I am well pleased," we ourselves heard this very voice borne from heaven, for we were with him on the holy mountain."*[8]

—2 Peter 1:16–18

*"...waiting for our blessed hope, the **appearing of the glory** of our great God and Savior Jesus Christ..."*

—Titus 2:13

Paul says we must wait to see Christ's appearance with our own eyes in the future. We would not need to wait if we were already "saved" today.

There are many passages that differentiate physical salvation from spiritual salvation. Appendix 2 provides a summary of salvation passages, categorizing those that refer to spiritual salvation in past or present verb tenses, as well as passages that refer to the resurrection in future tense.

Some of these passages mention both salvation in the past or present tense **and** future salvation (the event at which believers are resurrected); these passages tend to emphasize the resurrection over the spiritual salvation already attained. The gifts of salvation that we receive today often mention the tie into hope for the second coming.

---

8. Ref. Matthew 17 transfiguration vision of the second advent.

Sealed by the Spirit

In 1 Timothy 6:13–16, Paul urges his readers to persevere "until the appearing" of Christ, assuring them that "he will display at the proper time." We can only reconcile salvation passages with the "now and not yet" concept. When we first become born again, God seals us and fills us with his Spirit. From that moment on, we have hope based on the physical salvation we will receive at Christ's future appearing.

John 6:40 shows the belief aspect of faith in the gift of Christ's nature working in the present tense to achieve salvation later through resurrection:

"For this is the will of my Father, that everyone who looks on the Son and believes in him should have eternal life, and I will raise him up on the last day."

Here we see Christ associating presently held faith with the transmission of eternal life at the last day. Notice what Christ doesn't say: at no point does he say we are saved today, nor that we have eternal life today, nor that we are eternally secure today, nor did he put any special focus on the present tense.

Peter says we are "kept in heaven," while Paul describes seals and guarantees of the Spirit, which are related to what Christ is preparing in heaven to reveal on earth on "that day" (2 Timothy 1:12). Hope in future redemption is not hope if we already have it (Romans 8:24). We patiently wait for fulfillment (Romans 8:25).

Passages about waiting on earth or heavenly storage of blessings to be brought to earth don't make sense if we receive a spirit body in heaven immediately upon death. If we had a soul that went to bliss in heaven when we died, there would be no need for all these passages urging us to patiently wait for Christ's return. These passages would instead tell us to put our hope in what we receive when we get to heaven upon our death. Not one passage in Scripture contains such a teaching.

We need to be careful of the eternal security message of "once saved, always saved." We have security today, but we need to fully understand the meanings of "soul" and "spirit" in comparison to a resurrected body. Hope is one of the key aspects of faith; waiting for the future demonstrates our faith. If we stop keeping watch, our faith will likewise deteriorate.

If we interpret resurrection passages in figurative terms, whether we expect a spiritual or physical return of Christ, we have the same potential issue to deal with regarding future verb tenses in the texts. We wouldn't have to wait for the second advent or any rapture or appearing if we were to be absent from the body and immediately "present" with the Lord.

The temple of the Holy Spirit is our body today; as we see in Ephesians 2:19–22, this is a work in progress. We do not see clearly yet ("face to face") as Paul describes in 1 Corinthians 13:8–12. We must wait for the appearing—for the moment when "the perfect comes."[9]

The Spirit we receive from Christ guarantees our future

---

9. See Philippians 3:10–14 and Hebrews 11:40 for "perfect" language; to be made perfect is to obtain a resurrected body.

resurrection. 2 Corinthians 5:5 speaks of immortality in the context of the resurrection, and Paul uses very similar language in Ephesians 1:13–14. We don't receive guarantees for things that are already perfect or that we've already obtained. We are not perfected yet.

We are "comforted" by the guarantee of the Spirit in 2 Corinthians 1:20–22 based on the blessings in store on the "day of the Lord" (2 Corinthians 1:14). The Comforter is prophesied extensively in John 14:15–31 and John 16:4–14. The explanations the disciples were looking for when Christ was physically present with them did not come until after the Comforter entered into them at Pentecost. The answer they received was to spread the gospel and wait longer for the kingdom to appear (or to be revealed) and for God's blessings to be fully established.

"...knowing that he who raised the Lord Jesus will raise us also with Jesus and bring us with you into his presence."

—2 Corinthians 4:14

Second Corinthians 4 and 5 draw significantly from 1 Corinthians 15, which deals with the resurrection extensively. Paul uses different terms in 2 Corinthians to describe the same event he taught about in his previous letter. The word "tent" in 2 Corinthians 5:1 refers to our body. Paul speaks of the upgrade we get by moving out of a mortal tent into a heavenly building—that is, an immortal body.

"For we know that if the tent that is our earthly home is destroyed, we have a building from God, a house not made with hands, eternal in the heavens. For in this tent we groan, longing to put

on our heavenly dwelling, if indeed by putting it on we may not be found naked. For while we are still in this tent, we groan, being burdened—not that we would be unclothed, but that we would be further clothed, so **that what is mortal may be swallowed up by life.** *He who has prepared us for this very thing is God, who* **has given us the Spirit as a guarantee.** *So we are always of good courage. We know that while we are at home in the body we are away from the Lord, for we walk by faith, not by sight. Yes, we are of good courage, and we would rather be away from the body and at home with the Lord. So whether we are at home or away, we make it our aim to please him. For we must all appear before the judgment seat of Christ, so that each one may receive what is due for what he has done in the body, whether good or evil."*

—2 Corinthians 5:1–10

Paul wanted to shed his earthly body and be with his Lord. This is Paul's confession, not an argument for a new doctrine. He provides many details in other passages that explain the resurrection (especially 1 Corinthians 15), and never does he describe an afterlife in heaven, harp in hand or otherwise. He simply states the preference of being immortal with the Lord over being mortal. Everyone should want the same thing. Timing is not stated specifically in this passage as it was not necessary since he previously stated timing in his first letter to the Corinthians.

The Pauline passages must be considered as a whole; in light of the order of the Big Three events he defines elsewhere, this individual passage must not be advocating a private rapture or private judgment scenario. A similar verse often taken out of context is Philippians 1:23, in which Paul again expresses his desire "to depart and be with Christ." We should not read this as an argument for an "absent from the body, immediately present with the Lord" afterlife. Paul clarifies both passages in another passage using very similar terminology.

In 1 Corinthians 5, he explains how the body and spirit are related. While the passages above talked about being with the Lord in spirit upon death, here Paul describes being with other believers in spirit while still alive. Basically, Paul was in two places at the same time. His body was absent, but his spirit was present in the assembly. This explains how Paul's body could be in the grave upon death and his spirit in heaven. There is no mention of a body or soul entity going to heaven.

"For though absent in body, I am present in spirit; and as if present, I have already pronounced judgment on the one who did such a thing. When you are assembled in the name of the Lord Jesus and my spirit is present, with the power of our Lord Jesus..."

—1 Corinthians 5:3–4

There is no theological problem with Paul stating he wanted to be preserved with Christ upon his death, as he certainly knew his spirit returned to God upon death. Paul was an expert in the Old Testament. He was well versed in the resting-state passages of Sheol.[10] Paul never taught that a person might bypass judgment and receive instant bliss in the heavenly realm. The very fact that these passages of Philippians 1:23 and 2 Corinthians 5:8 are used so often

---

10. Even the New Testament writers understood Sheol to be the place where spirits rest after death. See Acts 2:22–35, for instance, regarding the spirits of David and Christ.

to justify mythology should warn us against forcing preconceived beliefs onto biblical texts; a better practice is to read the surrounding passages, to search for more details, and to allow what we read to challenge our assumptions.

To make the context clear regarding Philippians 1:23, a little later in Philippians 2:16, Paul says he is *"holding fast the word of life, so that **in the day of Christ I will have reason to glory.**"* Paul then begins to lead into a discussion of the resurrection in chapter 3. Paul's hope was in the resurrection that only happens at the second coming of Christ (stated as the "upward call"). Philippians 3:20–21 describes how we wait on earth for Christ's appearing, at which time we will be resurrected and given a glorified body.

Philippians 3:10–21 completes the theme that began in chapters 1 and 2, but many people take Philippians 1:23 completely out of context. The main theme of the epistle focuses on the end times, not merely death and what comes after. It just took Paul a few chapters to develop his resurrection theme.

The Old and New Testaments both emphasize the importance to see with our own eyes what appears before us. This is a Hebrew or eastern way of thinking where physicality is central. A western or Greek way of thinking focuses more on spiritualization. Plato in particular promoted idea that the physical realm is corrupt and only the spirit realm is good.

From the verb tenses in Philippians 3:10–14, we know that

perfection will come in the future when the resurrection takes place. Verse 12 states, *"Not that I have already obtained this [resurrection of the dead] or am already perfect, but I press on to make it my own, because Christ Jesus has made me his own."*

People who believe they have an immortal soul that will go to heaven either at death or at the rapture must not understand what 1 Corinthians 13:12 means. That future moment of clarity of vision does not take place in another realm; Paul describes a "face to face" encounter on earth. Throughout his epistles, Paul focuses on being sealed now, with perfection to come at the resurrection.

2 Corinthians 5:7 is wedged in the middle of a resurrection passage. *"We walk by faith, not by sight"* at this time. But in the future, we will indeed see. This passage is not obvious to those who believe in a soul going to some celestial heaven, as they may think that faith is a completed work. Yet hope is attached to faith, so we need to understand salvation as a work in progress to be realized in the future.[11]

The concept of something mortal putting on immortality (as in 1 Corinthians 15:54) is repeated in 2 Corinthians 5:4 with the phrase "so that what is mortal may be swallowed up by life."[12] Then verse 5 states the Spirit is our guarantor for what comes in the future at the second advent when God saves his people. Romans 8:11 also speaks to the future event of the mortal gaining immortality but being preserved in the Spirit today.

God wants us to know we are secure today (sealed now)

---

11. See Romans 8:23–25 for the clear message.
12. See Isaiah 25:8.

through the continual gifts of the Holy Spirit through his Word and institutions. He provides hope for the future when we will see him "fully," face to face.[13] The concept of partial vision today, then full vision tomorrow, is extremely important.

Our salvation is presently secure. That's the first half of the gospel message, but many people stop at that point. As a result, we see multiple gospel messages being preached or evangelized today:

1. **Saved today:** If a person gives his life to Christ today, he is "saved." If that person died today, he would be in heaven today. This partial gospel has two offshoots: the "once saved, always saved" argument for eternal security, and the idea of conditional salvation in which a person can lose his salvation if he rejects God later.

2. **Time dependent:** A person's claim to salvation isn't determined until she dies. Constant vigilance, confession, and other continual acts must be performed to be kept in God's grace. One can hope by the grace of God that salvation remains in the end (whether a spirit body or physical body is saved).

3. **Paradox:** A person is sealed yesterday and kept today to be saved in the future. This is the biblical model under the literal interpretive method. Since the resurrection is a cornerstone, we absolutely will be ultimately saved in the future. The Bible is also very clear that we have blessed assurance to know we are kept, preserved, comforted, and sealed today. All

---

13. See Job 19:26–27; Psalm 17:15; 1 John 3:2.

guarantees. These terms are primary works of the Spirit.

Necessity of Physical Resurrection

Without absolute resurrection, our hope is in vain, as Paul states. The faith Abraham and everyone else had throughout the Bible was misplaced if faith is only spiritualized and doesn't fulfill God's physical plans. If Abraham doesn't rise from the dead to enter into the Promised Land, God's irrevocable promise will not be fulfilled. The resurrection also facilitates God's plan for the earth to be inhabited.[14] God could just take us in spirit to heaven when we die, but this would not fulfill his promises to his people nor his intentions for his creation. And so he will bring heaven to earth for us to enjoy in his presence (glory) at the restoration of all things.

Scriptural promises are consistent in stating that God will bring gifts, crowns, and preparations with him on the day of resurrection. New Jerusalem is coming to earth; we are not going to some other realm or planet. See how the promised city in Hebrews 11:16 is brought to God's people in Revelation 21:2 and not the other way around. People and place are connected. New Jerusalem is not a city by itself without the saints, and the saints are not New Jerusalem without a place to inhabit. Over-spiritualizing the heavenly city diminishes the prophecy that people will dwell with God in glory.

Ephesians 1:10 and 1 Corinthians 15 lay out the Master's plans for the physical–heavenly merger. Either there is a

---

14. See Isaiah 45:18.

physical resurrection, or God's plans fail. There is no middle ground. It is all or nothing.

*"Now if **Christ is proclaimed as raised from the dead**, how can some of you say that there is no resurrection of the dead? But if there is no resurrection of the dead, then not even Christ has been raised. And **if Christ has not been raised**, then our preaching is in vain and **your faith is in vain**. We are even found to be misrepresenting God, because we testified about God that he raised Christ, whom he did not raise if it is true that the dead are not raised. For if the dead are not raised, not even Christ has been raised. And **if Christ has not been raised, your faith is futile and you are still in your sins**. Then those also who have fallen asleep in Christ have perished. **If in Christ we have hope in this life only, we are of all people most to be pitied.**"*

—1 Corinthians 15:12–19

First Corinthians 15 is one of the best salvation chapters in the Bible, as it explains the physics behind Old and New Testament understanding. Paul asks in essence, "Why bother being a Christian if you don't believe in the resurrection of the dead for salvation?" Paul finds it pitiful to focus on spiritual meaning alone in this lifetime. It never occurred to him that he might simply receive a spirit body in heaven when he died. He would have found no hope in such a concept. The physical resurrection was the only hope he knew of; otherwise, a person remained as "perished." He anticipated the future merger of the physical and heavenly realms, as we will see in other verses he wrote here in chapter 15 and elsewhere.

Without the resurrection of the dead, our faith is in vain.

There is no justifiable reason to be a believer if Christ didn't rise from the dead, or if we don't believe we will rise from the dead. Christianity would be just another philosophy or belief system to compete with every other religion that offers an afterlife for the soul in heaven. But Paul never describes a "spirit-body"—he assumed a dead person stays dead until the resurrection (an "in this life only" philosophy).

Differing concepts of the resurrection result in different versions of Christianity.

1. **Spiritual focus:** There is no physical resurrection. Our spirit or soul goes to heaven when we die, so we don't really need a physical body or transformed body. We get some kind of spirit body or become a spirit being. Resurrection language in the Bible is assumed to be figurative.

2. **Physical focus:** Our body will be physically raised, just as Christ's body was raised. Our spirit goes back to God upon death and is kept until resurrection day. Bible language uses "resting" language to describe that interim period as we wait for resurrection. The Holy Spirit is a seal or a guarantee that preserves us until that day.

3. **Hybrid:** Resurrection happens in phases. We obtain a new spirit-body in heaven when we die, entering a state of bliss. Later, we will receive some other type of glorified body. This may take place at the rapture, the day of judgment, or resurrection day.

The hybrid option is not mentioned in the Bible, except

in one highly symbolic passage in Revelation that will be discussed in Volume II.

CHAPTER 8.

RESTING AND WAITING

What does it mean to be raised physically, to appear with God in glory, or to see God as he is? What will our bodies be like in the resurrection? Like the bodies of angels.[1] Our bodies will be transformed to be just like Christ's resurrected body, as Paul taught in 1 Corinthians 15 and here in Philippians:

*"But our citizenship is in heaven, and from it **we await** a Savior, the Lord Jesus **Christ, who will transform our lowly body to be like his glorious body**, by the power that enables him even to subject all things to himself."*

—Philippians 3:20–21

If these passages mean to say that we'll get a new spirit-body in heaven, then what is the waiting for? It makes no sense to wait for Christ to come if we'll receive a spirit-body when we die. But of course these passages teach nothing of the sort. Paul never speaks of this spirit-body concept.

---

1. See Matthew 22:30 and Luke 20:36.

The appeal of this spirit-body concept likely comes down to a lack of patience. People want salvation now, forever asking, "Are we there yet?" But Scripture states we are to wait for judgment and the resurrection; only then will we receive our rewards. The crown of life (eternal life) is the main prize that we receive.

Many end-time passages stress the need to wait. This waiting takes place on earth, not standing in line outside the pearly gates.

Once the waiting period finally ends, then rewards will be handed out.[2] This too will happen on earth.

*"For the **creation waits** with eager longing **for the revealing** of the sons of God."*

—Romans 8:19

*"And not only the creation, but we ourselves, who have the firstfruits of the Spirit, groan inwardly as **we wait eagerly for** adoption as sons, **the redemption of our bodies.**"*

—Romans 8:23

*"...so that you are not lacking in any gift, as you **wait for the revealing** of our Lord Jesus Christ."*

—1 Corinthians 1:7

*"Therefore do not pronounce judgment **before the time**, before **the Lord comes, who will bring** to light the things now hidden in*

---

2. See "Rewards at the second coming" in Appendix 3.

darkness and will disclose the purposes of the heart. **Then each one will receive** *his commendation from God."*

—1 Corinthians 4:5

"But our citizenship is in heaven, and ***from it we await*** *a Savior, the Lord Jesus Christ."*[3]

—Philippians 3:20

"...and to ***wait for his Son from heaven****, whom he raised from the dead, Jesus* ***who delivers us from the wrath to come****."*

—1 Thessalonians 1:10

*"...****waiting for*** *our blessed hope,* ***the appearing*** *of the glory of our great God and Savior Jesus Christ."*

—Titus 2:13

"So Christ, having been offered once to bear the sins of many, ***will appear a second time****, not to deal with sin but* ***to save those*** *who are eagerly* ***waiting for him****."*

—Hebrews 9:28

*"...****waiting*** *from that time* ***until*** *his enemies should be made a footstool for his feet."*

—Hebrews 10:13

*"...****waiting for*** *and hastening* ***the coming of the day of God****, because of which the heavens will be set on fire and dissolved, and the heavenly bodies will melt as they burn!"*

---

3. Here we are waiting on earth, not preparing to go to a different realm. The gift of the resurrection comes from heaven to earth.

—2 Peter 3:12

*"But according to his promise we are **waiting for** new heavens and **a new earth in which righteousness dwells**. Therefore, beloved, since you are waiting for these, be diligent to be found by him without spot or blemish, and at peace."*

—2 Peter 3:13–14

Many books have been written about the state of the dead and the spirit state. It is interesting to see the historical progression of different religious views and mythologies regarding the dead, along with resurrection and spirit-body concepts. At first there were two main competing viewpoints, and then one emerged as the dominant Church view. By viewing the historical record, we can see clearly just how things got so far off track from the original biblical teaching.

The Bible is very clear as to the state of the dead: asleep until the resurrection. William Tyndale made a very simple, logical argument about the resurrection and the state of the dead that summarizes the biblical concept very concisely. Tyndale starts with sarcasm in this dialogue but then ends with very sound statements. Notice the last sentence in particular.

"Nay, Paul, thou art unlearned; go to Master More, and learn a new way. 'We be not most miserable, though we rise not again; for our souls go to Heaven as soon as we be dead, and are there in as great joy as Christ that is risen again.' And I marvel that Paul had not comforted the Thessalonians with that doctrine, if he had wist [known] it, that the souls of their dead had been in joy; as he did with the resurrection, that their dead should rise again. If the souls

be in Heaven, in as great glory as the angels, after your doctrine, shew me what cause should be of the resurrection."[4]

The old English is a little rough, so here is a modern summary:

What need is there for the resurrection if a person believes he goes to heaven when he dies and then immediately receives a glorified spirit-body? Why have a resurrection at all? Why didn't Paul comfort the Thessalonians with statements like "Don't worry, your loved one is now in bliss enjoying heaven in a spirit-body"?

Paul clearly stated the only hope the Thessalonians had was to wait for physical resurrection—the same resurrection Christ had received. Yet today we tell people at a funeral, "Uncle Joe is in a better place now playing golf with St. Peter and Aunt Josephina," or something along those lines. We say this to make the bereaved feel better. This is our culture.

The idea that Uncle Joe is conscious right now with a new body that doesn't have cancer is very comforting. However, this perpetuates a mythological way of thinking. Doesn't this bypass judgment day? Should any good person be entitled to receive a spirit-body immediately upon death, or does such a reward violate the biblical order?

It doesn't sound as good to say, "Uncle Joe is at perfect rest now waiting for the resurrection when Christ comes again." Most of the western world believes in the spirit realm as

---

4. William Tyndale. *An Answer to Sir Thomas More's Dialogue*, bk. 4, ch. 4, p. 118. Parker 1850.

the immediate destination for "good" people, whereas the literal biblical scenario is by far a minority position today.

We are inclined to think as the world does in believing our soul will go to heaven upon death, given how eager we are to be with the Lord. But this hybrid concept of resurrection undermines the importance of physical resurrection and diminishes God's key promises to his people.

The Old Testament clearly identifies Sheol as the resting place of the soul; the New Testament uses the Greek word "Hades" to refer to the same place. Repeated over and over again throughout both Testaments is the promise of physical resurrection of the dead. The bodies lying in the grave will be awakened from rest by a voice. Christ will bring the preserved spirits of the saints to earth and restore our bodies on resurrection day. This is the clear message of ultimate salvation.

But what about other traditional ideas about the afterlife? Won't our soul float to heaven after death? What about our meeting with father Abraham or St. Peter, our heavenly mansion, our golden harp, or our place in the heavenly chorus? If these traditional beliefs about the afterlife do not come from Scripture, what are their historical sources?

Beliefs about an immediate afterlife in the heavenly realm are derived from Egyptian, Babylonian, and Greek sources (see citations to follow). These first made their way into the Babylonian Talmud, then into the Church through the cultural influence of Alexandria, Athens, and Rome. No Bible passage states any joyous spirit-body activity—or any other type of activity at all. The person is simply "resting." Scripture is literally silent otherwise.

So what happens at death? We don't have enough space here to go over the detailed history of all the differing traditional viewpoints. But we can look at some key passages to get the literal biblical perspective. This biblical perspective is of course informed by a focus on the resurrection of the dead, not an immortal spirit-body or floating souls.

The Bible states that, upon death, a person's spirit goes back to God. The Bible is mostly non-descriptive about what happens to consciousness during the period between death and just prior to the resurrection. "Sleeping" or "resting" are by far the most used terms. In some cases, Scripture states outright that the dead don't do anything. The body is still a corpse in the grave during this period.

A good clarifying passage is found in Isaiah 38:9–20. Here King Hezekiah describes what he expects to experience in Sheol; this is the typical Old Testament perspective.

What does the New Testament have to say about the current status of Hezekiah and other Old Testament saints?

"God raised [Christ] up, loosing the pangs of death, because it was not possible for him to be held by it. For David says concerning him,

"'I saw the Lord always before me,

for he is at my right hand that I may not be shaken;

therefore my heart was glad, and my tongue rejoiced;

my flesh also will dwell in hope.

For you will not abandon my soul to Hades [Sheol],

or let your Holy One see corruption.

You have made known to me the paths of life;

you will make me full of gladness with your presence.'

"Brothers, I may say to you with confidence about the patriarch David that he both died and was buried, and his tomb is with us to this day. Being therefore a prophet, and knowing that God had sworn with an oath to him that he would set one of his descendants on his throne, he foresaw and spoke about the resurrection of the Christ, that he was not abandoned to Hades, nor did his flesh see corruption. This Jesus God raised up, and of that we all are witnesses. Being therefore exalted at the right hand of God, and having received from the Father the promise of the Holy Spirit, he has poured out this that you yourselves are seeing and hearing. For **David did not ascend into the heavens**, but he himself says,

"The Lord said to my Lord,
'Sit at my right hand,

until I make your enemies your footstool.'"

—Acts 2:24–35

It is very hard to read this passage in a figurative sense or imagine that Peter is describing resurrection in a spiritual sense, knowing that Christ physically rose from the dead. Peter knew and preached after Pentecost that the following details about David were true:

- David's corpse was still in the grave;

- David did not ascend into heaven (as of the day of Pentecost, resurrection had yet to occur);

- David was resting in the state of Sheol ("Hades" in Greek);

- David received the promise that the Messiah would be his Descendant;

- David's only hope was that the Messiah would defeat death (to make an enemy one's footstool was to gain total victory over that foe).

The main enemies of God are death, sin, and the devil. The Bible prophesies that each of these will be destroyed.[5] Christ is to reign until all enemies are defeated.

Isn't David in heaven right now playing a harp or singing in the heavenly choir? This concept is nowhere to be found in the Bible. None of the Old Testament saints have been resurrected yet. The last enemy to be destroyed is death, but that has not happened yet for us. (Spiritual death is another matter.) Romans 6:5–9 explains that Christ defeated death for himself, and we believers will be resurrected like him when death is finally eradicated in the future.

If Sheol is the resting place for the spirit or soul, why would David state confidence that his soul would not remain there? Because David believed in the resurrection.[6] Why did

---

5. See 1 John 3:8; Revelation 21:4.
6. See Psalm 16:10; 17:15; and 49:15.

David state that Christ's body would not see corruption? Because David knew of his resurrection.

We should appreciate that biblical beliefs are unique among other modern religions in regard to the state of the dead. We need to look at cultural foundations to determine where we obtained our information. One would need to go back prior to the *Epic of Gilgamesh* to find the most ancient beliefs of the afterlife. The Mesopotamian culture that produced *Gilgamesh* believed in an afterlife trapped in the underworld. Later, Egyptian, Babylonian, and Greek mythology began to popularize the idea of a soul going "up" to heaven for the average person.

Immortality of the Soul?

Some people have reported a "floating soul" experience during an operation—an apparent separation from the body during a near-death incident. I myself once experienced something like this. But it is impossible to obtain empirical evidence about the immortality of the soul, regardless of the observations. This is a matter of belief, not a fact. We should differentiate between these sorts of claims and the Bible's consistent message—the same theme repeated over a 1,000 year period. Near-death experiences are inherently subjective, colored by the individual's prior knowledge and beliefs. There is no consistency found.

The "floating soul" and spirit-body concepts have made their way into Judaism and Christianity, culminating in today's popular view that each person has an immortal soul. But we must be very careful. God alone is the true God, he alone is immortal, and God alone grants immortality. Anything else is heresy.[7]

"Behold, I tell you a mystery: **We shall not all sleep**, *but we shall all be changed—in a moment, in the twinkling of an eye, at the last trumpet. For the trumpet will sound, and* **the dead will be raised incorruptible**, *and* **we shall be changed**. *For this corruptible must put on incorruption, and* **this mortal must put on immortality**. *So when this corruptible has put on incorruption, and this mortal has put on immortality, then shall be brought to pass the saying that is written: '***Death is swallowed up in victory**.*'"*

—1 Corinthians 15:51–54

There is a huge difference in believing a person has an immortal soul or spirit versus believing God has the power to grant immortality at the resurrection. First Corinthians 15 is very clear that we are mortal ("a body of death"). Our only hope is in God to raise us. Our bodies will be redeemed at the resurrection.[8]

The soul finds its definition in the relationship between the body and the spirit. We can find some helpful background in the creation narrative:

"Then the Lord God formed man of the **dust** *of the ground, and breathed into his nostrils the* **breath** *[spirit] of life; and man became a living* **soul**.*"*

—Genesis 2:7, KJV

---

7. See 1 Timothy 1:17; 6:16; and John 17:1–3.
8. See Romans 8:11, 23.

God put "spirit" into Adam. Now living, Adam's soul came into being.

The same formula is true in us. Our bodies, comprised of dust (physical elements), combine with breath (spirit) to form a soul (a living being).[9]

When breath leaves a body, the soul retreats and we are left in the state of Sheol; the body becomes a corpse. You do not *have* a soul. You *are* a soul—so long as you have the breath of life.

God's Life-giving Spirit

Many people confuse "soul" with "spirit," or use "soul" as a metaphor for their inner being, as in "my soul is troubled." In English, "soul" and "spirit" are basically interchangeable. But biblically speaking, these do not have the same meaning. There is complete confusion about who we really are as beings.

To repair our understanding of what it means to be a living being, let's look at a biblical teaching on death:

"Then shall the dust return to the earth as it was: and the spirit shall return unto God who gave it."

—Ecclesiastes 12:7

What returns to God here is the spirit—God's animating

---

9. Though we tend to amend this definition to a living *human* being, the Bible doesn't explicitly exclude nonhuman life. For example, Genesis 1:21 tells of the "souls" with which God populated the seas, though most English translations render this "living things" or "living creatures." And in Revelation 8:9, we read, "A third of the creatures which were in the sea and had life, died" (NASB); *psyche*, the word translated as "life" in this passage, appears elsewhere as "soul."

breath. According to the ancient concept of breathing, breath wasn't just proof of life—breath *was* life. Death was the absence of breath. This concept features in Ezekiel's vision of dry bones (Ezekiel 37:1–14): God's breath of life re-enters the dead, and life resumes. This vision closely resembles the creation account of how human life began. Before exploring any potential figurative meanings of this passage (such as the restoration of Israel as a geopolitical entity in 1948), we must acknowledge the literal image of the promised day of resurrection.

Just before Jesus' death on the cross (Luke 23:46) and Stephen's martyrdom (Acts 7:59), each asked God to receive his spirit. These accounts are perfectly consistent with Old Testament descriptions of the spirit leaving the body (as in Ecclesiastes 12:7 above).

Creation of life and salvation of life are similar in that each is granted by the Spirit. This is no coincidence.

The Spirit gives life physically and spiritually. We are saved today spiritually and saved physically at the resurrection—due to the same Spirit of God. We see this concept clearly in Romans 8:11.

Physical death and spiritual death are both examples of the absence of God's Spirit. In physical death, his animating breath is gone. And so long as the Holy Spirit does not dwell within us, we remain in spiritual death. We are dead physically and spiritually without the Spirit. The Spirit is the breath of life, and the Spirit is the provider of faith for our salvation (and also provides our ability to do good works).

Here James compares physical death to spiritual death:

*"For **as the body apart from the spirit is dead**, so also faith apart from works is dead."*

—James 2:26

As breath animates our body, good works animate our faith once we are sealed with the Holy Spirit (that is, born again and baptized). We receive the Spirit, both physically and spiritually, as a gift. Grace always comes before works of the law.

God spoke, exhaled his breath, then creation of physical matter happened. God breathed his Spirit into that physical matter—the dust of the ground—and then life happened. He will breathe into the dust from our corpses on resurrection day—then eternal life will happen.

We do not need to understand all of this on a scientific level. We need not propose how God might recover all the scattered saintly dust from millennia past, nor debate whether any dust will do. The breath of God is a mystery of our faith, a bridge between the heavenly and earthly realms. Looking to science for clarification is futile, as science has no idea how life truly began; scientists continue to ask for tax dollars or charitable donations to fund their search for answers.

Like the ancient saints, we can only accept these mysteries by faith.

The root words in Hebrew and Greek for "spirit" in the Bible would be translated most literally as "breath."

Speaking and breathing are closely related to life itself in most ancient myths and cultures.

Are writings in Ecclesiastes and Genesis just poetry with metaphors or other analogous language? Should we embrace the ancient concept of divinely delivered breath as literally accurate? How might mythologies from ancient cultures be coloring our preconceived notions of the nature of the world? Do we unconsciously try to make the Bible fit our preexisting beliefs? These are all vital questions. Inerrancy holds that all biblical writings are essentially true, but there is a wide gap between believing the Bible holds subjective truth and actually discovering what objective truth is. The main difficulty, as we've explored before, is determining whether a particular biblical writer meant to record history, record the future, or express spiritual truths through poetic or figurative language. Inerrancy of the Bible depends on the existence of an objectively accurate interpretation.

If you believe the Bible is inerrant, you shouldn't claim that the symbolic language is open to personal interpretation. If there is only one Word of God, there must be one corporate interpretation for us to discern. We may have some disagreements about minor doctrinal points, but God only meant for us to preach a single gospel. And the gospel collapses without the promise of bodily resurrection.[10] So strict adherence to a physical, bodily resurrection is a necessary unifying trait in the body of believers.

Be careful not to add your personal beliefs or preferences to the gospel message. By fitting in with the world, you water

---

10. See 1 Corinthians 15:12–19.

down the truth. Do not dilute the complete gospel message that the justified dead are raised to eternal life on the day of resurrection.

Dust is a word that doesn't carry as much weight today as it did for ancient cultures. They associated dust (or earth, clay, ground, or land) with the creation of humanity—an event that connected the physical realm and the spiritual realm. The foundation of who we are is based upon physical matter and Spirit. It doesn't matter if dust is a metaphor for physicality—it has physical meaning to convey. According to the oldest records available to us, the ancient view was that humans were created from out of the earth.

Redemption through Resurrection

As you read the following passages, try applying both physical and spiritual interpretations. Is this literal, physical dust, or a symbol expressing a spiritual truth?

"*For I know that my Redeemer lives,*

and at the last he will stand upon the earth.

And ***after my skin has been thus destroyed,***

yet in my flesh I shall see God,

whom I shall see for myself,

and my eyes shall behold, and not another.

My heart faints within me!"

—Job 19:25–27

"When you hide your face, they are dismayed;

when you take away their breath, they die

and **return to their dust.**

When you send forth your Spirit, they are created,

and you renew the face of the ground."

—Psalm 104:29–30

"Your dead shall live; their bodies shall rise.

You who dwell in the dust, awake and sing for joy!

For your dew is a dew of light,

and **the earth will give birth to the dead.**

"Come, my people, enter your chambers,

and shut your doors behind you;

hide yourselves for a little while

until the fury has passed by.[11]

For behold, **the Lord is coming out from his place**

to punish the inhabitants of the earth for their iniquity,

and the earth will disclose the blood shed on it,

and will no more cover its slain."

---

11. This verse is speaking of Sheol rest.

—Isaiah 26:19–21

"I shall ransom them from the power of Sheol;

I shall redeem them from Death.

O Death, where are your plagues?

O Sheol, where is your sting?

Compassion is hidden from my eyes."

—Hosea 13:14

God plans to unite us with him, but first he must redeem us from eternal death and release us from Sheol (or Hades[12]). In Hosea's words, God must "ransom" us out of the ownership of death. To redeem is to gain possession.

Humanity is under the power of death and the devil. Someone needs to pay our ransom to release us from captivity. Through Christ's death on the cross and his fulfillment of the law, God has indeed paid the price.[13] He will finalize the transaction at the resurrection.

Under the law we are destined to die, but we are no longer under the law (Galatians 5:18) once we are gifted the promise of our inheritance. Christ paid our fines at the cross as a gift to us, thus fulfilling the promises and prophecies we encounter from Genesis 3:15 and onward.

---

12. Hades is used as the Greek equivalent of Sheol in the Bible, but Greek thinking actually associates Hades with hell or the underworld. So although we talk about Christ "descending into hell" in the Apostle's Creed, Christ didn't go to Dante's Inferno but to Sheol, the resting place of the dead.
13. See 1 Corinthians 6:20; Hebrews 9:15.

God's redemption plan is to give the inheritance to us so that we can have an everlasting relationship with him as part of his family. He calls us heirs, children, and brothers and sisters in Christ. His master plan is to reunite the family.

God spells out his plan through his promise to Abraham—the promise that is for all peoples of all points in history. Abraham believed in God's promises—even trusting God to deliver his son Isaac from the dead—and God credited this faith as righteousness. Before Abraham could demonstrate his belief, God had already given him the unconditional promise through grace. So Abraham's faith was itself a gift, and not a righteous work for salvation. God graciously declared Abraham righteous—Abraham didn't prove his righteousness or earn his own salvation.

Our faith is focused on God, the one who gives us our faith. Faith is a gift from God, not something we create through belief. Belief is secondary. It is important, but not the key aspect of faith.

*"Now to the one who works, his wages are not counted as a gift but as his due. And to the one who does not work but believes **in him who justifies** the ungodly, his faith is counted as righteousness."*

—Romans 4:4–5

Notice that belief is not what justifies a person; only God justifies.

Faith comes by hearing God's Word and then believing in his promises, just as Abraham did long ago. We receive faith as a pure gift. Grace needs to come first, then we can believe. Faith follows grace just as the law follows grace. God gave grace to the nation of Israel by taking them out of Egypt (as stated in his preamble to the Ten Commandments in Exodus 19:4). They were then supposed to live out their faith based upon a belief in grace; unfortunately, the people of Israel focused on works, relying on their own imperfect obedience to God's law for their salvation.[14]

"Repent, then, and turn to God, so that your sins may be wiped out, that times of refreshing may come from the Lord, and that he may send the Christ, who has been appointed for you—even Jesus. **He must remain in heaven until the time comes for God to restore everything, as he promised long ago** *through his holy prophets."*

—Acts 3:19–21

Peter turned out to be quite an evangelist after receiving the Holy Spirit at Pentecost. Three thousand were baptized after his previous sermon (Acts 2:14–41). He knew Christ was coming back, having seen the Transfiguration vision of glory that would fulfill the promise of the kingdom on the earth and restore everything back to God's original intent. This is why the disciples asked if the kingdom promises were going to be restored after Christ's resurrection (Acts 1:6). They knew the promises to Abraham were not yet fulfilled. But they did not yet realize that God had a bigger plan for the Old Testament saints—a plan that would be fulfilled with us.[15]

God's plan to bring the kingdom to earth implies a return

---

14. See Romans 9:31–33 and Hebrews 4:2.
15. See Hebrews 11:10–16, 39–40.

to the unspoiled Eden. He will restore everything back to a state of perfection; the world will be as it was before humanity's fall into sin, but without the existential threat of death and the devil. Such a resolution will fulfill God's promises to Adam and Eve, the patriarchs, and humanity itself.

But this ultimate fulfillment is yet to occur. What about the thief on the cross? Wasn't he promised paradise on the day of his death? For that matter, what is paradise? Is it the geographical coordinates of earthly Eden? Is it God's heavenly realm, not yet come to earth? Is it a kingdom to be established in the Promised Land?

"And [the thief] said, 'Jesus, remember me when you come into your kingdom.' And he said to him, 'Truly, I say to you, **today** you will be with me in paradise.'"*

—Luke 23:42–43

Regarding the asterisk above, it is important to remember that our English translations of the Bible are derived from ancient texts that do not include punctuation. So while this comma preceding "today" is a common choice among the various English translations, it could just as easily have been placed after "today" instead.[16] [17] That little comma

---

16. See "The Comma of Luke 23:43" by Grace Communion International. (www.gci.org/articles/the-comma-of-luke-2343, accessed June 4, 2019). This article addresses the need to interpret the passage without relying on the arbitrary comma, though it ultimately equates "paradise" with Sheol. That conclusion poses its own problems, as we see below.

17. It is worth noting the Greek renderings of Luke 4:21 (biblehub.com/text/luke/4-21.htm) and 19:9 (biblehub.com/text/luke/19-9.htm). In both verses, Jesus announces an event that has unambiguously happened in that moment: "Today this Scripture has been fulfilled"; "Today salvation has come to this house." The Greek conjunction *hoti* appears in each verse to connect "today" to the event. But Luke

significantly impacts the meaning of Jesus' statement. Let's look at the two variants.

1. *"Truly, I say to you, today you will be with me in paradise."*

According to this rendering, on the day of Christ's death, the thief and Christ went together to a place called "paradise"—which Jesus implied was equivalent to his kingdom. Yet we know from other passages that Christ went to Sheol and the grave, not heaven, immediately upon his death.

Did the thief also "descend into hell" as the Apostle's Creed would say? Even if we define hell as Sheol in this instance, could that be paradise—a picture of Christ's kingdom?

By placing a comma before "today," we force a figurative interpretation of at least one element of the passage. Clearly paradise, Sheol, and the kingdom cannot literally refer to the same place. So Jesus couldn't have been speaking of paradise as a literal place in the earthly or heavenly realms because he himself did not go to such a place at that time. A non-literal paradise is deeply unsatisfying, and an immediate fulfillment is the whole point of insisting on this comma placement, so we are left awkwardly isolating "with me" as the single figurative clause in an otherwise literal passage. In other words, "Today you will be in paradise, and I'll be there too just as soon as I descend to hades, rise from the grave, spend another 40 days with my disciples, and then ascend to heaven."

2. *"Truly, I say to you today, you will be with me in paradise."*

23:43 does not contain this conjunction. By declining to use *hoti* in this instance, Luke decided not to explicitly connect "today" to the fulfillment of Jesus' promise.

According to this rendering, Christ assured the thief that he could have confidence of salvation. "Today" marked the initiation of the promise. The thief's fate was assured but not to be completed at that moment. Every other person throughout history receives the same "now and not yet" salvation message. Christ meant for the thief to have assurance "today" that he would enter the future kingdom on the day of resurrection. Every part of this passage is thus literally true.

The word translated here as "paradise" is *parádeisos*, an ancient Persian word meaning "garden" or "park." The garden paradise concept is repeated many times in the Bible, often with references to a future "tree of life" echoing Eden (We will study these references in greater detail in Volume II). The paradise awaiting the thief—or any "good" person—must look like one of these two options:

1. A person's soul floats to a heavenly afterlife upon death, but we don't know what exactly happens because the Bible doesn't state specific details about paradise or Sheol. According to popular imagination, we might receive some sort of heavenly body with which to play golf with St. Peter or sing in the heavenly choir.

2. Following the resurrection event, believers will live together with Christ in the Promised Land, the kingdom of heaven on earth. Christ did not mention details on the cross, but many other passages of Scripture describe what God has in store.

There are plenty of ideas of what a pre-resurrection paradise might look like, and some allow for a future "completed" paradise of resurrected bodies on a fully restored earth. But these hybrid approaches still rely on the immortal soul myth. Scripture does not promise us a spirit-body prior to the resurrection of the dead. We must take care not to supplement biblical promises with mythological teachings of instant gratification.

God can create, sustain, or destroy a person if he wants. It is nonsense to think ourselves immortal. Angels and other created beings can die if God elects. The fallen will die, as we see in Psalm 82:6–7.[18] God can do anything he elects within his nature. His immortality and power over mortal creatures is absolute. Any view of the afterlife that insists on the immortality of human souls contradicts that truth, and is therefore myth, not the true gospel.

---

18. Christ quoted this Psalm for another purpose in John 10:34–36.

CHAPTER 9.

CULTURAL MYTHS OF LIFE AFTER DEATH

Greek mythological influence has infiltrated Christianity since its origins. In the early days of the Church. Since Gnosticism and other beliefs were pronounced as departures from biblical teaching, early leaders of the Church easily quelled and discarded such heretical arguments. But Greek culture continued to quietly influence the Church, to the point that some of the traditional teachings we uncritically accept today have mythological underpinnings.

One of the early sources of direct Greek influence on Christianity was Athenagoras (born AD 127 in Athens). In his early days as a philosopher, he practiced Platonism (which contains a belief of the soul's natural immortality). He initially opposed the claims of Christianity; in an effort to develop his counter-arguments, he studied Christian writings, only to find himself persuaded by what he read. Following his conversion to Christianity, he continued to cling to a belief that the soul outlives the body. In chapter 31 of his *A Plea for the Christians*, he says, *"We are persuaded that when we are removed from the present life we shall live **another***

life…as heavenly spirit*…or, falling with the rest, a worse one and in fire; for God has not made us…that we should perish and be annihilated."* [1]

Perhaps never before in orthodox Christianity had it been taught that we live as a heavenly spirit in the next life. While the Gnostics were denounced for demonizing the body, this softer teaching of a post-body afterlife had a lasting imprint on orthodoxy.

Although an early adopter, Athenagoras was not the most influential Christian leader to draw from Platonic teachings and Greek myths. Clement of Alexandria was one key figure, along with his student Origen, who is quoted below:

"We shall be caught up in the clouds to meet Christ in the air, and so shall we ever be with the Lord. We are therefore to suppose that the saints will remain there until they recognize the twofold mode of government in those things which are performed in the air.…

"I think, therefore, that all the saints who depart from this life will remain in some place situated on the earth, which holy Scripture calls paradise, as in some place of instruction, and, so to speak, class-room or school of souls, in which they are to be instructed regarding all the things which they had seen on earth.…

"If anyone indeed be pure in heart, and holy in mind, and more practiced in perception, he will, by making more rapid progress, quickly **ascend to a place in the air***, and reach the kingdom*

---

1. For more information on the competing concepts of natural and conditional immortality, see *The Doctrine of Immortality in the Early Church* by Dr. John H. Roller, AB, Th.M, Ph.D. www.truthaccordingtoscripture.com/documents/death/immortality-early-church/John%20Roller%20--%20Doctrine%20of%20Immortality%20in%20the%20Early%20Church.pdf. Accessed May 12, 2019.

of Heaven, through those 'mansions,' so to speak, in the various **places which the Greeks have termed spheres, i.e., globes, but which holy Scripture has called heavens.**"

—Origen, *De Principis*, II, ch. xi

Notice the hybrid relation of Greek myth and Scripture. Origen was a major contributor to western Christianity. His influence is still realized today; many major sects and denominations of Christians continue to believe in this hybrid model. Most people do not realize how much the Church borrows from Plato, who himself was influenced by Egyptian and Babylonian myths. We struggle to notice these mythological influences because our secular western culture has been fashioned by the same influences.

This is the main crisis of the Church in the west: a mythological worldview led formative Church leaders to skew their interpretations of the Bible, thereby changing the gospel. Unbelievable? It happened.

In very ancient texts, only gods could rise again after death; when a mortal or demi-god died, they had no chance of a risen afterlife.[2] The person's spirit or soul would be trapped in the underworld forever. We do not find a mythological reference to a heavenly afterlife for regular mortals until Pythagoras, who recounted an Egyptian myth about floating souls aboard solar ships. Plato took it from there, and his philosophy made it into Jewish and Christian theology. Paul is rolling over in his grave.

---

2. See the ending of the *Epic of Gilgamesh* in which Gilgamesh steals, and promptly loses, a rejuvenating plant from the underworld. Text available at www.ancienttexts.org/library/mesopotamian/gilgamesh/tab11.htm. Accessed on May 20, 2019.

Christians and Hellenized Hebrew scholars developed a belief in the immortality of a person's soul or spirit through contact with the Greeks (and other pagans who carried mythological influences). The Greeks had fashioned their mythologies from Babylonian and Egyptian views of Orphic mystery religions. Plato's philosophy in particular blended these beliefs into a concept that is widely held today in Christian and secular circles alike within the western world.

"When the concept of the soul was further developed in the Greek world, a sharp distinction was made between the mortal body and the immortal soul which originates in the divine world. Only the latter journeys in the world to come. The idea of a journey of the soul now makes its appearance in Greek literature. According to the Orphic writings (6th – 5th century [BC]), which introduce the idea, the goal of souls is to return to their heavenly home after long travels. Hades now becomes the place of punishment, hell. Plato introduced into Greek philosophy the belief of the immortality of the soul and its many [re]incarnations up to the goal of final purification. According to the myth ... the soul goes to the place of judgment after leaving the body. There the judges order the righteous ... to ascend to Heaven ... The idea gradually changes from a descent of the soul to the underworld, to an ascent of the soul into Heaven."

—Gerhard Kittel[3]

The historian George Ladd shows that these non-biblical concepts of the spirit and soul were introduced in the interim period between the writing of the Old and New Testaments.

---

3. Kittel, Gerhard. *Theological Dictionary of the N.T.*, Vol. VI, p. 568.

"In the intertestamental period, a distinct development is to be noted; both pneuma [spirit or breath] and psyche [soul] are conceived as entities capable of separate existence. The Pauline usage of psyche is closer to the Old Testament than is the intertestamental literature. Paul never uses psyche as a separate entity in man, nor does he ever intimate that the psyche can survive the death of the body. Psyche is 'life' understood against a Hebrew background." [4]

The *Dictionary of Paul and His Letters* (DPHL) says this about Paul's beliefs regarding the resurrection:

"Paul's teaching about the bodily resurrection arises out of a Jewish anthropology in which the 'soul' [Hebrew: nephesh; Greek: psyche] is the animating principle of human life. In mainstream Jewish thought human beings do not have souls, they are souls....

"Given this background it is perfectly understandable how in Romans 8:23 Paul describes the effects of the resurrection in terms of the ultimate 'redemption of our bodies.'" [5]

The literal biblical concepts of body, soul, and spirit are different from the westernized version brought to us by the Greeks.

We also need to bear in mind that Platonism includes the idea that the physical realm is bad and the spirit realm is superior. Notice how current western thinking echoes that theme by fixating on an end to the world in which everything physical is destroyed. Even within western Christianity, the idea persists that only heaven exists

---

4. George Eldon Ladd. *A Theology of the New Testament*, 459–60. 1974
5. *Dictionary of Paul and His Letters*, p 810. InterVarsity Press, 1993.

eternally, while all physical matter will either disappear or be destroyed through God's end-time wrath. This contradicts the land promise and the new (regenerated) earth concept that appear throughout the Bible.

Many prophecies declare that God will bring "new heavens and a new earth."[6] This end-time event is associated with restoration, redemption, regeneration, renewal, and cleansing after judgment takes place.

Why would Christ create and inherit the earth only to blow it up? Isaiah 45:17–18 tells us that Christ has a purpose for the earth. Fire does feature in end-time prophecy, but the lasting images are of an earth restored to its unspoiled state—not a world destroyed.[7]

"The restoration of all things" implies that in a literal sense all things will return to an Edenic state. Whether you want to call this new world the Promised Land, heaven, the Garden of Eden Part II, paradise, or the kingdom of heaven—God's restorative work has begun but is not yet completed.

God's great love drives him to redeem his creation; through his master plan, he will fulfill his desire to live with us forever. We see this plan summarized in Ephesians 1:10 and realized all throughout the Bible from Genesis to Revelation.

It is very important to come to a correct understanding of the Old Testament in light of the promises built into the

---

6. See Isaiah 65–66; Matthew 19:28; 2 Peter 3:13; and Revelation 21:1.
7. We will discuss Revelation's treatment of fire in Volume II. See Deuteronomy 29:29.

new covenant; this foundational knowledge ensures that we preach the genuine gospel message. Once we understand the promises and covenant foundation in relation to the Big Three end-time events and the receipt of our inheritance, we will see a common and coherent theme throughout the entire Bible.

It would be nice if Christians could send a consistent message to the world. Mixed messages yield mixed reception. Why can't there be just one gospel? It has been too long since Christians have rallied together from different walks of life around a common literal understanding of the Bible.

If you take only one thing from this book, it should be this point: Scripture clearly states that a bodily resurrection is our only hope. We can disagree on the details of what precedes the resurrection event, or what follows, but the vital point is that we will be with Christ on the restored earth.

Will a "millennial" earthly kingdom serve as prelude to Resurrection Day? Will the resurrection mark the beginning of God's eternal kingdom on earth? These debates only matter if the kingdom is established on earth, not some celestial realm or mystical place.

Abraham is the first person of any significant record shown to anticipate resurrection; previous religious myths held that resurrection was only for gods. Adam and Noah likely had some awareness of God's ability to resurrect their bodies; however, nowhere in their biblical accounts does this topic arise. Stemming from Abraham's influence, the main monotheistic religions all shared the belief that common people had access to God's gift of physical resurrection of the dead (modern monotheists have strayed from their roots in this regard). Abraham also offers us the main biblical example of faith in the gospel plan as initiated in Genesis 3:15.

If God can create life in the womb (Ecclesiastes 11:5), he can sustain life. If God can raise "dry bones" from the dust they came from and knit them into a newly restored body (Ezekiel 37:1–14), he can also bring back consciousness that is stored in the resting place of Sheol. If God created mankind in the beginning, he can certainly resurrect physical matter (Psalm 104:29–30) and give us glorified bodies as he glorified Christ's resurrected body. The resurrection may sound foolish, but if we have faith to believe in a literal creation, we have enough to accept the resurrection. There are many truths we wish to understand, but God only reveals some.

The substance and timing of the end-time events described in the book of Revelation are far less important to understand than the gospel of the end times. It is of the utmost importance that we understand God's offer of salvation to us and to the world.

Ancient and Modern Opposition

Is Christianity like all other religions in the world that pose the myth of a soul floating to heaven (or down to hell)? Or does a literal understanding of the Bible compel the belief of a physical resurrection into a glorified body? Is the Bible a symbolic book that invites interpretation based on individual preferences? Or is it a revelation from God that is meant to have one collective interpretation?

In the Hindu epic *Mahabharata*, Krishna argues for a form of resurrection via reincarnation, telling Arjuna, *"Never was there a time when I did not exist, nor you, nor all these kings; nor in the future shall any of us cease to be."*

The eastern pantheistic religions share a belief in an eternal cosmic collectivity. Interestingly, these religions trace back to an early form of monotheism. We see traces in early Indian and Chinese written records of a monotheistic supreme creator God who rules over lesser "gods" (similar to the biblical treatment of God's supremacy over the gods of the Egyptians and the Philistines).[8]

The rise of quantum physics in our modern age raises again the ancient eastern idea that we are all part of the same consciousness. Proponents of New Age mysticism point to these scientific theories as evidence—even though quantum physicists themselves aren't trying to promote a religious belief system.

Even though quantum physics suggests some level of human connectivity, this does not mean you and I lack an individual nature. Scientists cannot prove whether we

---

8. As far back as the 23rd century BC, the Chinese offered sacrifices to ShangDi, the "heavenly ruler." For more information, see "The Original Unknown God of China" by Dr. Ethel Nelson (June 1, 1998. answersingenesis.org/genesis/the-original-unknown-god-of-china/#a1. Accessed June 4, 2019). And ancient India believed in a "God of gods" known as Rudra, the eternal, unified One who contained everything seen and unseen in the universe. Rudra's attributes are described in the Atharvashiras Upanishad, a text dated to roughly the 5th century BC. For an excerpt, see *Researches Into the Nature and Affinity of Ancient and Hindu Mythology* (pg 443. 1831) by Vans Kennedy (books.google.com/books?id=bU1OZhGq8qUC&pg=PA443. Accessed June 4, 2019).

exist as separate individuals or as part of the combined consciousness shared by all matter residing in the entire universe.

Quantum physics would tell us that dust doesn't really exist in any specific location at a final level—rather it "moves" in cosmic consciousness. Since everything is connected somehow within this quantum realm, there is some new reality we are yet to perceive. However, these cutting-edge scientific ideas are not new at all; eastern religions have promoted the idea of cosmic collectivity for thousands of years. Scientific progress merely allows us to use different words to describe our big ideas about the universe. There is little we can prove. Science cannot displace faith.

No human (aside from Christ when he was on earth) has ever proven anything substantial about how God created or sustains the universe. Without proof, there can be no claims. We only need to read Job 38–41 to see an explanation of God's understanding compared to humans. Either God has revealed it, or we can't know it.

After God spends those four chapters reminding Job of everything he doesn't understand about the world, Job replies, *"Therefore I despise myself, and repent in dust and ashes"* (Job 42:6).

Job's summary says it all. Most of the book seems to point to the wisdom and righteousness of Job. But in the end, he repents and turns to God, confessing that he really didn't know or comprehend much at all. Job was humbled. God favors humble people who turn completely to him.

As Christians, we shouldn't need scientific proof of God's

existence or other matters of faith because we have our answer already. Faith is the evidence of the unseen (Hebrews 11:1–3). In faith, we read passages about the outpouring of the Spirit (such as Galatians 4:6) and receive these spiritual gifts from the heavenly realm.

A person who has received grace by the Holy Spirit knows it came from an unseen source, so this person has "proof" of the faith God provided. But a nonbeliever who wants proof of the unseen needs to have an open, humble heart like a child or they will reject God before he has a chance to supply the "proof."

"Truly, I say to you, whoever does not receive the kingdom of God like a child shall not enter it."

—Luke 18:17

This verse has created a lot of confusion. Many think it means that a person needs to have a simple, very basic faith—like a child's naïve belief in Santa Claus. But faith is not a belief. Jesus' main point is that a child brings nothing to the table. Children simply trust in something else, not themselves or their own degree of belief. There are no degrees of faith itself, as it is 100 percent based on grace. There are only degrees of humility based upon how much we trust in God versus our own understanding. Belief is secondary to the gift itself.

Though Peter spent three years at Jesus' side, he stated God did not distinguish between his faith and that of a newly converted Gentile (Acts 15:8–11). God requires us to humble ourselves and adopt a child-like attitude if we wish to obtain faith to be saved into the kingdom of God.[9]

God cannot enter and merge with a sinful heart. So God gives us a new, clean heart instead.[10] We are to be born again, not simply scrubbed clean. We are a new creation.[11]

First comes an encounter with the Word (gospel); then we either believe or reject the message. We need to embrace God's gift of faith without relying on our senses or any scientific method. Proof comes through the experience of the Spirit working in our lives in an ongoing relationship. God wants us to believe and trust in him alone, not in our own understanding or in our ability to make choices. He will let us test and prove his goodness (1 Thessalonians 5:21), but we won't be able to prove certain things (for one example, see Ecclesiastes 11:5).

We certainly know from Scripture that God wants to be connected to us through his Word and Spirit. God approaches us in his paradoxical manner, offering to help us begin anew as a spiritual creation in an old physical body. Then we experience the paradox of many-yet-one, becoming part of the one body of believers. This isn't the eastern cosmic collective, but we do share the same Spirit and the same baptism.[12] One of Christ's great priestly prayers is found in John 17.

"I do not ask for these only, but also for those who will believe

---

9. See Matthew 18:3–4.
10. 2 Corinthians 6:14–16 teaches that we also should refrain from mixing good and evil.
11. See 2 Corinthians 5:17.
12. See Ephesians 4:4–6.

in me through their word, that they may all be one, just as you, Father, are in me, and I in you, that they also may be in us, so that the world may believe that you have sent me. The glory that you have given me I have given to them, that they may be one even as we are one, I in them and you in me, that they may become perfectly one, so that the world may know that you sent me and loved them even as you loved me. Father, I desire that they also, whom you have given me, may be with me where I am, to see my glory that you have given me because you loved me before the foundation of the world."

—John 17:20–24

Science, mythology, philosophy, and religious clashes have not affected the substance of this gospel message in the several thousand years that have passed since its inception. The gospel message predates even Sumerian culture. No other message has traveled further through time, and it has withstood challenges from other religions and beliefs all the while.

This message remained constant through numerous prophets, messengers, and biblical authors. Perhaps our perceptions of what the Bible says have changed over time, but the Bible is not at fault for our own misinterpretations.

Hidden in plain sight is the oldest message in history, repeated through countless passages of the most widely published book of all time.

We know from the Creator's record that there are multiple realms of existence, the earthly and the heavenly, the seen and unseen. Science has long focused on that which can be seen, while downplaying what cannot be measured or observed. But now quantum sciences are trying to understand the unseen elements of the universe. What is the relationship of the seen to the unseen? Some eastern religions state that the unseen and the seen are one. Platonism teaches that everything that can be seen is bad and only the unseen is good. The Bible teaches that what is seen will be restored and the unseen will merge with it someday (see Ephesians 1:7–14, especially verse 10). This teaching culminates in the ending of Revelation.

Sometimes it is easy to spot age-old lies. But when you find it difficult to distinguish the truth, instead of relying on your own understanding (invention), rely on the Creator's words (revelation) found in the Bible. All will finally be revealed on "the last day."

Here are some verses to consider:

"How you are fallen from heaven,

O Day Star, son of Dawn!

How you are cut down to the ground,

you who laid the nations low!

You said in your heart,

'I will ascend to heaven;

above the stars of God

I will set my throne on high;

I will sit on the mount of assembly

in the far reaches of the north;

I will ascend above the heights of the clouds;

I will make myself like the Most High.'"

—Isaiah 14:12–14

Created beings have always wanted to live forever and ascend to heaven; even before the creation of humanity, angelic beings faced the same urges. Satan, for one, fell. And when humanity had its turn, we quickly fell into sin also.

*"But the serpent said to the woman, '**You will not surely die**. For God knows that when you eat of it your eyes will be opened, and you will be like God, knowing good and evil.'"*

—Genesis 3:4–5

Let's get to the heart of the matter:

"Son of man, say to the prince of Tyre, Thus says the Lord God: Because your heart is proud, and you have said, 'I am a god, I sit in the seat of the gods, in the heart of the seas,' yet you are but a man, and no god, though you make your heart like the heart of a god."

—Ezekiel 28:2

"But when his heart was lifted up and his spirit was hardened so that he dealt proudly, he was brought down from his kingly throne, and his glory was taken from him."

—Daniel 5:20

As we can see, God does not like it when his created beings

do not listen to his Word and become proud. When we claim immortality of our soul or try to climb our own way into heaven, we fall for age-old tricks that only lead to more false beliefs. So we need to be very careful to match our beliefs to what is clearly stated in the Bible.

The devil lured Adam and Eve with the promise of immortality; today, 79 percent of Americans today believe they have an immortal soul.[13] This cannot be a coincidence. Humanity, as ever, is being deceived.

Many thorough studies have been published about the similarities and differences of Hebrew beliefs compared to other ancient cultures. Given God's direct revelation, the biblical perspective should differ considerably from the majority cultural viewpoint regarding immortality in particular. But the devil tricks us into following worldly wisdom instead of sticking to God's true gospel message.

If we can get back to the unvarnished biblical concepts, we'll find an extremely unique perspective on eternal life and how to pass into the afterlife. Once understood, the biblical concept is seen to bear few similarities to the teachings of other religions. In fact, each of the other major religions treats the afterlife in a manner very similar to the others—which is to be expected, as they are based upon human understanding, not divine revelation.

We should be able to spot manmade belief systems with relative ease. Each will have established its own justice

---

13. "Americans Describe Their Views About Life After Death." October 21, 2003. The Barna Group. www.barna.com/research/americans-describe-their-views-about-life-after-death/. Accessed May 20, 2019.

system, declaring which deeds, laws, rules, or steps will result in salvation.

In contrast, God reveals a paradoxical justice system in which law and grace work together in tandem because of just and merciful nature. He judges our deeds, yet he forgives us our sins. He hates evil, yet he showers us with goodness. As we saw in previous chapters, God saves us through his gift of grace, then satisfies his law through the righteousness of Christ.

We may wish to improve our nature, but we cannot sufficiently improve ourselves to meet God's standards. Rather, it is belief in God's nature that initiates our faith. Judgment is part of the law, and God is justly against all things that violate his nature. However, the law is also a gift and is part of God's Word (gospel).

As easy as it is to fixate on the idea of obtaining immortality, our first priority is to achieve total reliance on God. Without his Spirit, we cannot sustain life or obtain eternal life. We are dead eternally without the Spirit. When we stop breathing, we have no hope unless the breath of God returns to us and transforms us into a new body. Only by his Spirit breathing into the dust of the physical realm can we enter eternal life. But God only resurrects those who have had Christ's righteousness imputed to them. Only these will be able to pass judgment.

CHAPTER 10.

HUMAN NATURE

Before we can be judged, we need an examination. God examines our condition to see if we are "good." This is the quickest test ever.

As Christ said, *"No one is good except God alone"* (Luke 18:19b).

We pass the examination if we are deemed perfect.[1] But ever since the fall of Adam from his state of innocence, not one of us has been able to claim perfect righteousness. We can only pass if we obtain Christ's perfect goodness as a gift.[2]

Below are verses of advice relevant to every person throughout history since the fall of mankind. This is a longer test to examine our condition in comparison to the righteousness of God. Are there degrees of righteousness?

*"The Lord saw how great the wickedness of the human race had become on the earth, and that **every inclination of the***

---

1. See Matthew 5:48.
2. See James 1:17.

thoughts of the human heart was only evil all the time. *The Lord regretted that he had made human beings on the earth, and his heart was deeply troubled.... But Noah found favor [grace] in the eyes of the Lord."*

—Genesis 6:5–6, 8, NIV

"Can mankind be just before God?

Can a man be pure before his Maker?"

—Job 4:17, NASB

"But how can a man be in the right before God?"

—Job 9:2b, NASB

"Who can make the clean out of the unclean?"

—Job 14:4a, NASB

"What is man, that he should be pure,

Or he who is born of a woman, that he should be righteous?"

—Job 15:14, NASB

"The Lord looks down from heaven on the children of man,

to see if there are any who understand,

who seek after God.

"They have all turned aside; together they have become corrupt;

there is none who does good,

not even one."

—Psalm 14:2–3

"Behold, I was brought forth in iniquity,

and in sin did my mother conceive me."

—Psalm 51:5

"And do not enter into judgment with Your servant,

For in Your sight **no man living is righteous."**

—Psalm 143:2, NASB

"Who can say, 'I have made my heart pure;

I am clean from my sin?'"

—Proverbs 20:9

"We have all become like one who is unclean,

and all our righteous deeds are like a polluted garment.[3]

We all fade like a leaf,

and our iniquities, like the wind, take us away."

—Isaiah 64:6

"This is what the Lord says:

'Cursed is the one who trusts in man,

---

3. Translated "filthy rags" in the KJV.

who draws strength from mere flesh

and whose heart turns away from the Lord.'"

—Jeremiah 17:5

"What then? Are we Jews any better off? No, not at all. For we have already charged that **all***, both Jews and Greeks,* **are under sin***, as it is written:*

*'****None is righteous****, no, not one;*

no one understands;
no one seeks for God.

All have turned aside; together they have become worthless;

no one does good*,*
not even one.'"

—Romans 3:9–12

"But now the righteousness of God has been manifested apart from the law, although the Law and the Prophets bear witness to it—the righteousness of God through faith in Jesus Christ for all who believe. For there is no distinction: for **all have sinned and fall short** *of the glory of God, and are justified by his grace as a gift, through the redemption that is in Christ Jesus."*

—Romans 3:21–24

Christ stated in Matthew 4:4 (quoting from Deuteronomy 8:3) that we are to live by the Word of God, so we need to trust his definition of our nature.

Humans cannot self-generate even a minor scale of

goodness according to Scripture. By nature, our hearts are not up to the task. When God looks at our heart,[4] he sees the sin that stems from within.

But we are not without hope.

"And the Lord your God will circumcise your heart and the heart of your offspring, so that you will love the Lord your God with all your heart and with all your soul [life], that you may live."

—Deuteronomy 30:6

"Circumcise yourselves to the Lord

And remove the foreskins of your heart,

Men of Judah and inhabitants of Jerusalem,

Or else My wrath will go forth like fire

And burn with none to quench it,

Because of the evil of your deeds."

—Jeremiah 4:4, NASB

One of these passages summarizes grace, the other the terms of the law; our nature must be changed if we wish to live according to God's law, and only God can make the necessary changes within us. This truth has never changed. We need to approach God with a humble and broken heart. Our "self" needs to be drowned in baptismal waters, crucified with Christ, and buried. God freely provides grace through an ongoing process in which his Spirit is poured

---

4. See 1 Samuel 16:7; Romans 2:28–29; 1 Corinthians 4:5.

out continually into "our" heart. He first carves out a location to live (circumcision), then by the gift of God's Spirit we can keep his law.

Do we really have a sinful nature, or does sin change our nature? Who are we really in our innermost being? What happens to our heart when we turn to Christ? Do we still "own" it? Sometimes the Bible describes God pouring out his Spirit into our heart, and sometimes God promises to give us a new heart. Sometimes he circumcises our heart (a gift of grace), and sometimes he urges us to circumcise our own heart (keep the law).

So the heart presents us with another paradox of law and grace. As elsewhere in the gospel, grace must come first, then the law follows. All seemingly contradictory passages are nonetheless correct. Some passages speak to God's gift of a new heart, and some speak to the law in our heart. We need to understand the proper sequence. We first need a new heart given to us; only then, through his indwelling nature, can we keep his commands.

When we analyze our heart condition, there are only two states: sinful or clean. Either our heart exists in its own human nature, or it is transformed according to Christ's divine nature. The two do not mix.

When God gives us his heart, we become "one" with him and with each other as Christ described in the priestly prayer of John 17. We have the same heart. God's heart becomes ours—we may call it "our" heart because it was a gift—yet it continues to belong to him to share with others. This is yet another divine paradox. Note that we can reject

God at any moment and operate from our original sinful heart that still resides in us. We will have two hearts until the last day. As Adam gave us his fallen nature, the "second Adam" (Christ) gives us God's Spirit.[5]

Because it is Christ's nature at work that enables us to keep his law, he gets all the glory when we succeed in doing good. We can only take credit for the sin we commit when we stumble and indulge in our old sinful nature.

We don't keep the law to obtain salvation. We keep the law because that is the natural output of God's Spirit at work in us. God's Spirit motivates us to love others as he loves, and as Christ showed by example—but we cannot do this through our own measure of goodness.

Many people think life is like a test where they must do some work to get a good grade. If there are more good works than bad, they pass the test or tip the scales of justice to their favor, and heaven will be their reward.

"Getting at orthodoxy (or, rather, heterodoxy) among the American population, most (55%) agree that if a person is generally good, or does good enough things for others during their life, they will earn a place in heaven."

—The Barna Group[6]

According to another Barna survey, *"a large majority of*

---

5. See Romans 5:12–18; 1 Corinthians 15:42–50.
6. "The State of the Church 2016." The Barna Group. September 15, 2016. www.barna.com/research/state-church-2016. Accessed May 20, 2019. Note - this link may be broken.

Americans (79%) agreed with the statement 'every person has a soul that will live forever, either in God's presence or absence.'"[7]

Barna and other research surveys have reported that these ways of thinking represent the majority views for Americans in general, not just American Christians. Culture has promoted the immortal soul myth and legalism, the idea that we can achieve righteousness through our own works.

Can we be good enough to earn our way to heaven? The biblical argument for humility says no. Will our soul live on forever? The Bible is clear regarding our mortal condition. We must take care not to believe the lies spread by our culture—even, in some cases, within the walls of our churches.

"The heart is deceitful above all things,

and desperately sick."

—Jeremiah 17:9a

The biblical view is that we are in a desperate condition; we will die unless we undergo spiritual heart surgery. God first circumcises our heart, then through his Spirit gives us a new heart. This new heart is a gift to be believed in, not to be earned by keeping rules, making choices, or performing surgery on ourselves.

This heart transplant is part of the free, eternal healthcare program. The fees are paid out of our inheritance. Christ

---

7. "Americans Describe Their Views About Life After Death." The Barna Group. October 21, 2003. www.barna.com/research/americans-describe-their-views-about-life-after-death. Accessed May 20, 2019.

paid for everything, so we don't have any dues to worry about. We simply need to believe in it; the law does not oblige us to contribute anything to the payment Christ made on our behalf. By following the prescription plan of redemption, we will receive our inheritance.

God's Word gives us both commands and promises, based upon his nature of being just and gracious at the same time. His Word delivers the gift of baptism by the Holy Spirit. This gift bestows a new nature upon us; we are born again. In Paul's famous words, *"It is no longer I that live, but Christ who lives in me"* (Galatians 2:20). Here we see a distinction of the two natures in each Christian. There is a nature of life and a nature of death, and both reside in us.

The new nature we receive through the Spirit was originally God's, but now it is ours as well; we have a shared nature with him. This does not transform our human nature but is a separate nature altogether.

Once born again, we have two hearts, two competing natures within us. We must embrace the new heart and reject the old heart, as it cannot contribute anything toward grace or salvation.

Once we believe in the promises given to us by the Spirit, faith begins to form. The next step is to act out in obedience; this completes our faith. Faith is the bridge that takes us from receiving the gift to living by the gift. Belief is not a true belief unless we act on it through the power of the Spirit given to us. Otherwise we are hypocrites, saying we believe one thing but doing another. Having received the Spirit, should we neglect to follow the Spirit?[8]

When Paul says, "It is no longer I that live, but Christ," he is clearly talking about his spiritual life, not his physical life. He rejected his previous attempt to save himself by keeping the law, deeming it an impossible task. He drowned, crucified, and buried his sinful heart after his conversion and repented of his former self-righteousness.

Paul received grace and repented afterward. He did not take the initiative in turning to God, nor did God decide to save Paul based upon one of Paul's good deeds. In being sealed spiritually, Paul experienced the second birth (as Christ discussed with Nicodemus in John 3:3–7). An interesting lesson to note is that God told Paul he would meet Ananias and then receive the Spirit. So Paul was filled with the Holy Spirit and reborn before he could carry out any specific righteous acts to demonstrate repentance. Paul did not "make a decision to follow Christ" in order to receive the Spirit.

> *"[Ananias] said, 'Brother Saul, the Lord Jesus who appeared to you on the road by which you came has sent me so that you may regain your sight and be filled with the Holy Spirit.' ... Then he rose and was baptized."*

—Acts 9:17, 18b

Spiritual salvation comes before physical salvation. We are spiritually sealed when we accept God's gift of a new heart, but we do not receive physical salvation from death until

---

8. See Galatians 5:25.

the resurrection. We must continue to wait alongside all people who are kept by faith in God's grace, anticipating the ultimate fulfillment of God's promises of redemption. Our hope is based on Christ's fulfillment of the law, and our faith flows out of God's Spirit within us. We do not contribute anything at all toward either the grace that saves us or the faith that sustains us.

The Scales of Justice

Many biblical concepts sound strange from a human perspective; our beliefs and biases continue to be warped by ancient mythological concepts. Yet we all have a common sense of justice; a moral code of law is ingrained into every person.[9]

As human beings, we have a figurative scale in the back of our mind that weighs the good things we do against the bad. We all feel the need to do something to earn justice or favor. According to human reasoning, good deeds must be rewarded and bad deeds must be punished. If we sense the scale tipping toward bad deeds, we may redefine what good and bad mean to get the scale back on our side. Some people go so far as to reject the very idea of evil, seeking to eliminate the counterweight altogether. But in rebelling against justice, such people cannot help but acknowledge the intrinsic nature of the concept. They use justice to remove the future need for justice.

Our mythological concept of justice says that if, upon death, a person's good deeds tip the scale of justice against the bad-deeds counterweight, then the person's soul can float

---

9. See Romans 2:14–16.

to heaven. Reliance upon good works and belief in an immortal soul combine to form the most common belief system in America today. This is an ancient myth dressed up in modern language and sensibility, and the majority of western people, Christian and non-Christian alike, have bought in.

We all have the ability to reject God's plan of salvation. But we have no ability to save ourselves. Through our free will, we can decline God's offer of redemption and remain mired in eternal death. We can say "no" to God's gift and say "yes" to our own plan of salvation. If we think we need to do even a little to help earn our own salvation, this is evidence of pride. We need to shake free from the belief that we can balance our own scales.

The world often tells children to have self-esteem and "believe in yourself." Sometimes we deliver this message ourselves. But this is not the gospel message. From a human perspective, we want our kids to appreciate and develop their own talents and abilities, but it is even more important that they humbly believe in God and let his Spirit equip them to serve others. Promoting a child's sense of pride is a slippery slope. God has already deemed us worthy of his love. We can't add to our worth by our own good works, beliefs, or choices.

God places more worth on us than we can know.[10] But the devil asks, "Would God let bad things happen to you if he truly valued you?" When we adopt such a perspective, we misunderstand God's love and justice. We often assume that we anger God with our sin, causing him to withhold

---

10. See Luke 12:7.

blessings or deal out punishments. But God doesn't give blessings as a reward for good behavior; these blessings are undeserved grace. And while some of our sinful actions do have earthly consequences, God's discipline is an expression of grace, not a lawful punishment.

"Know then in your heart that, as a man disciplines his son, the Lord your God disciplines you. So you shall keep the commandments of the Lord your God by walking in his ways and by fearing him."

—Deuteronomy 8:5–6

It should be noted that "disciple" and "discipline" have the same root meaning relating to a student. Both words connote learning. Having received our new heart from the Spirit when we are born again at our baptism, now we need the Spirit to continually teach us how to live as God's people and follow in his ways.

Discipline is not well understood by the one being disciplined. But we need to realize God is perfecting us through his Spirit living in us. God is holy and expects us to be holy.[11] We need to humbly fear God before we can live through him. And we need to love others to keep in step with God's intent. We spend our lives in a transformational process (Romans 12:1–2) until we are fully transformed on the last day (Philippians 3:21).

Human thinking is not God's way of thinking.[12] Judgment Day can't be understood under the law of justice alone, as

---

11. See Ephesians 1:4.
12. See Isaiah 55:8.

that seems to leave no room for grace. We think of grace as an all-or-nothing concept, but what about justice? In our earthly justice system, we expect judges to mete out sentences of varying severity based on the level of the offense. But does God judge by degrees? We first need to look at God's nature to understand his mode of judgment. We already know we are sinful by nature and by actions, but how does God really judge us?

The Law is Love

God is love. Love is directly associated with law, righteousness, and good works. Love is not a feeling or emotion, even if we often think of it this way. So God is in fact lovingly giving of himself when he gives us his law, drawing from his just, fair, and righteous nature.

He gives us his grace and his law through the gospel; both are gifts to us. His plan has always been to transfer his nature to us so we can be givers as well. In other words, we keep his law by loving others. The devil disrupted this exchange when he came onto the scene in the garden. He continues to do all he can to promote selfish acts over the giving relationships God intended for us to experience.

First John 4–5 states God is love and he gives his love to us:

*"Beloved, let us love one another, for **love is from God**, and whoever loves has been born of God and knows God. Anyone who does not love does not know God, because **God is love**."*

—1 John 4:7–8

We are to love (thus keeping God's law) because God first gave us his lawful nature:

*"**We love because he first loved us.** If anyone says, 'I love God,' and hates his brother, he is a liar; for he who does not love his brother whom he has seen cannot love God whom he has not seen. And this commandment we have from him: **whoever loves God must also love his brother.**"*

—1 John 4:19–21

We are to believe in Christ and be born again, and then we are to love:

*"Everyone who **believes** that Jesus is the Christ has **been born of God**, and everyone who loves the Father loves whoever has been born of him. By this we know that we love the children of God, when we **love God and obey** his commandments. For this is the love of God, that we keep his commandments. And his commandments are not burdensome."*

—1 John 5:1–3

The law is to love; we receive this law after we are born again. Love is obedience to God.

"For the one who loves another has fulfilled the law."

—Romans 13:8b

God's gifts are unidirectional—the gospel message passes from God to us. Goodness is not inherent in us, so we need to receive it. God graciously puts a new heart within us.

But the love that flows out of our new heart is bidirectional, passing freely between all parties. The law defines how we are supposed to live in relationships. We can only love after we receive the gifts of God's grace and the commands given in his Word.

It should be clear that God wants a relationship with us and that we are to act justly with our neighbor. The law is not a burden.[13] If we live by the Holy Spirit, we keep the law. Having already received grace, we do not have the burden of trying to keep God's law through our own strength.

God's promises to Abraham demonstrate his grace, while the terms of the Mosaic covenant demonstrate God's law. Abraham didn't have to keep any law to receive the promises, only believe and trust in God. Later, he displayed his belief by trusting God to raise Isaac from the dead. Abraham's faith was considered complete only after he obeyed God's command.[14] God was testing Abraham by commanding the sacrifice of his son. God tests us today by commanding us to obey his word. Our faith is not complete until God tests it.[15]

Israel needed to exhibit the same belief and trust as Abraham. They verbally agreed to love God and their neighbor, but they often neglected to rely on faith as the basis of their lawful living. They did not follow the example Abraham set forth for them.[16]

God reveals himself and his attributes through law and

---

13. See Galatians 6:2.
14. See James 2:21–22.
15. See 1 Peter 1:6–7; James 1:2–3.
16. See Romans 9:31–33; Hebrews 4:2.

justice. We often do not associate love with law, but God's primary work is to give us his loving nature—and that includes the grace-giving law. When God demands perfection under the law, he is not being unreasonable. He is perfect and requires us to be perfect.[17] We are called to be holy just as he is holy.[18] But grace precedes the command as God gives his perfect nature to us; he knows we can't generate perfect righteousness on our own. Yet our obedience is required.[19]

Law and grace are two key elements of God's nature—the very nature he wishes to put within us. And so we see throughout Scripture two distinct aspects of God's gospel message:

1. God will save us by grace. Salvation is something we receive, not achieve.

2. We are to live by God's nature, a gift we receive through His indwelling Spirit.

We see in Scripture that belief in God is only the starting place of faith. Belief alone cannot complete our justification by faith. John 3:16 does not contain the entirety of the gospel message. Belief must culminate in obedience. Reading on in John 3, Jesus explains for us how the gospel message retains the law, but we tend not to memorize this part of the chapter:

*"Whoever **believes** in the Son has eternal life; whoever does not*

---

17. See Matthew 5:48.
18. See 1 Peter 1:15–16.
19. See Romans 10:16; 1 Peter 4:17–19.

obey *the Son shall not see life, but the wrath of God remains on him."*

—John 3:36

Here we see belief as a direct conduit for obedience. Are we to believe in the gospel and not act upon its grace? Are we to have faith without works?

Why does Scripture (and Jesus himself in the verse above) insist we need to do good works if we are saved by grace through faith?

The answer goes back to God's nature of being righteous and gracious at the same time.

- We can say we love God because he first loved us (1 John 4:19), yet it goes deeper than that. We can't self-generate a loving response to God, so he gave us his loving nature, which enables us to respond.

- God's law is a loving gift to us. We first receive this gift of God's very nature at our baptism in the Holy Spirit. This is what it means to be born again, to be born of God.

- We can't love God or our neighbor until we are born again (1 John 5:1).

First John 5:1–3 is very similar to John 3:36. Both show the connection of belief to obedience. When God graciously gives his gospel message to us, we receive the seeds of faith. We must then believe in this message and finally act upon it, which makes our faith complete. We have no strength in our own nature to save ourselves, but we do have the strength in God's nature to "obey the gospel" per his will.

Acts 5:32 and other verses about obedience can be taken out of context. The phrasing of this verse makes it seem as if obedience prompted God's gift of the Spirit, but in light of Scripture as a whole, we see a different meaning. We can't take any verses out of context. We can't focus on grace passages while ignoring law passages, or vice versa. All Scripture works together.

The law is useful as a curb to our selfish impulses and as a mirror to reflect the ugliness of our own nature. It shows us how to please God and how to engage in civil obedience. But while the law is very useful in all these ways, perhaps its ultimate purpose is to spread God's message of grace. As we act in obedience, we allow God's light to shine on the earth.

When people claim to be saved by grace yet display disobedience, they send a contradictory message. We are to reflect the light of God's word. If our "job" in the Great Commission is to spread the gospel (Matthew 28:18–20), should we show the gospel by good works or verbally communicate the message? The truth, of course, is that both methods are required.

People see good works, so our lives help to display the transformative power of God's nature. We are to live according to the law; words can also be helpful, but we know that actions speak louder than words as we demonstrate God's love.[20]

---

20. See Deuteronomy 4:5–9; Matthew 5:16; 2 Corinthians 4:4; Philippians 2:14–15; Titus 2:7, 2:14.

Relationships are the key to unlocking the law-and-grace paradox. We love in obedience to God's law, using the heart we receive by God's grace.

God's law is focused on nurturing good relationships. We love God in return (by the Spirit, not the flesh) since he first loved us; and we love our neighbor (by the same Spirit) since God loves them too. Love is the intended basis for every relationship. To show us how to live in this kind of relationship, God first dwells with us.

"For thus says the One who is high and lifted up,

who inhabits eternity, whose name is Holy:

*'**I dwell** in the high and holy place,*

*and **also with him who is of a contrite and lowly spirit**,*

to revive the spirit of the lowly,

and to revive the heart of the contrite.'"

—Isaiah 57:15

Scripture does not present the concept of a "mutually beneficial" relationship with God wherein God needs our worship; he does not wait for us to obey him in our own flesh before agreeing to save us or bless us. God knows we can't generate anything pleasing to him on our own. We need to rely on him and the teachings of his Word.

"The God who made the world and everything in it, being Lord of heaven and earth, does not live in temples made by man, nor is he

served by human hands, **as though he needed anything,** *since he himself gives to all mankind life and breath and everything."*

—Acts 17:24–25

God does not need our worship or sacrifice. Psalm 50:7-15 presents the same idea: God made everything and doesn't need sacrifices. This is not why he created us. He can set up a heavenly worship choir any time he so chooses. No, God desires our love and obedience.

"And Samuel said,

'Has the Lord *as great delight in burnt offerings and sacrifices,*

as in obeying the voice of the Lord?

Behold, **to obey is better than sacrifice,**

and to listen than the fat of rams.'"

—1 Samuel 15:22

"For **I desire** *steadfast love and not sacrifice,*

the **knowledge of God** *rather than burnt offerings."*

—Hosea 6:6

God wants us to know him—to have a relationship.[21] True knowledge comes by experience. We experience God by listening to and obeying his Word. This proper sequence reflects the order of grace before law. We should read the Bible and agree with it, but we will only obtain full

---

21. See Isaiah 58:2.

knowledge as we share the message with others and receive the message from others. First we receive God's blessings, then his commandments follow. Once blessed, we can be a blessing to those around us.

God's nature contains absolute grace and law; the sequence in which these work has never changed, as God doesn't change.[22]

Luke 6:27–36 shows us that God is full of grace and mercy (note verse 36 in particular). We are to be the same. Our first priority is to emulate God's grace. God designed the Ark of the Covenant so that the "mercy seat" would rest atop his testimony and law (Exodus 25:20–22); likewise, in our own lives, grace is seated over love.

Good works are not optional; God's laws are absolute. Even the secondary Mosaic laws (regarding ceremonies, cleanliness, and other details) either remind us of our need to trust in God and obey his Word, or point to God's future works in Christ.

Creation and the Fall

Isaiah 45:18, Colossians 1:16, and Hebrews 2:10 give us good glimpses of insight into why God created the world.

*"He is the image of the invisible God, the firstborn of all creation. For by him **all things were created**, **in heaven and on earth**, visible and invisible, whether thrones or dominions or rulers or authorities—**all things were created through him and for him**."*

—Colossians 1:15–16

---

22. See Malachi 3:6; Hebrews 6:17; James 1:17.

*"For it was fitting that he [Christ], **for whom and by whom all things exist**, in bringing many sons to glory, should make the founder of their salvation perfect through suffering. For he who sanctifies and those who are sanctified all have one source. That is why he is not ashamed to call them brothers, saying,*

'I will tell of your name to my brothers;

in the midst of the congregation I will sing your praise.'"

—Hebrews 2:10–12

God created the world for his own purpose in the person of Christ. Does this seem selfish? Remember that God is the ultimate giver; he proves his generosity by making us co-inheritors of the earth and giving us eternal life with him. It would not make sense for God to make himself the sole heir of the Abrahamic promise. Why bother?

God could have just made the earth, kept it, and set up a worship choir. Why go through the trouble of making covenants and promises? Why go to the cross? He did all these things for our benefit. He is a giver, not a taker like the devil.

To accomplish his plan, God had to do something first. Before he could justify us under his law, he had to come into the world in human flesh to live amongst his creation; he needed to have a relationship with us at our human level. By becoming like us, God could redeem our human experience. He could accomplish on our behalf everything that our human natures never could: Christ defeated death, did good works, demonstrated faith, and lived out the relationship with the Father we were always supposed to enjoy.

See Hebrews 4:15 for the short version of God's strategy. The full details are spelled out in Hebrews 2:

*"Since therefore the children **share in flesh and blood, he himself likewise partook of the same things**, that through death he might destroy the one who has the power of death, that is, the devil, and deliver all those who through fear of death were subject to lifelong slavery. For surely it is not angels that he helps, but he helps the offspring of Abraham. Therefore **he had to be made like his brothers in every respect**, so that he might become a merciful and faithful high priest in the service of God, to make propitiation [atonement] for the sins of the people. For because he himself has suffered when tempted, he is able to help those who are being tempted."*

—Hebrews 2:14–18

God gives himself freely to us. He is a constant giver.[23]

*"Have this mind among yourselves, which is yours in Christ Jesus, who, though he was in the form of God, did not count equality with God a thing to be grasped, but **emptied himself**, by taking the form of a servant, being born in the likeness of men. And being found in human form, **he humbled himself by becoming obedient** to the point of death, even death on a cross."*

—Philippians 2:5–8

---

23. See Matthew 20:28; John 10:11; 2 Corinthians 8:9; Galatians 1:4; Ephesians 5:2; 1 Timothy 2:6.

Christ became humble and obeyed the Father's law as an example for us.

"[Christ] **gave himself** *for us to redeem us from all lawlessness and* **to purify for himself a people** *for his own possession who are zealous* **for good works.***"*

—Titus 2:14

After receiving the gift of Christ's Spirit, we are able to imitate his attributes, as summarized in 1 Corinthians 13. And in fact we are commanded to do so.[24]

God alone is holy and eternal. We were meant to be holy as well, but the devil and the sin he inspires have mired us in mortality. Since the Fall, our nature has been poisoned by the devil; we are now enslaved to sin and death. We inherited death through a bad gift from the worst giver ever. Our only hope is to receive baptism of the Holy Spirit and new life in Christ.

"The **one who practices sin is of the devil***; for the devil has sinned from the beginning. The Son of God appeared for this purpose, to destroy the works of the devil."*

—1 John 3:8

If we are born of the Spirit, we will act in love. When we act sinfully, these acts flow out of our old sinful nature, the one enslaved to the devil. Our old nature is simply not capable of love. The flesh we are born into is entirely selfish.

---

24. See Matthew 5:48; John 13:12–16; Ephesians 4:32, 5:1–2; Hebrews 6:12; 1 Pet 1:15–16; 3 John 1:11.

"Or do you suppose it is to no purpose that the Scripture says, 'He yearns jealously over the spirit that he has made to dwell in us'? But he gives more grace. Therefore it says, 'God opposes the proud but gives grace to the humble.' **Submit** *yourselves therefore* **to God. Resist the devil, and he will flee from you."**

—James 4:5–7

Submission is obedience and denial of self.

Until we receive God's gifts, we remain in our sin (1 Corinthians 15:17), self-righteousness (2 Timothy 3:5), self-love (2 Timothy 3:2–4), selfishness (James 3:15–16), and ambition (Romans 2:8). These are traits of the devil. We will continue to reflect our human nature by acting selfishly until we become born of God; then we will begin to reflect his nature.

"Never again will I curse the ground because of humans, for ***every inclination of the human heart is evil from childhood.*** *And never again will I destroy all living creatures, as I have done."*

—Genesis 8:21

The Bible clearly states that we are fully sinful when we are born.[25] The process God uses to save us from sin starts with his Word. Through the Holy Spirit, we obtain his nature, which is embedded directly into his Word. But we don't lose our nature.[26] Two natures (two hearts) now compete within us. What will determine which nature wins out? How can we put the old self in remission?

---

25. See Psalm 51:5.
26. See Romans 7:25.

The Mind of Christ

"Whoever is of God hears the words of God. *The reason why you do not hear them is that you are not of God."*

—John 8:47

We need a faith infusion.

Faith comes by hearing the Word of God.[27] Abraham heard God's Word in person, but we hear it by the Spirit. We can't hear God's Word or begin to understand Scripture without the Spirit embedded in us.[28] After receiving God's Word, there can only be two final outcomes—submission or rejection. So how do we hear God's Word if we start out "of the devil" (as described above in 1 John 3:8)?

*"For who knows a person's thoughts except the spirit of that person, which is in him? So also no one comprehends the thoughts of God except the Spirit of God. Now we have received not the spirit of the world, but the Spirit who is from God, that we might understand the things freely given us by God. And **we impart this in words not taught by human wisdom** but taught by the Spirit, interpreting spiritual truths to those who are spiritual. **The natural person does not accept the things of the Spirit** of God, for they are folly to him, **and he is not able to understand** them **because they are spiritually discerned**. The spiritual person judges all things, but is himself to be judged by no one. 'For who has understood the mind of the Lord so as to instruct him?' But **we have the mind of Christ."***

—1 Corinthians 2:11–16

---

27. See Romans 10:14–17.
28. See Galatians 3:2–6.

Can we even begin to understand God's plan if we are operating out of our flesh's sinful nature? How can we grasp the plan with human understanding? If God's salvation plan doesn't make sense to our human intelligence, how can we agree to submit to it? It seems foolish from a human perspective that we should reject our own intellect in order to gain deeper understanding.

This is the divine genius of God's plan. We can't accept the Word of God, understand it, know it, or apply it without his Spirit coming into our life. We need the mind of Christ, not the mind we inherited from Adam.[29]

Faith is not completed at a singular event; we don't receive faith as a realized product and then move on. Faith exists as a constant outpouring of the Spirit through God's Word over our lifetime. We need to repeatedly hear God's Word and believe in it as stated—never changing, misinterpreting, or rejecting his clear revelation. Faith develops gradually over time by the grace of God and through his Word.

The starting point of faith arrives when we humbly receive God's Word. We see how the process begins in Peter's first sermon after Pentecost.

"When the people heard this [the gospel], they were cut to the heart and said to Peter and the other apostles, 'Brothers, what shall we do?' Peter replied, 'Repent and be baptized, every one of you, in the name of Jesus Christ for the forgiveness of your sins. And you will receive the gift of the Holy Spirit.'"

—Acts 2:37–38

---

29. See Romans 8:5–9, 12:2; 2 Corinthians 4:4; Ephesians 2:1–3, 4:17–24; Titus 3:4–7; 1 John 5:19.

All the main concepts for beginning the process of salvation are contained in these two verses.

1. The gospel was preached and heard. Faith comes by hearing.
2. The hearers were cut to the heart (humbled). The circumcision of their hearts began.
3. As spiritual infants, they asked what to do to be saved. They brought nothing to the table and needed discipleship.
4. Peter said, "Repent," or turn to God. They did not need to make a choice to count towards repentance or keep a law of repentance.
5. They needed to receive the gift of the Spirit. Unless they actively rejected God's plan for salvation through baptism of the Spirit, this gift would be theirs. Three thousand were baptized that day, so we know they did not reject this gospel message.

They repented and embraced God's grace; they did not turn back to themselves. Grace flows in one direction; they could not offer good works to God until they believed in the message and accepted it as a pure gift.

In the next chapter, we will look at the implications of the second element of Peter's invitation: the call to be baptized.

CHAPTER 11.

BAPTISM AND REBIRTH

Before ascending into heaven, Christ told his disciples to go and baptize all nations (Matthew 28:18–20). The early Church often baptized whole households.[1] Today, we tend to baptize individuals. But in all cases, the ceremony is a symbol of baptism of the Spirit, which brings salvation through God's Word.

These passages do not say whether the apostles themselves baptized children, but catacomb records show that this was indeed a practice within the first century and afterward of the early Church. Early Church fathers such as Justin Martyr and Irenaeus in particular were proponents of infant baptism.[2] This is controversial in some denominational circles. Why not stick to adult baptism?

The early Church didn't share the modern concept of the "age of accountability," the stage at which an individual can

---

1. See Acts 16:14–15 and Acts 18:8.
2. W.H. Withrow. *The Catacombs of Rome and Their Testimony Relative to Primitive Christianity*, pp 532–533. Nelson and Phillips, 1874. This book has entered the public domain and is available at archive.org/details/cu31924074296439/page/n535. Accessed May 21, 2019.

make his own decision whether to be baptized and commit to a life of faith.

According to human understanding, we may assume that a baby is born good—made not only in God's image but with a godly nature—only to learn evil over time. This idea may sound reasonable at first, but it is not biblical.

The Bible states that everyone is enslaved to sin and death. Little Joseph, Big Joey, and Uncle Joe have the same destiny. Age is irrelevant. All are destined to die.[3] Resurrection is the only hope for ultimate salvation. Baptism of the Holy Spirit represents the first step, saving us and sealing us. Resurrection is the final step.

Baptism of the Spirit happens when the Word of the gospel is delivered. No matter the age of the person being baptized, all receive the exact same gift. What happens after baptism is a different matter. Hearing the Word is our starting place, but the baptism act itself does not nurture faith or cause obedience or ensure lifelong belief. This is why there is a second command within the Great Commission. Not only is the Church supposed to baptize people, but we are also called to lead those same people into maturity—to make disciples out of new believers.

In giving the Commission, Christ didn't include a list of instructions for the baptism ceremony; he didn't weigh in on whether it's better to immerse converts in water or sprinkle water on a child's forehead. The Levitical purity laws and *mikveh* cleansing offered a rich history of water-based ceremonies; then came John the Baptist, who

---

3. See Genesis 3:19–24; Hebrews 9:27.

baptized with water. Each of these practices foreshadowed the baptism of the Holy Spirit.[4] It is clear throughout the New Testament that the baptism of the Holy Spirit leads to salvation, while the ceremony of water baptism is merely a symbol of what God is doing in the spiritual realm.

Instead of fixating on the ceremony of baptism, the Church should focus on the ongoing mission of discipleship. Getting the Holy Spirit into someone's life is very important, but keeping him there is just as vital. We must lead new believers in discipleship and help to keep them in the faith. Salvation comes later, but sanctification is happening today.

"But now that you have been set free from sin and have become slaves of God, the fruit you get leads to sanctification and its end, eternal life."

—Romans 6:22

While we await eternal life, we are set apart today. God is preserving us for use in his spiritual kingdom today and the physical kingdom to follow the merger of heaven and earth.

New disciples don't know a lot; they are spiritual infants. We must nurture them through a continual process that is realized through the delivery of the Word; we preach and teach, and they hear God's message over time.

Should we withhold baptism until a certain point when a person is "ready"? How might we tell when a person ready? The truth is, it shouldn't be up to us to judge the hearts

---

4. See Acts 11:14–18.

of others. Our task is simply to preach, baptize, and teach; only the Holy Spirit can see into the heart.

The belief described in Mark 16:16 is ongoing and constantly engaged. In contrast, water ceremonies represent a one-time event: the baptism of the Spirit and the corresponding receipt of our new, clean heart. But despite the symbolism of drowning our old sinful nature, the flesh doesn't stay smothered. We need daily drowning thereafter.[5]

A major dividing line about baptism relates to the question of what is baptized: a mortal or immortal soul? If we believe in an immortal soul, we are more liable to have a "once saved, always saved" (or "once baptized, always baptized") mentality. But if our soul is mortal, it must be continually preserved then finally saved at the resurrection. A one-time event of baptism would not be adequate.

We can experience the power of the Word through the Holy Spirit at any age. We in our flesh do not choose to pursue the Spirit, but God chooses to give himself to us; nothing we do can affect when God approaches us. Baptism is not a choice we make. It is a gift we receive from the Spirit.

Most of our debates over ceremony come down to a misunderstanding of free will as it relates to salvation in general. It is not presumptuous to baptize an infant because even adult believers must continually choose to remain in Christ. This ceremony does not ensure that the child will do so. By the same token, there should be no issue for the congregation in waiting for a family or person to be

---

5. See Luke 9:23.

baptized if the congregation is already engaged in relaying God's Word (and by extension God's Spirit). Salvation doesn't hinge on the application of water, but on the outpouring of God's Spirit. The power of the Word will convict the person or the head of a family.

Salvation: Our Choice or God's?

Belief is trust in God's Word alone. Is choice the same concept as belief?

Choice can be considered a work that we must do under the flesh while belief is trust in the work of Christ. This is why the Bible focuses on words like "believe" or "confess," not words like "choose" or "decide."

We cannot credit our choice to believe in God for salvation through our old nature, as this would mean that we contributed toward our own salvation. We cannot produce our own righteousness or good works, not in any amount; God alone is righteous, and only God can give us righteousness.

To make a choice, we weigh the options, then select what we think is best. Since we are sinful by human nature, our old heart can only make a selfish decision. Even if we say we are choosing to follow Christ, our motivation is to win something for ourselves: eternity in heaven; happiness; an alliance with a powerful God. Whenever we make a decision or choice, no matter how good we think our intentions are, we are following our own judgment and operating under the law of the flesh.

"But if you are led by the Spirit, you are not under the law."

—Galatians 5:18

We are saved by grace through the Spirit, and we must be led by the Spirit, not our human judgment. Our belief flows out of the grace we have received, not an idea we find persuasive.

The idea that we choose to become saved is generally tied to a mythological free will. According to this perspective, we in our human nature invite God to come in and clean our heart of its sin—or at least as much of it as possible. The result is a mixed nature, a merger of God and man. But this idea is not in the Bible. Our sinful nature can only be crucified, drowned, and buried--not cleaned. God does cleanse us but with the gift of a newly created heart.[6]

Remember, we do not *have* a literal soul; rather, we *are* a soul, which is the living combination of spirit and "dust." Our soul is not immortal, and isn't "ours" at all. We *are* a soul only when alive. As a mortal soul, we need the Holy Spirit to continually work in us after our baptism to sustain us.

After baptism, discipleship and discipline kick in. We all are spiritual infants when we first receive the Holy Spirit. We need a continual outpouring of the Spirit. Everyone needs this. The very term "born again" implies that a new nature has been given to us; no matter our age or maturity, we all have the starting point.

Baptism in the Holy Spirit marks the initiation of our salvation, and the continual outpouring of the Spirit

---

6. See Psalm 51:10–17; Ezekiel 36:26–27.

maintains our salvation. Discipleship keeps us engaged in obedience, and therefore growing in faith. The Spirit is continually engaged, the new believer must be continually engaged, and Christ commands the Church to be likewise committed to the ongoing work of teaching and training new disciples.

The making of a disciple in Matthew 28:19 is a singular, intermittent event, but teaching in Matthew 28:20 is an ongoing activity.

Due to the "now and not yet" nature of salvation, biblical verbs regarding salvation appear in a variety of tenses.

- **Past tense:** We were sealed at our baptism in the Holy Spirit. The Word came first. The Church gave us the gift of the Holy Spirit by relaying God's Word. We could not baptize ourselves, but after grace came, the Church followed God's law of institution. Nothing we did contributed to our own baptism; it was a gift from Christ through the Church.

- **Present tense:** We are kept, preserved, comforted, and sanctified by the continual saving work of the Holy Spirit. Salvation is a gift today.

- **Future tense:** We will ultimately be saved when the Spirit breathes life back into our corpse (or dust) at the resurrection. Salvation will be a gift in the future.

When we look at verb tenses within all salvation passages, we notice that there is a special focus on the future for ultimate salvation. There are also a lot of verses that speak to the present salvific effects of the Holy Spirit that keep us preserved until the resurrection. Of course, many passages speak to the past saving work of Christ. Some passages even depict all three tenses of salvation.

Ephesians 1 shows us a progression from past to present to future. Here the whole salvation process is summarized in just two verses.

*"In him you also, when you **heard** the word of truth, the gospel of your salvation, and **believed** in him, were **sealed** with the promised Holy Spirit, who **is** the guarantee of our inheritance **until we acquire** possession of it, to the praise of his glory."*

—Ephesians 1:13–14

In this passage, Paul arranges many key points in the proper sequence.

1. The gospel was **heard**; by grace, we heard the good news of the gift of eternal life.
2. Faith was formed; we **believed** this message (through humility, not analysis).
3. We were **sealed** with the Spirit; he **is** now the guarantee of our inheritance.
4. We **will acquire** the inheritance of the promise to Abraham on the day of resurrection.

Salvation in this passage is in the future. Paul didn't have it yet. He wasn't totally saved.

We can't "hear" this gospel under our old sinful nature. Wanting the matter to be settled, we will grasp for something we can do to ensure our salvation. But what is required of us is contriteness, broken-heartedness, and humility (Isaiah 66:2b); these attributes convey the correct attitude with which to hear the gospel. We need to be like a child who brings nothing to the table before God. We can't bring our decisions, prayers, petitions, pleas, or sacrifices to God as a first step. God does invite us to call upon his name and continually confess, yet these are not singular events that establish our relationship. We are not asked to respond to "altar calls" or offer up a "sinner's prayer."

"For You do not delight in sacrifice, otherwise I would give it;

You are not pleased with burnt offerings.

The sacrifices of God are a broken spirit;

a broken and contrite heart, O God, You will not despise."

—Psalm 51:16–17, NASB

Let's again look at infant baptism as a way to examine our attitudes regarding salvation and free will. In every case, no matter the age of the person involved, the following aspects of baptism are true:

- Baptism conveys God's gift;
- No one can baptize himself;
- Only the Church can administer baptism;
- Baptism does not produce a perfected faith; and so
- Continual discipleship must follow.

Depending on the age of the person being baptized, she may or may not comprehend what baptism means. Obviously an infant would be oblivious, while confusion in an adolescent would be perfectly understandable—but even an adult might have some misconceptions about what is happening in the spiritual realm.

The reason some people get bent out of shape over infant baptism is reason itself. Can a person be baptized without understanding baptism? Put another way, is it acceptable to baptize now and then train and disciple the child until he is ready to confess his faith later on?

Can confession and baptism occur separately?

The Bible, the early Church Fathers, and the catacombs reveal that early Christians practiced both infant and believer's baptism. Why should we pick one or the other? Our clear mission is to build the corporate Body of Christ by following the means he instituted. Our primary concern should not be how people in our community receive the Spirit's baptism, but how we nurture each other in the Spirit and are united together in Christ.

Common Misconceptions

As we've seen, many of our widely held beliefs about God and his creation do not align with Scripture. Let's take a closer look at a few common ideas regarding our human nature that ought to be reconsidered.

1. **Immortal soul:** the idea that we have a soul that will never die. Branching off from this concept is the idea of eternal security, or "once saved, always saved."

2. **Free will to accept God:** the idea that we must make a decision to follow God as a primary step of

salvation. Accepting God by faith is different from making a decision to accept God through our own free will.

3. **Individualism:** the idea that we can go look for God on our own.

Eternal Security

When an adult is baptized, is he eternally secure? When an infant is baptized, is she eternally secure? If she becomes confirmed in the faith as an adolescent, should we consider her salvation secure at that point?

Salvation is not completed at baptism, nor at confirmation, nor at any other rite or ceremony available to the Church. Salvation is only made complete at the second advent. No graduation ceremony, no event, no single act of any person or group of people can make an individual's salvation permanent. We can turn away and reject the gift of the Holy Spirit at any time. Free will is always present within our old nature, fully capable of rejecting God.

Free Will to Accept God

While we can use our free will to reject God, we cannot use that same will to accept Christ as savior. Under the law of flesh, we cannot choose to accept God into our heart, or else we would be able to secure our own salvation through our good actions.

Salvation requires our continual belief. We are kept secure as long as we don't reject God or interrupt the work he is doing in us through his Spirit. Obeying his commands demonstrates that we haven't rejected his Word or his will.

God's grace is unconditional in the sense that the whole world is offered forgiveness and salvation, but conditional in the sense that we need to believe and trust in him. Accepting his will means that we do not change, add to or take away from his plans. We leave them "as is".

Where is the Bible passage that says we must choose God to be saved? As soon as we make salvation hinge on our own actions, we end up in the parable of the Rich Young Man (Matthew 19:16–24). We can't say that we like some of what the Bible has to say, then only follow the teachings we like. It is all or nothing with God. We either live by every word that comes out of his mouth, or we end up adding to his Word or taking away from it. After the ending of the parable, Christ tells us that mankind does not possess the will to do what is necessary to be saved.

*"When the disciples heard this, they were greatly astonished, saying, 'Who then can be saved?' But Jesus looked at them and said, **'With man this is impossible**, but with God all things are possible.'"*

—Matthew 19:25–26

We do see one passage in the Bible that describes making a choice for salvation. In Deuteronomy 30:11–20, Moses relays God's message to his people as they prepare to enter the Promised Land. Verse 19 states that Israel should choose life over death. But this passage rests within the context of the Mosaic covenant. Israel needed to agree to God's conditional terms; by stating that they would keep his laws, they would be blessed to enter the land. This teaching is not repeated in the New Testament but is for our instruction that we cannot choose life or earn eternal life. It is a gift that we can only accept by faith.

We often talk about making a choice or decision to follow Christ. But the key element of salvation is Christ choosing us, calling us. Let's look at the apostles' election as an example. In John 15:16–17, Christ reminds his disciples that he chose them, not the other way around.[7] People are "elected" for salvation. (After we study free will further, we'll come back to the concept of election.)

Individualism

Although individualism is a strong cultural value in our society, this is not a biblical value. God intends for us to live in Christian community, and this begins with baptism. We cannot baptize ourselves; only the Church can deliver this gift through the Word by the Holy Spirit. God's goal is to form a larger Church body. The Church is not effective in its work for Christ when we isolate ourselves and try to operate alone.

Baptism of the Spirit is a corporate gift that an individual can reject at any time after receiving it. We can "lose" salvation by rejecting God's methods. Comprehension of the gift may come later through discipleship, or we may grasp God's plan of salvation on the day of our baptism. But there is no need for us to fully comprehend baptism *before* receiving the gift of the Holy Spirit.

As Christians, we must continually believe in God's grace as it is poured out over time. The initial event of baptism

---

7. His instruction in this verse to abide in good works relates to his earlier teaching to abide in God's love (John 15:10). Good works flow out of God's nature, not our own.

is very important, but the Bible puts much greater focus on the ongoing process of sanctification through which the Spirit keeps us in the faith. Like baptism, the process of sanctification is carried out within Christian community, not on our own.

New Life in the Spirit

Here Paul offers us some insight into the salvation process:

"But what does it say? **'The word is near you**, *in your mouth and* **in your heart'** *(that is, the word of faith that we proclaim); because, if you confess with your mouth that Jesus is Lord and* **believe in your heart** *that God raised him from the dead,* **you will be saved**. *For with the heart one believes and is justified, and with the mouth one confesses and is saved. For the Scripture says, 'Everyone who believes in him will not be put to shame.' For there is no distinction between Jew and Greek; for the same Lord is Lord of all, bestowing his riches on all who call on him. For 'everyone who calls on the name of the Lord will be saved.'"*

—Romans 10:8–13

So the Word comes first to enter the heart. This is a new heart *in* us, not a merger of the Word into our old heart.

This passage can be taken out of context, so let's look closely. We need to understand what "believes" means, so let's examine other appearances of this word in Romans.

"For I am not ashamed of **the gospel**, *for it* **is the power of God for salvation** *to everyone who believes."*

—Romans 1:16a

*"May the **God of hope fill you** with all joy and peace in believing, so that **by the power of the Holy Spirit** you may abound in hope."*

—Romans 15:13

Belief itself doesn't contain anything of intrinsic value without the power of God. We do need to believe in God and not reject him, but our belief is nothing compared to his power, which is contained in his Word.

Salvation begins when God puts a new heart within us and imbues it with the power of the Word of the Spirit (see Romans 10:8 above). The gospel is planted (or embedded) inside of us. Only then can true belief occur. It does us no good to try to believe God with our old nature. The original heart of our sinful nature either rejects God's Word outright, or tries to change it or modify it to fit our preconceived beliefs.

When we believe in God's gifts with our new heart, we receive the seeds of faith. This gift of faith is the beginning of justification. As Paul puts it, we are saved "through faith" in Christ.

*"Yet we know that a person is not justified by works of the law but **through faith in Jesus Christ**, so we also have **believed in Christ Jesus**, in order to be justified by faith in Christ and not by works of the law, because by works of the law no one will be justified."*

—Galatians 2:16

A common view is that justification begins when we in our human nature become persuaded to believe in the gospel. Were this true, many Scriptures would no longer make sense. True belief is the result of God coming into our heart, not a mechanism that prompts his arrival. As we will see in Acts 15:11, Peter states that he and a new Gentile believer have each received the same grace. What matters is God's generosity, not the relative intensity of our belief or convictions.

Is our faith in itself a gift from God? Or is our belief contributing to the primary gift, with faith sprouting from that belief? Each interpretation seems to have its own supporting passages.

Some passages describe belief as coming from our old heart. But even evil demons believe in God.[8] Belief itself is not the whole message, as we can see. True belief must flow out of a contrite heart after the gift of the gospel is delivered.

We need to pay close attention to verb tenses as we seek to understand salvation in general and the faith-by-grace concept in particular. In Romans 10:8–13 (quoted above), Paul twice uses the future tense "will be saved." This is to be expected; salvation will be made complete at the second advent when we are resurrected and welcomed into the Promised Land.

But in Romans 10:10, Paul switches to the present tense: "With the mouth one confesses and **is saved**." According to this English translation, full salvation occurs in the present,

---

8. See James 2:19.

which contradicts several other passages we've already studied. It is possible that Paul is referring to spiritual salvation, not bodily resurrection. On the other hand, a more literal rendering of this sentence would read, "With the mouth one confesses "**unto salvation**." This phrase (used in such translations as the New King James Version) depicts an ongoing salvation in terms of a preservation effect. With this more literal translation, the textual conflict is resolved.

Salvation is presented in different verb-tenses in Scripture as we have seen. But we also see some movement in the understanding of salvation—not in terms of when, but for whom.

"But some men came down from Judea and were teaching the brothers, 'Unless you are circumcised according to the custom of Moses, **you cannot be saved.***'"*

—Acts 15:1

According to traditional understanding of the Mosaic covenant, salvation was for the people of Israel and converts to this originally Hebrew nation. Only such people could hope to receive resurrection and enter into the Promised Land.

"But we believe that we [Jews] **will be saved** *through the grace of the Lord Jesus, just as they [Gentiles] will."*

—Acts 15:11

Peter's simple response in this second passage covers two extremely important topics.

1. **Salvation is in the future.** Peter believes he isn't saved yet but will be saved at the second advent. We receive the promise by grace today, but the promise is not fulfilled until the day of resurrection.

2. **The true Promised Land is heaven on earth.** This passage doesn't explicitly mention the Promised Land, but verse 1 sets the context with a discussion of circumcision and salvation. Circumcision is a covenant reminder of the blessings given to Abraham—in particular, that he would live eternally in the Promised Land. So Peter here declares that God is bringing Gentiles into the same covenant promise; they too will enter heaven on earth.

There are many examples in Scripture of present-tense gifts that lead to future-tense salvation verbs; that is, grace today leads to eternal life on the last day.[9]

In Acts 16, Paul offers present-tense baptism and preaches future-tense salvation. Notice the jailor's contrite heart; also see how "the word of the Lord" was the means through which he and his family came to believe.

*"Then he brought them out and said, 'Sirs, what must I do to be saved?' And they said, **'Believe in the Lord Jesus**, and **you will be saved**, you and your household.' And **they spoke the word of the Lord** to him and to all who were in his house. And he took them the same hour of the night and washed their wounds; and he was baptized at once, he and all his family."*

—Acts 16:30–33

---

9. See Acts 11:18; Romans 6:22–23.

We are to believe in the Word of the Lord to be saved. The Word comes first; only then can we believe in God's promise to save us in the future.

Here is a similar passage that shows how Gentiles received the same gift (Word and Spirit) as the Jewish apostles.

*"'And he told us how he had seen the angel stand in his house and say, "Send to Joppa and bring Simon who is called Peter; he will declare to you a **message by which you will be saved**, you and all your household." As I began to speak, the Holy Spirit fell on them just as on us at the beginning. And I remembered the word of the Lord, how he said, "John baptized with water, but you will be baptized with the Holy Spirit." If then God gave the same gift to them as he gave to us when we believed in the Lord Jesus Christ, who was I that I could stand in God's way? When they heard these things they fell silent. And they glorified God, saying, "Then to the Gentiles also God has granted repentance that **leads to life**."'"*

—Acts 11:13–18

These passages from Romans and Acts feature the same concepts about baptism of the Holy Spirit. The Spirit of Christ's Word was delivered; then belief in the Word enabled salvation in the future.

Present-tense verbs of salvation are also very important in that we need to be sealed today by the Holy Spirit. Throughout Scripture we encounter words like "keeps" and "preserves." This work of preservation is ongoing. Sanctification follows justification as a process over time.

Unfortunately, a lot of people just use the past tense to describe salvation. For example, someone might say, "I was saved on June 3, 1967," or "I was baptized on..." But salvation is an ongoing process, something we experience in the present and realize in the future.

Freedom in the Ever-Present Spirit

*"And those who belong to Christ Jesus have crucified the flesh with its passions and desires. If we **live by the Spirit**, let us also **keep in step** with the Spirit."*

—Galatians 5:24–25

*"...that according to the riches of his glory he may grant you to **be strengthened** with power **through his Spirit** in your inner being."*

—Ephesians 3:16

*"[W]**alk** in a manner worthy of the Lord, fully pleasing to him: bearing fruit in every good work and **increasing** in the knowledge of God; **being strengthened** with all power, **according to his glorious might**, for all endurance and patience with joy; giving thanks to the Father, who has qualified you to share in the inheritance of the saints in light."*

—Colossians 1:10–12

*"Do not lie to one another, seeing that you have put off the old self with its practices and have put on the **new self**, which **is being renewed** in knowledge **after the image of its creator**."*

—Colossians 3:9–10

*"The Spirit of God has made me; the breath of the Almighty **gives** me life."*

—Job 33:4

Job declares his life is being sustained in the present tense.

*"And I am sure of this, that he who began a good work in you **will bring** it to completion at the day of Jesus Christ."*

—Philippians 1:6

Salvation is ongoing, a promise yet to be fulfilled.

*"[F]or **it is God who is at work in you**, both to will and to work for His good pleasure."*

—Philippians 2:13

The good works that come out of our lives are God's doing. We cannot do the good that God desires.

*"Do not quench the Spirit.... Now may the **God of peace** himself **sanctify** you completely, and may your whole spirit and soul and body **be kept** blameless at the coming of our Lord Jesus Christ."*

—1 Thessalonians 5:19, 23

The ongoing work of sanctification is carried out by the Spirit. God himself sets us apart from the world and our old sinful nature. We are not saved once, and then free to go on sinning.

The famous passage of Ephesians 2:8–9 describes how grace leads to faith. But if we put too much focus on grace, we may not read or practice verse 10. Grace enables us to join God in doing good works that were established for us long ago.

*"For we are his workmanship, **created in Christ Jesus for good works**, which God prepared beforehand, **that we should walk in them.**"*

—Ephesians 2:10

God predestined us to do good works—to keep his law and love others. God's election contains a general plan that he has for us all, but he also has an individual plan for each of us.

God desires to have a continued relationship with us—to "walk" with us, not just deliver a one-time gift of grace. When we are faithful in our relationship with God and our obedience to his will, the result is our sanctification.

Sanctification means to be set apart for holy use. We need to be set apart from the world and our sinful nature because the Holy Spirit now dwells in us.[10] Transformation is a process of steady separation.

Our human flesh is only sinful and cannot save itself. There is no conversion of the old nature, as it is considered dead, crucified, drowned, and buried.[11]

*"In him also you were circumcised with a circumcision made without hands, by putting off the body of the flesh, by the circumcision of Christ, **having been buried with him in baptism**, in which you were also raised with him **through faith in the powerful working of God**, who raised him from the dead. And you, who were dead in your trespasses and the*

---

10. See 1 Corinthians 6:19.
11. See Mark 8:34; Romans 6:1–15; 7:4; 2 Corinthians 5:17; Galatians 2:20; 5:24; 6:14; Ephesians 4:20–24; Colossians 3:9–10.

uncircumcision of your flesh, God made alive together with him, having forgiven us all our trespasses, by canceling the record of debt that stood against us with its legal demands. This he set aside, nailing it to the cross."

—Colossians 2:11–14

The concepts of drowning, burial, crucifixion, and denying oneself to take up the cross are all perfect analogies of what needs to happen to the old heart.

"That which is born of the flesh is flesh, and that which is born of the Spirit is spirit."

—John 3:6

Flesh connotes self, our sinful nature, enslavement to death and the devil.

Spirit connotes Christ, God's nature, new birth, eternal life.

The Bible often relates concepts and entities to one other, such as death and the devil, or Christ and life. Opposing natures or concepts are only pitted against each other, never mixed—unless to demonstrate an abomination. The Bible never promotes lukewarm faith, hybrid gospels, or mixing truth with myths.[12]

We often struggle to define our own sinful nature. We can get as far as acknowledging that Adam sinned, thus putting us under the death curse. But we resist associating our mortality with an inherent sinfulness. We were created good in the image of God, after all. Free will was meant to

---

12. See Mark 8:33.

be a blessing, physical nature was perfect—even our dust will be resurrected someday. If all other aspects of life are good, how can we be lumped into an all-bad sinful-nature scenario?

The short answer is that even one small imperfection makes the whole lump unholy as seen in God's eyes. The death curse is the unholy ingredient.

We need to focus on the new nature. Our new identity is life in Christ, who saved us and continues to live in us through his Spirit. But the death nature still resides within us, even though we consider it crucified with Christ and know it will be destroyed. The ceremony of baptism illustrates our hope, the water drowning our old nature as we rise to new life with our resurrected savior. We are born again with God's Spirit. We are alive in Christ and dead to the flesh.

However, all enemies are not yet destroyed. Death no longer has its sting, but death remains.

"The last enemy to be destroyed is death."

—1 Corinthians 15:26

We are born into sin and remain in it until we are born of the Spirit. Our sinful (mortal) nature is described by Christ in John 3:36 as wrath remaining in us.

Wrath in this case refers to the curse of death that God put on Adam and Eve and their descendants (including us).

"...among whom we all once lived in the passions of our flesh,

carrying out the desires of the body and the mind, and **were by nature children of wrath**, *like the rest of mankind."*

—Ephesians 2:3

Everyone is cursed to die.

"Behold, I was brought forth in iniquity,

and in sin did my mother conceive me."

—Psalm 51:5

Did this person's sin come upon him through his own thoughts or actions? No. All are cursed before they are born.

Since the Fall, every person starts off life in sin and remains in sin. Born into death, we must be made alive in the Spirit.

"For **God has consigned all to disobedience**, *that he may have mercy on all. Oh, the depth of the riches and wisdom and knowledge of God! How unsearchable are his judgments and how inscrutable his ways!*

'For who has known the mind of the Lord,

or who has been his counselor?'

'Or who has given a gift to him

that he might be repaid?'

"For from him and through him and to him are all things. To him be glory forever. Amen."

—Romans 11:32–36

We need to read the entirety of God's Word to understand the "depths of his wisdom and knowledge." The concept of being "consigned" or born into sin doesn't make sense from a human perspective, yet it's true.

On what basis does God condemn our nature? What good is our free will if we cannot choose righteousness?

Free will is not true freedom. We cannot choose whether to sin or do good, as it is our nature to sin. It is automatic. In following our nature, we cannot help but choose the sinful path (until we are born again). This is imprisonment, not freedom. The Spirit must set us free from our sinful nature and empower us to do good through God's nature.

The freedom we have in Christ is true freedom. However, we are not free to choose sin in the Spirit, which means our new situation is the exact opposite of free will in the flesh. We can "choose" to sin under the flesh, or we can exercise our freedom in Christ to do good. God's nature cannot produce sin, and our human nature cannot produce righteousness.

A common assumption is that God converts our old human nature by rinsing out most of the sin, allowing us to merge with the Spirit and become holy ourselves. We imagine we must choose to seek God's forgiveness so we can go to heaven. The truth is that we first need the mind of Christ (1 Corinthians 2:16) that comes by his Word. Our human mind is bound by the curse and fixated on selfish desires.

Instead of trying to choose to act righteously, we need to

trust in the God who is righteous. He is the one who does good works; we were planned from the foundation of the world according to his will to be a conduit in the Spirit. With humility we submit to God's power at work in and through us. Instead of trying to make our own good decisions, we need to follow God's commands. His Word tells us all we need to do.

God's Word clearly spells out his plans, instructions, laws, and commands. We have nothing to debate or decide upon. We should simply obey. Adam was designed to live by the Word of God.[13] We share the same design.

Human nature cannot help but believe the lies of the devil, who is the father of lies.[14] His first lie convinced us to doubt God and trust in our own supposed immortality. Because of this sin, we live under the death curse.

The devil continues to tell this same lie today, but Christ's nature binds us to eternal life and truth. Hidden in Christ who cannot lie (Hebrews 6:18), we have access to every truth necessary for life.

Christ is literally *"the way, the truth, and the life"* (John 14:6a)—the antidote to our curse of death and sin.

Christ is the founder of salvation (Hebrews 2:10), the source of salvation (Hebrews 5:9), and the perfecter of our faith (Hebrews 12:2). Only by his gifts can faith be completed. Christ calls us to act out our faith through his Spirit; these are the good works we can participate in.

---

13. See Matthew 4:4, which is quoting Deuteronomy 8:3.
14. See John 8:44.

*"But someone will say, 'You have faith and I have works.' Show me your faith apart from your works, and I will show you my faith by my works. You believe that God is one; you do well. Even the demons believe—and shudder! Do you want to be shown, you foolish person, that faith apart from works is useless? Was not Abraham our father justified by works when he offered up his son Isaac on the altar? You see that faith was active along with his works, and **faith was completed by his works**; and the Scripture was fulfilled that says, 'Abraham believed God, and it was counted to him as righteousness'—and he was called a friend of God. You see that a person is justified by works and not by faith alone."*

—James 2:18–24

The flesh cannot produce good works, so James is speaking here of good works done in tandem with the Spirit through his nature. He clarified in the previous chapter that everything good comes from God (James 1:17).

God's promises to Abraham were unconditional (Genesis 12 and 15); once Abraham received God's grace, commands followed (Genesis 17 and 22). Abraham believed in the promise, initiating his faith (Genesis 15:6), but his faith was only completed after he obediently acted out his belief (Genesis 22:1-18).

How did Abraham's belief in God's unconditional promises compare to him acting out his trust that God would raise Isaac from the dead? The promises God made to Abraham in Genesis 12 and 15 did not depend on Abraham making a choice to believe in God. Abraham merely received these gifts. God bore all the responsibility in the blood oath he initiated (Genesis 15:13–20). Abraham offered Isaac to God based upon his previous belief in the gifts; this completed his faith.

Our own faith begins when God reaches out to us in forgiveness. Faith is included with the gift like a hand to grab on to. If we believe the gift is true, we will act out in obedience to complete our faith according to God's guidance. Many people stop at belief. This is making a handshake agreement only to fail to follow through. Carrying out the work fulfills the contract. But even in faithfulness, we must maintain proper perspective and humility.

*"What then is Apollos? What is Paul? Servants through whom you believed, as the Lord assigned to each. I planted, Apollos watered, but God gave the growth. So neither he who plants nor he who waters is anything, but **only God who gives the growth**."*

—1 Corinthians 3:5–7

Our belief is an important step in the salvation process, but belief does not count as a work towards righteousness. Rather, Christ grants us his own righteousness and power. We get "credit" for our belief only when we trust God enough to act in faith with God's spiritual resources. This results in our justification, completing the work of Christ.

Christ completed the universal work on the cross for all; when we believe in him, we can live through the power of his work in us.

CHAPTER 12.

DUELING NATURES

Until God puts his nature within us, we cannot love God. Even if we in our human mind agree with the concept of a loving God, we are not able to respond with love in our human nature. Only God is capable of love, though he does share this ability when he gives us his Spirit. Then we can love God and love others with God's own heart.

We are either "of God" (John 8:47) or "of the devil" (1 John 3:8, 10). There is no such thing as a "sort-of-good person" or a single nature containing both evil and righteousness.

We often think of moral dilemmas in terms of the angel-and-demon concept. We imagine a demon on one shoulder, speaking lies into one ear, and an angel on our other shoulder, speaking the truth in our other ear. We then decide which advice to act upon. Such a concept is pure mythology, located nowhere in the Bible.

This myth has been constantly repackaged since the fall of mankind. Another popular version of this myth goes like this:

A Chief is talking with his grandson. He says, "There are two wolves inside of us which are always at battle. One is good and represents things like kindness, bravery, and love. The other is bad and represents things like greed, hatred, and fear."

The grandson asks, "Grandfather, which one wins?"

The Chief replies, "The one you feed."

According to the biblical model, we are the evil one. The human nature that we received in our inheritance from Adam is hopelessly spoiled. There is no such thing as a neutral person who decides between good or evil. Either we become linked to the Spirit of life or remain linked to our flesh that is mired in death.

Flesh can only choose evil. We imagine that we have some potential to do good or make good choices, but our original sinful nature is fully self-centered. Even if we do good, give to charity, help our neighbor, and other acts of kindness under the flesh, we always do these things to satisfy our own desire for justification as our "contribution" towards eternal life.

Truth and Lies

We see all throughout the Bible that only God is good (Luke 18:19) and God only speaks truth (Hebrews 6:18). The opposite concept is that the devil is the father of lies (John 8:44). Lies led to our enslavement to sin.

We know faith starts with hearing God's truth; likewise, evil starts with hearing Satan's lies. Adam and Eve first heard the devil's lies, then believed in the lies, putting trust in the devil. In turn, we have inherited a human nature prone to believing lies. Nobody likes to think they are of the devil, but if we hear lies and believe them, we prove our enslavement.[1]

Although we may say we reject the devil, we cannot escape his influence. Perhaps we do not intentionally follow the devil, but when we follow our own thoughts, listen to our own heart, or believe in ourselves to make the right decisions, we are nonetheless deceived; we remain in sin.

Free-will gospel says we make a decision to "let" God into our life. But the Spirit cannot enter our sinful heart even with permission. Our heart needs to be cut before God can enter. Circumcision of our inner being is the first step of receiving a new identity. This comes by the Word.

Once our sinful nature has been circumcised (Colossians 2:11), there is room for the gift of God's nature (2 Corinthians 5:17). But at any point during the sanctification process, we can choose to reject God's Word and Spirit and return to our old sinful nature.

Salvation is conditional. Christ stated that there is an unforgivable sin of speaking against the Holy Spirit.[2]

"And whoever speaks a word against the Son of Man will be

---

1. Though our corrupted human nature is inclined to believe the devil's lies, we were designed to live by every word that comes from the mouth of God (see Matthew 4:4, which quotes Deuteronomy 8:3).
2. Christ does not condemn the sin of speaking against himself. But remember that Christ emptied himself of the fullness of God in the incarnation. Since Christ regained this fullness upon his resurrection, this warning against blasphemy likely extends to all Persons of the Trinity.

forgiven, but whoever speaks against the Holy Spirit will not be forgiven, either in this age or in the age to come."

—Matthew 12:32

Rejection of God's Word and speaking against the Holy Spirit are essentially the same sin. The Spirit and the Word go hand in hand. Our salvation has one essential condition: we can't reject God's Word. Most believers don't dare do this outright. But many believers do adjust their interpretation of Scripture to fit their biases instead of letting God's Word speak clearly and directly.

Notice the conditional underlined words in the passages below; these relate to the actions we must take to keep the faith.

*"The ones along the path are those who have heard; then the devil comes and **takes away the word** from their hearts, so that they **may not believe** and be saved."*

—Luke 8:12

*"They [Israel] were broken off because of their unbelief, but you [Gentiles] stand fast through faith. So do not become proud, but fear. For if God did not spare the natural branches, neither will he spare you. Note then the kindness and the severity of God: severity toward those who have fallen, but God's kindness to you, **provided you continue in his kindness**. Otherwise you too will be cut off. And even they, if they do not continue in their unbelief, will be grafted in, for God has the power to graft them in again."*

—Romans 11:20–23

"**By this gospel you are saved, if you hold firmly** to the word I preached to you. Otherwise, you have believed in vain."

—1 Corinthians 15:2

"Examine yourselves, to **see whether you are in the faith.** Test yourselves. Or do you not realize this about yourselves, that Jesus Christ is in you?—**unless** indeed **you fail to meet the test**! I hope you will find out that we have not failed the test."

—2 Corinthians 13:5–6

"And those who belong to Christ Jesus have crucified the flesh with its passions and desires. **If we live by the Spirit, let us also keep in step with the Spirit.** Let us not become conceited, provoking one another, envying one another."

—Galatians 5:24–26

"Therefore, my beloved, as you have always obeyed, so now, not only as in my presence but much more in my absence, **work out your own salvation** with fear and trembling, for it is God who works in you, both to will and to work for his good pleasure."

—Philippians 2:12–13

"**Follow** the pattern of **the sound words** that you have heard from me, in the faith and love that are in Christ Jesus."

—2 Timothy 1:13

"[H]e has now reconciled in his body of flesh by his death, in order to present you holy and blameless and above reproach before him, **if indeed you continue in the faith**, stable and steadfast, not shifting from the hope of the gospel that you heard."

—Colossians 1:22–23a

"Take care, brothers, lest there be in any of you an evil, unbelieving heart, leading you to fall away from the living God. But exhort one another every day, as long as it is called 'today,' that none of you may be hardened by the deceitfulness of sin. For we have come to share in Christ, **if indeed we hold our original confidence firm to the end.**"

—Hebrews 3:12–14

"**[T]ake care that you are not carried away** with the error of lawless people and **lose your own stability**. But grow in the grace and knowledge of our Lord and Savior Jesus Christ."

—2 Peter 3:17b–18a

"**[B]e on your guard so that you may not** be carried away by the error of the lawless and **fall from your secure position**. But grow in the grace and knowledge of our Lord and Savior Jesus Christ."

—2 Peter 3:17b–18a, NIV

"As for you, **see that what you have heard** from the beginning **remains in you. If it does**, you also will remain in the Son and in the Father. And this is what he promised us—eternal life. I am writing these things to you about those who are trying to lead you astray."

—1 John 2:24–26, NIV

"But you, beloved, building yourselves up in your most holy faith and praying in the Holy Spirit, **keep yourselves in the love of God**, waiting for the mercy of our Lord Jesus Christ that leads to eternal life."

—Jude 20–21

Some passages assure us that God will keep us in his care by his Spirit (1 Thessalonians 5:23), but other passages implore us to keep in step with the Spirit (Galatians 5:25; Jude 20-–21). We saw a similar contrast earlier: some passages state that God circumcises our heart, while others instruct us to circumcise our own heart. In each case, the contrast illustrates the relationship between law and grace. Grace comes first, then we can keep the law.

Each set of verses is inspired and correct. They are not contradictory, but sequential. First comes justification, then ongoing sanctification. But if we stop exercising our faith by acting in obedience, we can disrupt the sanctifying work God is doing in our life. By rejecting God's truth, we reject his Spirit and put our salvation at risk.

The passages above are all addressed to existing believers, urging them to be on guard against Satan's lies, to remain in obedience. If we say we believe something yet act in a contradictory way, we disprove our own testimony. Lip service to Christian belief is essentially a lie.

"Therefore put away all filthiness and rampant wickedness and **receive with meekness the implanted word**, *which is able to save your souls. But be doers of the word, and not hearers only, deceiving yourselves. For if anyone is a hearer of the word and not a doer, he is like a man who looks intently at his natural face in a mirror. For he looks at himself and goes away and at once forgets what he was like."*

—James 1:22–24

Once we receive the gospel message, we can't take credit for the good works that follow. These are not a result of our good choices. Only through the implanted Word (God's Spirit in us) can we produce works that reflect God's nature. Humility and contrition are requirements; we must not indulge our human nature by taking even a little credit for helping God.

Here we read one of Paul's teachings on humility along with the fuller context of the Old Testament passage he quotes:

*"And **because of him you are in Christ Jesus**, who became to us wisdom from God, righteousness and sanctification and redemption, so that, as it is written, 'Let the one who boasts, **boast in the Lord.**'"*

—1 Corinthians 1:30–31

"Thus says the Lord: 'Let not the wise man boast in his wisdom, let not the mighty man boast in his might, let not the rich man boast in his riches, but let him who boasts boast in this, that he understands and knows me, that I am the Lord who practices steadfast love, justice, and righteousness in the earth. For in these things I delight, declares the Lord.'"

—Jeremiah 9:23–24

We cannot generate good works, so God puts his own righteousness-generating nature within us—if we submit to him.

*"For, being ignorant of the righteousness of God, and seeking to establish their own, they did not **submit to God's righteousness**."*

—Romans 10:3

A common theological debate is the question of whether salvation hinges on our free will or God's predestination. This conversation often supposes we have an immortal soul that will either be converted (through our will) or saved (by God's will).

As we've seen, neither side is biblically accurate. We contain a dual nature: our mortal soul with the immortal Spirit dwelling inside us. God has chosen to show us mercy, but his condition is that we keep his Word without altering any of his commands. It is that simple.

We can talk of "conversion" of our mortal soul, but we should clarify it is a conversion from our mortal nature to God's immortal nature, a transformation only made complete upon our resurrection. Our conversion is taking place now, yet we are mortal at this time.

Conversion does not indicate the renovation of our human nature. Sin and death cannot be fixed or cleaned, only defeated. We often misinterpret the following passage to show that there is one ongoing process of gradual conversion. But note that the passage states a denial of the world. Only having rejected our human nature can we be transformed. We do not repair our mind but rather take on the mind of Christ, the will of God.

*"I appeal to you therefore, brothers, by the mercies of God, to present your bodies as a living sacrifice, holy and acceptable to God, which is your spiritual worship. **Do not be conformed to this world**, but **be transformed** by the renewal of your mind, that*

*by testing you may discern what is the **will of God**, what is good and acceptable and perfect."*

—Romans 12:1–2

Transformation describes the ongoing process of sanctification through which our sinful nature is sacrificed, denied, crucified, circumcised, drowned, and buried over time. As our self decreases, the new self increases. We are to be set apart from the world. Our will is transformed into God's will.

*"We do not boast beyond limit in the labors of others. But our hope is that as your **faith increases**, our area of influence among you may be greatly enlarged."*

—2 Corinthians 10:15

*"[W]alk in a manner worthy of the Lord, fully pleasing to him: bearing fruit in every good work and **increasing in** the **knowledge of God.**"*

—Colossians 1:10

*"Now may our God and Father himself, and our Lord Jesus, direct our way to you, and may the **Lord make** you **increase** and abound in love for one another and for all, as we do for you."*

—1 Thessalonians 3:11–12

*"We ought always to give thanks to God for you, brothers, as is right, because **your faith is growing** abundantly, and the love of every one of you for one another is **increasing**."*

—2 Thessalonians 1:3

Some of these passages seem to instruct us to do the work or increase faith ourselves, while others describe the Lord providing the work or faith. As we've seen, the greater biblical context is that God is the source of all righteousness, and he equips us to join in what he is doing.

"His **divine power has granted to us all things** that pertain to life and godliness, **through the knowledge** of him who called us to his own glory and excellence, by which **he has granted** to us his precious and very great promises, so that **through them you may become partakers of the divine nature**, having escaped from the corruption that is in the world because of sinful desire. For this very reason, make every effort to supplement your faith with virtue, and virtue with knowledge, and knowledge with self-control, and self-control with steadfastness, and steadfastness with godliness, and godliness with brotherly affection, and brotherly affection with love. For if these qualities are yours and are increasing, they keep you from being ineffective or unfruitful in the knowledge of our Lord Jesus Christ. For whoever lacks these qualities is so nearsighted that he is blind, having forgotten that he was cleansed from his former sins. Therefore, brothers, be all the more diligent to confirm your calling and election, for if you practice these qualities you will never fall. For in this way there will be richly provided for you an entrance into the eternal kingdom of our Lord and Savior Jesus Christ."

—2 Peter 1:3–11

Here Peter shows us the big picture. He begins his epistle by establishing that all good things come from God's divine nature foremost, and we can become partakers of his nature when he grants the Spirit to us. Only then, through God's nature, are we asked to keep his laws.

Every time we see a passage about increasing our faith or doing good, we need to remember the wider biblical context: the writer is speaking to the new man, not the old.

God's Destiny for Us

God is not willing that any of his creation should perish but that all should come to him (2 Peter 3:9). First Timothy 2:4 similarly states that God *"desires all people to be saved and to come to the knowledge of the truth."*

His will is truth. His Word is clear: our destiny is to obey God's will.

God has predestined everyone to be saved and to do good works. He gave us his Word, which provides all the instruction we require. Everything was established from the beginning; we see God's plan of salvation weaving throughout Scripture, starting with his promise to Adam and Eve in Genesis 3:15, then continuing with his promises to Abraham and Christ's fulfillment of the law. We see God's master plan in Ephesians 1:9–10, and see a glimpse of its resolution in Revelation. He desires all to be saved, and through his grace he provides the means for all to be saved.

The biblical concept of predestination does not neatly match up with our cultural idea of what destiny is. God created us with one destiny in mind. Following the corruption of our nature in Eden, God ordained the plan of redemption, making salvation possible for us all. This is the destiny God wants for us and has planned for us. But on an individual level, he does not force us to submit to these plans.

Many people ultimately reject God's Word and derail God's will for their redemption. Such people were not predestined to reject God. On the contrary, Christ has offered them a portion of his inheritance. But so long as we retain our human nature, we can choose to opt out of the destiny God has prepared for us.

All people who do not believe in the gospel remain under the law, even if they do not hear the message of the law. The curse remains in effect. Yet Christ fulfills the law on everyone's behalf to remove us from the penalties of the law (death and judgment). All people are destined to die under the law, which is the curse from the garden, unless they are first born again by the Spirit and sealed until they are born again in the body to eternal life at the resurrection.

"For all who have sinned without the law will also perish without the law, and all who have sinned under the law will be judged by the law. For it is not the hearers of the law who are righteous before God, but the doers of the law who will be justified. For when Gentiles, who do not have the law, by nature do what the law requires, they are a law to themselves, even though they do not have the law. They show that the work of the law is written on their hearts, while their conscience also bears witness, and their conflicting thoughts accuse or even excuse them on that day when, according to my gospel, God judges the secrets of men by Christ Jesus."

—Romans 2:12–16

In the verse below, Christ describes belief that comes from within a person's human nature. We can only obtain the truth from God.

"The one who speaks on his own authority seeks his own glory; but the one who seeks the glory of him who sent him is true, and in him there is no falsehood."

—John 7:18[3]

Pride is part of our sinful nature. We naturally want to take at least a little credit for salvation, pointing to our "choice" to follow God or invite him into our heart. But Scripture does not support any works-based interpretation of the gospel.

We simply cannot invent a private interpretation of Scripture.[4] A prophet, apostle, or average Joe cannot take liberties with a given passage to make it fit an existing worldview. We do have many liberties and freedoms in Christ. Private interpretation is not one of them. Revelation through his Word is all we need.

When we compare the hybrid single-entity gospel (in which our immortal soul is reformed), the western humanistic gospel (in which all good people go to some kind of better place in the next life), and the biblical gospel message, we see that these all offer assurance; they all intend to give hope today and offer eternal life.

But unlike the biblical gospel, proponents of the hybrid message and the western world at large both believe that human beings possess a partially good immortal soul and can choose to act righteously.

According to our secular culture, every average, mostly

---

3. Also see John 8:44 and Romans 2:8 for similar messages.
4. See 2 Peter 1:20–21.

good person goes to heaven; according to the hybrid single-entity gospel, Christians go to heaven based on the same relative judgment. Both perspectives agree that everyone is immortal and must go somewhere. So good and/or saved souls must go to heaven. There is not much of a difference between choosing moral goodness versus choosing God's grace as the source of goodness. In either case, a person utilizes choice to obtain credit towards heaven.

Neither humanism nor the hybrid gospel considers the biblical dual-nature scenario; the focus on making choices through free will is ingrained into us. The dual-nature message must come from outside ourselves and pass into our hearts. How can anyone "hear" this message unless the unified body of Christ preaches the complete gospel?

The Christian presenting the hybrid gospel will argue that salvation is based entirely on grace and faith. Which is reasonable; grace does in fact lead to faith according to the biblical salvation message. But we are to be transformed over time, not converted instantly.

So it isn't enough to simply proclaim the gospel (Matthew 28:19); we are also called to facilitate the discipleship of fellow believers (Matthew 28:20), encouraging each other to persevere and grow in the faith.

The complete gospel as written in the Word sounds different from the modern hybrid gospel that is often preached today. The modern hybrid sounds better to modern ears and blends in with cultural preferences, which mostly eliminates worldview clashes. But how can the

Church preach such a convenient, inoffensive gospel and still be the salt or the light?

Some passages (such as Acts 17:30–31 and Hebrews 6:9–12) speak to spiritual salvation without mentioning the future resurrection, but these do not mention death at all; their purpose is to provide hope and assurance, not to argue for an immortal soul.

Present-tense salvation passages do not conflict with other Scripture, but some people take them out of context to promote the hybrid gospel. This is why people memorize Ephesians 2:8 (suggesting a competed salvation) and do not add 2:7 (looking forward to Christ's future demonstration of grace). Isolated verses such as John 3:16 can be used to justify the hybrid single-entity concept and belief in a spirit-body resurrection into heaven. However, John 3:16 does not contradict the many other passages focused on a future bodily resurrection on earth. The Bible differentiates between spiritual salvation today and physical salvation at the second advent. We can't focus on just one or the other; we need the Spirit today and tomorrow.

We were sealed when the Spirit came to give us a new heart, we are preserved today, and we will be saved in the future. Salvation is past, present, and future.

If we believe our soul is immortal and our human nature must be repaired, we will tend to believe in salvation as a past-tense work. But if we believe we are mortal, we will understand our need for continual reliance on God as he strengthens us, keeps us, preserves us, and sanctifies us before ultimately granting us immortality at the resurrection.

- Were we already immortal before birth (like Islam and Mormonism)?

- Did we receive an immortal soul at birth?

- Did we become retroactively immortal when we were born again?

- Do we become immortal when our mortal body dies?

- Do we become immortal upon the resurrection of our body?

The Bible only says yes to the last of these. Christ is waiting at the Father's right hand until the proper time.[5]

We need to wait until Christ comes again; then all enemies—including death—will be defeated. Christ will sit on the throne of glory in the kingdom where we will dwell together in glorified bodily form.[6]

Can we be 100 percent certain we don't need to do something to help save ourselves? Don't we have some choice or say in the matter, or does God just decide our fate on our behalf?

*"And when the Gentiles heard this, they began rejoicing and glorifying the word of the Lord, and as many as were **appointed to eternal life believed.**"*

---

5. See Acts 3:21, Romans 6:5–9, 1 Corinthians 15:26 and Hebrews 10:13.
6. See Matthew 19:28; 25:31; 1 Corinthians 15:23–26).

—Acts 13:48

On one extreme, we can insist on complete predestination to the point where God controls everything; according to some schools of thought, God even selects which people will remain in their wickedness and be damned to hell. On the other extreme, we imagine our free will is so potent that we can choose righteousness and save ourselves. And of course many belief systems fall in the middle. Here are some common perspectives on our role in salvation:

- We need to decide to follow Christ; our salvation is 100 percent dependent on our free will. Life is all about choices.

- God does the first work and reaches out to us, then we choose the next step(s).

- We take the first step as a spiritual seeker, then God agrees to enter our heart as requested.

- Salvation depends on God's choice. We cannot be saved unless we are predestined for salvation, and we have no ability to resist God's grace if we are among his elect.

- God does the first and only work needed, then we live by his Spirit. Our faith is not based on the strength of our belief, but on the consistency of our obedience. We are to be humble and contrite, rejecting our own sinful nature.

The Bible is very clear and objective. There is nothing subjective about the gospel. We need to understand all clear passages, first relating to God's plan of salvation; only then we can understand more difficult passages.

"For the mind that is set on the flesh is hostile to God, for it does not submit to God's law; indeed, it cannot. Those who are in **the flesh cannot please God.** *You, however, are not in the flesh but in the Spirit, if in fact the Spirit of God dwells in you.* **Anyone who does not have the Spirit of Christ does not belong to him.** *But if Christ is in you, although the body is dead because of sin, the Spirit is life because of righteousness."*

—Romans 8:7–10

"Such is the confidence that we have through Christ toward God. **Not that we are sufficient in ourselves to claim anything as coming from us,** *but our sufficiency is from God, who has made us sufficient to be ministers of a new covenant, not of the letter but of the Spirit. For the letter kills, but the Spirit gives life."*

—2 Corinthians 3:4–6

"And **you were dead** *in the trespasses and sins in which you once walked, following the course of this world,* **following the prince of the power of the air**, *the spirit that is now at work in the sons of disobedience—* **among whom we all once lived** *in the passions of our flesh, carrying out the desires of the body and the mind, and were* **by nature children of wrath, like the rest of mankind.** *But God, being rich in mercy, because of the great love with which he loved us, even when we were dead in our trespasses, made us alive together with Christ—by grace you have been saved."*

—Ephesians 2:1–3

We can reject God's grace using our natural free will. We can use our free will to sin—but not to choose to follow Christ. Faith flows out of the new nature we receive from God, not out of our old human nature.

"Are you so foolish? Having begun by the Spirit, are you now being perfected by the flesh?"

—Galatians 3:3

Human nature is to rebel against the Maker. He calls prodigals back, even though we lavishly spend our life away. We act as if we own our body, our soul, or our very life--when in reality all belongs to God. He simply wants to share his inheritance with us.

"For all the earth is mine."

—Exodus 19:5b

"For every beast of the forest is mine,

the cattle on a thousand hills.

I know all the birds of the hills,

and all that moves in the field is mine.

If I were hungry, I would not tell you,

for the world and its fullness are mine."

—Psalm 50:10–12

CHAPTER 13.

THE WAY TO GOD

Because God created the earth and everything in it, he has every right to decide the path we are to take. The created do not get to complain to the Creator.

"Woe to him who strives with him who formed him, a pot among earthen pots! Does the clay say to him who forms it, 'What are you making?' or 'Your work has no handles'?"

—Isaiah 45:9[1]

Although we should submit to God and honor his Word and his will, we tend to try to make our own way through life, putting our own ideas ahead of biblical teaching. Many Christians do this unintentionally by adhering to the concept of an immortal soul that can be saved through free will. Most other religious systems on earth throughout history have promoted similar ideas regarding salvation, nirvana, heaven, or some other type of afterlife. Each religion establishes the means through which a person can earn the afterlife—usually by making choices, passing a test, or accomplishing some task(s). Salvation is *not* a free ride.

---

1. A similar concept is found in Romans 9:20–21.

It must be earned based on the concept of justice that is ingrained into every person who ever lived.

Meanwhile, some dispense with religion altogether. Everyone goes to heaven; there is no hell.

Yet another option is nothingness, as Carl Sagan asserted in his final book:

"I would love to believe that when I die I will live again, that some thinking, feeling, remembering part of me will continue. But much as I want to believe that, and despite the ancient and worldwide cultural traditions that assert an afterlife, I know of nothing to suggest that it is more than wishful thinking."[2]

In *Cosmos*, perhaps Sagan's most famous book, he wrote, *"The Cosmos is all that is or was or ever will be."*[3]

Most religions and belief systems present one of the following perspectives:

1. Everything is good; there is no such thing as evil (or vice versa).

2. Only the spirit realm is good; the physical realm is evil.

3. There is only a physical realm. No unseen (unobservable) realm exists.

4. The physical, heavenly, and/or spiritual realms are intertwined. Both good and evil exist in the mix.

---

2. Carl Sagan, *Billions and Billions: Thoughts on Life and Death at the Brink of the Millennium* (New York: Random House, 1997).
3. Carl Sagan, *Cosmos* (New York: Random House, 1980), 4.

5. The heavenly realm is veiled from the physical realm but is linked through the spiritual realm.

Biblical Christianity embraces the fifth perspective. God's Word says the physical realm will be restored to its original state of perfection before the Fall—but this time the devil will be removed from the picture. In the future, the realms will merge so that the unseen will be seen on earth. God will physically dwell with us.

Before God gave Moses the Ten Commandments, his law had already been written on the hearts of humankind. It was ingrained into Adam, and by extension our human nature. And the law existed even before Adam's fall into sin. The law is a definition of God's love in action.

When Adam and Eve broke God's law in the Garden of Eden, they received the death curse: no longer would they have access to the fruit of the tree of life. But before God carried out this law-based sentence, he offered them the first message of grace recorded in the Bible.

"I will put enmity between you and the woman,

and between your offspring and her offspring;

he shall bruise your head,

and you shall bruise his heel."

—Genesis 3:15

The first message of grace is that Christ will "bruise" the devil's head. Undeserved grace also came to Noah before the justice of the flood: *"But Noah found favor in the eyes of the Lord"* (Genesis 6:8).

God first bestowed grace upon the nation of Israel by taking them out of Egypt; he reminded them of this gift as he was about to give them his law through the Ten Commandments:

*"You yourselves have seen what I did to the Egyptians, and how **I bore you on eagles' wings** and **brought you to myself**. Now therefore, if you will indeed obey my voice and keep my covenant, you shall be my treasured possession among all peoples, for all the earth is mine."*

—Exodus 19:4–5

Passages that describe God's names, nature, or attributes always trace back to his righteousness and/or graciousness. Sometimes one quality is depicted, and sometimes both attributes are shown to be working together.

God "cannot lie," "does not change," and "does not tempt." We sometimes say that God "can do anything but sin." God doesn't seem to have, or want to have, free will to sin. A person can only choose according to his nature. God's nature is only good so he won't choose evil. We can only choose to sin based on our original nature (before being born again in the Spirit).

*"[P]ut on the new self, created after **the likeness of God** in **true righteousness and holiness**."*

—Ephesians 4:24

God is true righteousness. Our righteousness can only come from God.[4] God only produces righteous acts because his nature is purely and eternally righteous. However, we act inconsistently because we have two natures residing in us (God's Spirit and our sinful flesh).

*"So I find it to be a law that when I want to do right, evil lies close at hand. For I delight in the law of God, **in my inner being**, but I see **in my members** another law waging war against the law of my mind and making me captive to the law of sin that dwells in my members. Wretched man that I am! Who will deliver me from this body of death? Thanks be to God through Jesus Christ our Lord! So then, I myself serve the law of God with my mind, but with my flesh I serve the law of sin."*

—Romans 7:21–25

As we have seen, "heart" is generally a metaphor for the mind, conscience, or inner being. Scripture tells of the Spirit coming to dwell in each; some passages speak to the heart metaphor, while the passage above speaks to Paul's mind and inner being (which have the same meaning in this passage).

Paul's "flesh" means the same thing as his "members"; both had been afflicted by the death curse. His flesh was his inherited nature, including his will and emotions. Paul wrote, "I want to do right," but he could not. This is because he had a (cursed) "body of death." The cursed body affects our human nature, causing our free will to chooses selfish acts. We can't escape it.

---

4. See 2 Corinthians 5:21 and Philippians 3:9.

The body will not be transformed until the resurrection, when Christ shall return and lift our curse. Paul described elsewhere how his mind was being transformed to the mind of Christ in an ongoing process (Romans 12:1–2). Our own transformation is a similar work in progress.

Paul called his mind "the mind of Christ" in 1 Corinthians 2:16 and "my mind" in the passage above from Romans 7. Paul had the same mind as Christ. They were of "one" mind, sharing the same thoughts and concerns. In the same way, we may call our heart "God's heart" or "my heart." It is a shared heart; though it is a gift of God, it still ultimately belongs to him.

Paul associated his human will with his selfish desire to good. Like Paul, we try to please God in the flesh. But we can't. Paul understood his death nature was completely corrupted by sin and restrained from doing good.

Romans 7 does not describe a single entity with a mixed nature or the ability to choose good. Paul could not detach himself from both his godly and human natures and decide whether he would do good or evil. He could only live fully in God's nature or in his own. All actions would either be informed by the mind of Christ or Paul's own flesh.

When Paul received the Spirit, his old nature did not disappear, even though in other passages he considered it drowned and buried. This is yet another echo of the "now and not yet" concept of salvation. Our sinful nature is "defeated" when the Spirit comes into our life, but we do not achieve our ultimate bodily purpose until the resurrection. In biblical language, when we drown and bury our sinful nature today, our sins are "covered" by God's forgiveness.[5]

This Romans 7 passage presents the two dueling natures—God's Spirit and Paul's flesh—not an individual deciding between good and evil options. Free will does not have the power to change our nature, nor can it change Christ's nature given to us. Nature wars against nature with no hope of reconciling the two.

Paul described a nature enslaved by death where "the law of sin" dwelt. Like Paul experienced, the old nature that we inherited from Adam is warring against the new nature in Christ that we received from God. There is a constant battle. There can be no merger between the Spirit and the "body of death."

We know Adam and Eve had the ability to choose to eat of the tree of the knowledge of good and evil, so choice in itself was created "good." Choice is good under the freedoms we have in Christ. These freedoms can't be used to obtain salvation, nor should they be used to promote our own selfish interests. Rather, our freedoms allow us to bless and serve others, building God's kingdom and enriching relationships. Our will is to be the same as God's will. This was God's intent. We should be devoted to truth, not enslaved to lies.

*"So Jesus said to the Jews who had believed him, '**If you abide in my word**, you are truly my disciples, and **you will know the truth**, and the truth will set you free.' They answered him, 'We are*

---

5. See Romans 4:7, which is based on Psalm 32:1–5.

offspring of Abraham and have never been enslaved to anyone. How is it that you say, 'You will become free'?"

"Jesus answered them, 'Truly, truly, I say to you, everyone who practices sin is a slave to sin.'"

—John 8:31–34

"For this purpose I was born and for this purpose I have come into the world—to bear witness to the truth. **Everyone who is of the truth listens to my voice.**"

—John 18:37b

In the passage above, Christ testified to the purpose of his life and ministry: Christ came to proclaim the truth. In response, Pilate asked, "What is truth?" Sinful nature can't "hear" truth or distinguish it from lies.

Although the Gospel accounts do not say whether Christ fully or directly answered Pilate's question, we know he gave his disciples the answer. Truth is God's Word. In the two passages above, Christ first instructed the disciples to "abide" in his Word to obtain truth, then stated that those who "listen" to his Word are of the truth.

When we tell kids to "listen" to what we say, what we really mean is that they should obey. "Listening" or "hearing" is a good start, but then the message must be believed and finally acted upon. Listening also means doing what God commands. Listening, hearing, and abiding all assume follow-through, not just lip service to belief that includes no action.

"Everyone who practices sin is a slave to sin." Forgiveness from sin does not give us freedom to sin further. Freedom *from* sin is God's desire for us. But until we receive God's Spirit and Word and then follow the explicit instructions Christ gave, we will remain in enslavement.

True freedom comes from following God's law.

*"If you **keep** my commandments, you will **abide** in my love, just as I have kept my Father's commandments and abide in his love."*

—John 15:10

This verse builds off of John 15:5, which states that we *"can do nothing"* without abiding in Christ. Christ offers an image where he is the "vine" and the Father is the "vinedresser" or gardener. We in turn must stay connected to the vine for nutrition and growth.

John 15:10 and its description of conditional law combines nicely with Ephesians 2:10, a teaching on the nonconditional election of grace. This is another paradox; both truths are contained within the same gospel.

We are destined to do good works that God has prepared for us. Grace by faith is also based on God's work.

*"For by grace you have been saved through faith. And **this is not your own doing**; it is the gift of God, not a result of works, so that no one may boast."*

—Ephesians 2:8–9

We have to be very careful that we do not interpret our belief as the element that completes our faith. Faith is completed by obedience, not belief. We do get credit for belief (Genesis 15:6) and it is necessary for salvation, but we must go farther.

Faith is a pure gift that flows out of God's righteousness. Our belief is based on God's work. In the verse preceding the passage above, Paul explains that we are saved by Christ's past work resulting in spiritual salvation at the present time. Verses 8–9 focus on grace and do not mention actions we must take to finalize faith, nor do they mention salvation at the second coming—but we can't take them out of context. These are bookended by verses that speak to these precise "missing" ideas. Make sure that you read Ephesians 2:8–9 along with its grounding verses, 2:7 and 2:10.

Faith is not complete until we act upon what we say we believe. Paul states that we are not saved by our works in Ephesians 2:9, but then adds in verse 10 that we were created to do good works. The truth is that Christ's work is given to us. His righteousness passes through us like a conduit; it is reflected by us like a mirror. Rather than trying to perform our "own" good works, we emulate Christ's perfection.

This is the intent of God's will for our lives, that we would love and keep his commandments. His Word states his will.

We should not be confused with the past-tense wording of "have been saved" in Ephesians 2:8. Paul is not speaking of the resurrection in the future. He is speaking of being "lifted" or "raised," as he mentioned earlier in verse 6. This is a spiritual resurrection that we receive at baptism when we are born again in the Spirit. But we will not receive physical resurrection until the "coming ages"; we must wait for the time when grace is fully shown (Ephesians 2:7).

Free Will and God's Image

Free will obviously relates to freedom. What else does Scripture say about it?

"Now the Lord is the Spirit, and where the Spirit of the Lord is, there is freedom."

—2 Corinthians 3:17

"For you were called to freedom, brothers. Only do not use your freedom as an opportunity for the flesh, but through love serve one another."

—Galatians 5:13

"Live as people who are free, not using your freedom as a cover-up for evil, but living as servants of God."

—1 Peter 2:16

There is a clear difference between spiritual freedom and freedom in the flesh. We should notice in these passages that freedom enables us to do good works. We do not receive total freedom to do literally anything, as God's nature cannot sin. Freedom also refers to our rescue from the slavery of death.[6]

"But the one who looks into the perfect law, **the law of liberty**,

---

6. See Romans 8:21 and Hebrews 2:14–15.

and perseveres, being no hearer who forgets but a doer who acts, he will be blessed in his doing."

—James 1:25

The law of liberty? This sounds crazy at first, but God's freedom is indeed constricted. Here we see law and freedom working side by side. Freedom in Christ comes from grace.

Biblical teachings about freedom state that we have a limited freedom of choice.

- We do not have a choice to change or add to God's gifts of grace.

- We cannot change the nature of Christ in us.

- God's will is displayed in his Word. His Word predefines our destiny.

- We do not have freedom in Christ to sin. We are predestined to do good.

- Once we believe the gospel as-is, God commands us to use our freedom to choose variations of good works within his nature.

- God is holy (or pure, perfect) and requires us to be holy by his Spirit.

Sin is considered slavery or bondage. We say that we have free will in human nature, but it only allows us to do evil and is the opposite of freedom in Christ.

- We do not have a choice to change our sinful nature nor to do good.

- Sinful nature can only be covered (or buried, drowned) by the new nature until our full transformation on the day of resurrection.

- Our sinful nature remains in us, causing us to choose selfish acts until then.

- Our nature only gives us the freedom to choose among sinful variations.

The flesh is not free to do good, and the Spirit is not free to sin. Once we believe the biblical concept of a dual nature residing in us, we can see that we are to live by the Spirit only and reject our sinful nature. This is true freedom. The "perfect law."

God shows us examples in his own nature. Is God free to lie or do evil? No, Scripture states God is only good and cannot lie. God does not have the freedom to choose sin, so how can we claim that our free will is able to choose good?

In Scripture, nature and will are connected. Nature defines who we are. We cannot change who we are by nature nor who Christ is. In Christ, we have the freedom to choose among variations of good works; in the flesh, we have the freedom to choose among variations of sin.

God's nature is purely righteous. His will is fixed, based upon his nature only to do good. Yet there is relational flexibility within the fixed will; he loves us and wants us to love, so he invites us to complete his desired will.

Galatians 5:24–25 kills a few birds with one stone. If we have been baptized (our flesh has been crucified, drowned, and buried), then we should live by the Spirit and keep in step with God's commandments.

Desire is part of our will in the flesh. It is what we want. Our desire is only selfish. But God calls us to keep in step with what he desires. God desires us to exercise humility (Psalm 51:16–17), to pursue knowledge of God (Hosea 6:6), and to obey (1 Samuel 15:22). His commands reflect his will.

God's law is perfect because he is just. God can't choose evil as it violates his will. Neither can we choose righteousness and violate our nature. Adam was punished for acting out his choice, and now we all live under the curse of death.

Adam was originally supposed to listen to God and act according to God's Word. Adam's free will in itself was not the problem. The problem was that he listened to and believed Satan's lies instead of believing every word that came out of the mouth of God. He used his free will and rejected God.

Today we are in the same situation. With the gift of God's Spirit inside us, we have the opportunity to listen to God's Word and believe and obey. Or we can choose to listen to the deceiver and attend to our own selfish desires. We must be a servant to truth or lies; we cannot choose freely between the two.

Since Adam rejected God's truth for Satan's lies, we have inherited his sinful nature. This is the "body of death."

Instead of violating his own law or removing our free will, God cursed us to die. Sin and death are now related.

The curse of death is paramount to understand. There was no curse when God created Adam and Eve; he called it into being as punishment for their sin. We inherited their mortal nature. Notice in Genesis 3 that God's main punishment was to evict humanity from the garden that held the tree of life. Only the fruit from this tree had been keeping humans from death. Sin itself is based upon a lie that we are inherently immortal, but only God can sustain eternal life. Adam did not have an immortal soul. He had conditional immortality, just as we now have in Christ.

"Then the Lord God said, 'Behold, the man has become like one of us in knowing good and evil. Now, lest he reach out his hand and take also of the tree of life and eat, and live forever—' therefore the Lord God sent him out from the garden of Eden to work the ground from which he was taken."

—Genesis 3:22–23

Christ came to destroy the works of the devil and will finally destroy the last enemy—death—after he returns. The devil's lie led to the death curse for all humanity. This prompted God to send Christ to earth.[7] Christ will redeem his people so that we may have an eternal relationship together (Revelation 21:3). Death and sin cannot exist if this is to happen (Revelation 21:4).

God cannot sin, God cannot choose evil, and yet Adam was given the ability to choose evil. Adam's nature was in the

---

7. See 1 John 3:8.

image of God, but he was not God replicated. Adam was not begotten of Spirit. Death came into humanity once Adam acted sinfully, but note that Adam had fallen into a deceived mindset before physically taking the bite. Sin is a result of believing lies and the one who spreads them. Adam's sin proved he was not God in human flesh; he had not received the "full" image of God. Christ, however, is called the second Adam, and he does indeed bear the fullness of the Father. Numerous passages speak to the fullness of Christ's divinity within his glorified body.

"For in him [Christ] **the whole fullness of deity dwells** *bodily, and you have been filled in him, who is the head of all rule and authority."*

—Colossians 2:9–10

We cannot know the mind of God (1 Corinthians 2:11–13) under human nature, but Scripture states that God cannot choose to do evil because his nature forbids it. His very nature defines what goodness is.

As God's righteousness begins in his mind and then moves to action, sin begins in our heart. We can sin through our thoughts (Matthew 5:27–28) or words (Psalm 59:12), not just our physical actions. All these self-centered thoughts and desires are sinful and lead to sinful actions. This pattern of sinful thought leading to sinful deed first played out with Satan himself before humans were ever created.[8]

Actions come from the heart, where motives are developed. An important part of any investigator's work is

---

8. See Isaiah 14:13.

determining the motive that led to a given crime. He must understand the mind of his suspect. Depending on the crime, this attempt at empathy may be a deeply horrifying exercise. How anyone could anyone conceive of such a thing?

In a positive sense, we are equally perplexed by the goodness of God. His motives are not our motives. His thoughts are not our thoughts.[9]

How are we motivated? Do we do good because we can choose to do good? Can goodness come from within our own heart? We would not need a new heart if we could obtain goodness from within our own nature or if God could rinse it clean. But the truth is that our heart is motivated to act selfishly. God's nature is entirely different. He is motivated to act righteously and to give us his righteousness.

We have the same type of free will that Adam possessed. He was created into his human nature, and we were born into ours, inheriting the curse of death that Adam first received.

Scripture teaches that we are sinners not because we choose to commit sinful actions, but because our human nature cannot produce anything else. How else does the nature into which we were born (Psalm 51:5) differ from God's nature?

God's Freedom from Temptation

We can be tempted to sin. God cannot be. This is because

---

9. See Isaiah 55:8–9.

God alone is good and cannot do anything but good. Goodness is inherent within God.

"Let no one say when he is tempted, 'I am being tempted by God,' for God cannot be tempted with evil, and he himself tempts no one."

—James 1:13

Christ, however, was tempted on earth before his exaltation. Let's consider Christ's example while on earth compared to the Father and the first Adam.

This comparison brings up a potential conflict. Christ is God, yet God cannot be tempted with evil. Christ was certainly tempted beyond anything imaginable in Gethsemane (deciding whether to accept or reject the cup of the wrath from the Father). Did God tempt his very own nature as the Son of Man?

To find the answer, we need context. While James 1:13 simply says God cannot be tempted, the surrounding verses provide much more information to help clarify the Spirit's message to us.

*"Blessed is the man who remains steadfast under **trial**, for when he has stood the **test** he will receive the crown of life, which God has promised to those who love him. Let no one say when he is tempted, 'I am being tempted by God,' for God cannot be tempted with evil, and he himself tempts no one. But **each person is tempted** when he is lured and enticed **by his own desire**. Then desire when it has conceived gives birth to sin, and sin when it is fully grown brings forth death. Do not be deceived, my beloved brothers. Every good gift and **every perfect gift is from above**,*

coming down from the Father of lights with whom there is no variation or shadow due to change. Of his own will he brought us forth by the word of truth, that we should be a kind of firstfruits of his creatures."

—James 1:12–18[10]

Our own desire is the real issue, as it begins in the heart, then gives birth to sin. The tempter is our self, not God. We need to resist temptation if we are to obtain eternal life; we must reject our desires and submit to God.

There was a short point in time where Christ *could* sin. This was before his glorification and during his earthly ministry. While God himself cannot sin, Christ's humanity prior to the resurrection (Philippians 2:6–7) was different from his current state of glory at the right hand of the Father.

Christ had the potential to sin because he felt the temptation to follow his own will. This does not mean the Christ did sin, nor that he had an evil human nature, nor that he ever would have elected to sin. He *could* have sinned. Simply, the potential to sin was there. We could also say the opposite: we have the potential to do good under our human nature, but we can't, don't, and won't do good by ourselves.

Christ's capacity to sin and our capacity to do good are related. We think theoretically we have potential to do good and keep God's commands, but no natural person under Adam has been able to do this because we are cursed and "consigned to disobedience" (Romans 11:32). Likewise,

---

10. Also see 1 Thessalonians 2:4.

Christ had free will to choose sin, but he was born of the Spirit, begotten of the Father, and ultimately couldn't resist doing the Father's will. We are begotten of Adam and will remain so until we are born again. We can't choose good until we are born of the Spirit.

If it were not possible for Christ to sin on earth, he could not have been tempted; he would not have legitimately shared in our human experience. Christ suffered greatly because he took on all sin for all mankind, but something deeper was happening beyond his suffering. Hebrews 2:14–18 and Hebrews 4:15 state that he had to be like us in every way in order to be the mediator between God and men. Christ was given the ability to reject the cup—to act upon a separate desire. However, he had learned obedience to the Father while "in the days of his flesh" (Hebrews 5:7–9) before he went to Gethsemane.

"For we do not have a high priest who is unable to sympathize with our weaknesses, but one [Christ] **who in every respect has been tempted** *as we are, yet without sin."*

—Hebrews 4:15

"We must not put Christ to the test, as some of them did and were destroyed by serpents, nor grumble, as some of them did and were destroyed by the Destroyer. Now these things happened to them as an example, but they were written down for our instruction, on whom the end of the ages has come. Therefore let anyone who thinks that he stands take heed lest he fall. No temptation has overtaken you that is not common to man. God is faithful, and **he will not let you be tempted** *beyond your ability, but with the*

temptation he will also provide the way of escape, that you may be able to endure it."

—1 Corinthians 10:9–13

"Beloved, do not be surprised at the fiery trial when it comes upon you to **test** you, as though something strange were happening to you. But rejoice insofar as you share Christ's **sufferings**, that you may also rejoice and be glad when his glory is revealed. If you are insulted for the name of Christ, you are blessed, because the Spirit of glory and of God rests upon you. But let none of you suffer as a murderer or a thief or an evildoer or as a meddler. Yet if anyone **suffers** as a Christian, let him not be ashamed, but let him glorify God in that name. For it is time for judgment to begin at the household of God; and if it begins with us, what will be the outcome for those who do not obey the gospel of God? And 'If the righteous is scarcely saved, what will become of the ungodly and the sinner?' Therefore **let those who suffer according to God's will** entrust their souls [lives] to a faithful Creator while doing good."

—1 Peter 4:12–19

As we saw in the earlier passage from James 1, God does not tempt anyone, yet he allows temptation to occur as a means of testing our faith.[11] The Father did not tempt the Son, but the Son was certainly tested. Temptations only come from the devil—or in this case, Christ could have tempted himself to reject the Father's will and follow his own will instead. The Father allowed Christ to suffer through the

---

11. See also the book of Job.

Good Friday trials, and Christ willingly accepted and obeyed.[12]

We can follow Christ's example of obedience and submission. Christ's examples should be our answers since he was made to be like us in every way. God tests us so that we may complete our faith and reject our sinful nature. Trials, tests, and suffering are part of God's plan, while temptations that arise from self-motivated desires are Satan's domain.

*"No one born of God makes a **practice of sinning**, for God's seed abides in him, and he cannot keep on sinning because he has been born of God. By this it is evident who are the children of God, and who are the children of the devil: whoever does not **practice righteousness** is not of God, nor is the one who does not love his brother. For this is the message that you have heard from the beginning, that we should love one another."*

—1 John 3:9–11

God tests those who wish to perform righteous acts to ensure that they will practice these within God's will. His will is defined in his Word, so not only is the test spelled out but he gives us the answer sheet as well. Passing the test is accomplished by following God's instructions. Though we may wish to rely on a grace "curve" to pass the test, we must not leave out any of the instructions written in God's law.

Evil is inherent within us. Goodness can only come from the outside, not from within.[13] Christ is our example. Christ

---

12. See Philippians 2:8.
13. See James 1:17.

gave up his life to achieve resurrection in a glorified body, just like we are called to do. We give up our life in a spiritual sense and receive a new nature by being born again.[14]

"Whoever seeks to preserve his life will lose it, but whoever loses his life will keep it."

—Luke 17:33

Why would we want to chase after our free will when it isn't useful for righteousness?

*"And he said to all, 'If anyone would come after me, let him **deny himself and take up his cross daily** and follow me. For whoever would save his life will lose it, but whoever loses his life for my sake will save it.'"*

—Luke 9:23–24

We need to **daily** deny our self. This passage goes against the "once saved, always saved" belief. If we don't drown our flesh on a continual basis, we risk losing our new life in Christ. As we practice obedience and exercise the faith we have been given, we strengthen that faith.[15]

Does any of this mean Christ was born into sinful human flesh? Christ was certainly a paradox, being Son of God and Son of Man at the same time. The Bible does not say much about the humanity of Christ at his incarnate birth; the clearest picture we get of Christ's humanity is his night of prayer and anguish in the garden. On that night, he passed

---

14. Of course, we are born again only in the Spirit, not in the flesh. Our body will not be transformed until the resurrection.
15. See 1 Corinthians 9:25.

his test, willingly taking and bearing our sins by accepting the Father's will. He resisted the temptation to serve his own will. By accepting the cup of the Father's wrath, Christ furthered the plan of lifting the death curse. He gave us the best example of submission by stating, *"Not my will, but yours, be done"* (Luke 22:42b).[16] Christ was obedient.

"For I have come down from heaven, not to do my own will but the will of him who sent me."

—John 6:38[17]

As Christ exemplified, we must not act out our own free will. This is an extremely important concept.

Resisting temptation means rejecting the free will that is directly connected to the self; when tempted, we will either yield to our flesh or submit to God. Christ did not yield to the flesh, and because his Spirit resides in us, we also have the strength to resist. But we can only tap into the Spirit's strength when we humbly submit to God like a child to a parent.

Matthew 7:21 tells us more. Here we see that "not everyone" who calls upon the name of the Lord will be saved. After all, even devils believe in God. It is right that we should confess our faith after receiving the gift of God's Word, but we have to bear in mind the context of all other salvation passages. Calling on God must lead to submission to God's will; if we do not turn to God and turn away from our self, our cry to God accomplishes nothing. True

---

16. Also see John 12:49–50, Philippians 2:5–8, and Hebrews 5:7–8.
17. Also see John 5:19, 30–31.

repentance results in us keeping God's commandments. Receiving grace, we then keep the law.

God's Way of Salvation

No one is saved simply by hearing the gospel. After hearing, we must believe God's Word and live out his will. Belief must lead to good works, as his will for us is to love.

"But I say, walk by the Spirit, and you will not gratify the desires of the flesh. For the desires of the flesh are against the Spirit, and the desires of the Spirit are against the flesh, for these are opposed to each other, to keep you from doing the things you want to do. But if you are led by the Spirit, you are not under the law [of the flesh]."

—Galatians 5:16[18]

We often think of babies as being totally innocent, yet from the earliest time of our life, we are already intensely focused on our needs and desires. This selfishness is perfectly natural, but sinful nonetheless. Nobody needs to be taught how to be selfish. It is our most foundational instinct. Selfish potential has been with us all along.

God knew what would happen before the foundation of the world; he knew even before the fall of mankind that his creation would need a Savior, someone to teach us how to live by the will of God. Everything was known and predestined in advance of creation. Our names were written in the Book of Life before the Fall. God's plan all

---

18. Romans 7 expands on this teaching.

along seems to have been to utilize a long transformation process to align us with his will.

Teaching and discipleship are very important parts of the process. While Adam received instant maturity, God has elected to develop our relational and spiritual maturity over time.

Christ looked to the Father constantly, prompting us likewise to look outside of ourselves, not within. Hebrews 5:8 says that Christ "learned obedience" while in the days "of his flesh." He humbled himself to an incredible extent while on earth. As Christ relied on the Father, we must rely on the gifts offered by the Spirit. We cannot generate from ourselves the strength we need to resist temptation and live righteously. Adam needed to listen to God's Word, and we must do the same.

God favors the humble and resists the proud (1 Peter 5:5–6). We have no reason to be proud because we cannot produce from within ourselves any good work to assist in salvation.

Christ conquered sin and thus has more right to boast than anyone—but he continues to be humble and gracious. As the inheritor of Abraham's promise, he grants us the opportunity to be co-heirs with him. Since he took on our human nature, he can mediate justice with the Father on our behalf. The Father is just and cannot violate his own law, but due to the righteousness of Christ, now the law has been kept. Christ is able and willing to justify our faith in him.[19]

---

19. See Romans 3:26.

God's commands and revelations are absolute and holy. We cannot debate or judge absolutes. They exist regardless of our opinions or wishes. In the same way that God is eternally "I am," his commandments just are. We receive his grace via his revelations so we can keep his law.[20]

God gave grace to Adam before commanding him not to eat of the tree, he gave grace to Noah before the flood, and he gave grace to the nation of Israel before giving them the law at Mount Sinai. We receive grace in the new covenant before we are asked to keep God's commandments, and grace is given to us before we are judged for our deeds. Grace is absolute.

Even with a focus on grace, we see that the law still exists within the new covenant. We were saved by grace to do good works; God wants us to spread the gospel, give generously, and love our neighbor. The New Testament is filled with commands to do good.

*"We know **that everyone who has been born of God does not keep on sinning**, but he who was born of God protects him, and the evil one does not touch him. We know that we are from God, and **the whole world lies in the power of the evil one.**"*

—1 John 5:18–19

Most modern people tend to think of the soul in terms of mixtures that can only equal 100 percent. For example, if a person is 75 percent good and 25 percent bad, she'll get to go to heaven because she is mostly good. But the literal biblical teaching seems paradoxical and nonsensical to the

---

20. See Deuteronomy 29:29.

human mind. How can a person contain a 100 percent good nature and a 100 percent sinful nature at the same time? Our instinctual understanding of justice doesn't know what to do with such a concept.

Some people favor justice or grace as their preferred way to heaven, but most tend to believe that the two work together simultaneously within a single soul. For example, Christ can come in to clean up or forgive the 25 percent that is bad, and we can keep the 75 percent that is good. An extra-sinful person with the opposite percentages would need Christ three times as badly. Of course this is not a biblical concept.

Most religions and belief systems offer a one-dimensional mixture of law and grace that skews heavily toward grace. Law is scaled back to a manageable degree, only somewhat necessary for salvation. But the Bible presents multidimensional levels of law and grace that confound our human mind. A few other belief systems do speak to extra dimensions of law and grace in concert, allowing for a higher level of reformation within the soul—but they still tend to treat the individual as an entity with a single nature. They do not consider the idea that an outside nature might dwell side by side with our original human nature.

Even a belief system that totally disregards the need for law and insists salvation depends fully on grace will require a justice system of some sort to set the ground rules for the grace on offer. A system where everyone receives grace and goes to heaven requires a law to establish the need for the donor in the first place. The donor will get to decide the plan for salvation, not the receiver.

There is no way to get around the laws of God. They are absolute even as we try to bend the rules he established. Our pitiful attempts to short-sell the evil in our heart are not based upon reality. The reality is that sin and death exist today, just as they always have since the Fall. No imagination or human invention can change this reality. Death has not yet been defeated.

We are beginning to see a new religious worldview gain in popularity in our western culture. The science of quantum physics is merging with eastern religious concepts to argue that there are many paths to get to the same place. The universe consists of a single consciousness, according to this thesis, and there are many ways we can come to realize our place within that whole.

We might find it inspiring to see scientists turn their art toward the supernatural. However, this "many paths" approach excludes the single path we find in Scripture. That is, the way to God is God's way. Only the biblical model presents a salvation formula that entails 100 percent law and 100 percent grace. It is a paradox of justice and mercy based upon God's nature.

There are many attributes of God. However, they all trace back to two recurring elements of his nature: law and grace.

In the following passage, God's nature of law and grace provides a physical place where he can unite with his people.

"The cherubim shall spread out their wings above, overshadowing the mercy seat with their wings, their faces one to another; toward **the mercy seat** *shall the faces of the cherubim be. And you shall*

*put the mercy seat on the top of the ark, and in the ark you shall put **the testimony** that I shall give you. **There I will meet with you**, and from above the mercy seat, from between the two cherubim that are on the ark of the testimony, I will speak with you about all that I will give you in commandment for the people of Israel."*

—Exodus 25:20–22

Even though we do not have the Ark of the Covenant today as a focal point of God's presence on the earth, we can still meet with our Creator. God's presence is now spread out throughout the whole earth; Christ is our mediator in heaven, so we no longer have need of a High Priest to mediate at a single location in a tabernacle or temple.

We see two important aspects of God's nature in this passage:

1. **The Mercy Seat:** this represents the grace of God, through which our sins are forgiven. Grace covers sin just like dirt on a coffin. Our old nature is buried here.

2. **The Testimony:** this includes the law of God that forms his commandments. God's law is part of the old Mosaic covenant with the nation of Israel and is part of the new covenant that is called the "law of Christ" in the New Testament. God's law has not fundamentally changed even though some conditional language changed to nonconditional.

God meets his people at his Mercy Seat, which sits over his law. This custom has not changed in thousands of years as God's nature does not change.

God's nature is both righteous and gracious. This is a paradox; two apparently opposite attributes are both true at the same time.

The Mercy Seat does not remove God's law, but it covers the law. We are thus able to approach God without fear despite our sinfulness. His forgiveness covers our sins. Grace always comes first before the law.

"But I say to you who hear, Love your enemies, do good to those who hate you, bless those who curse you, pray for those who abuse you. To one who strikes you on the cheek, offer the other also, and from one who takes away your cloak do not withhold your tunic either. Give to everyone who begs from you, and from one who takes away your goods do not demand them back. And as you wish that others would do to you, do so to them.

"If you love those who love you, what benefit is that to you? For even sinners love those who love them. And if you do good to those who do good to you, what benefit is that to you? For even sinners do the same. And if you lend to those from whom you expect to receive, what credit is that to you? Even sinners lend to sinners, to get back the same amount. But love your enemies, and do good, and lend, **expecting nothing in return***, and your reward will be great, and you will be sons of the Most High, for he is kind to the ungrateful and the evil.* **Be merciful, even as your Father is merciful.***"*

—Luke 6:27–36

It is impossible to do all that Christ commands of us under our nature. The only way we can do these things is to "be merciful" as God is merciful.

God's merciful nature is given to us. First comes grace—also described as mercy in many places in Scripture—then come works of grace called love.

We are to "expect nothing in return" for the love we show others. If we did expect payment, this wouldn't be grace at all. So we look to God's example and see how he is constantly giving his love and his Spirit to the world. He does not need anything in return, not even our worship.[21] He does not need us to provide our own sacrifice (Genesis 22:14), nor does he expect us to generate good works. He knows we can't do anything good without relying totally on him.

---

21. See Acts 17:24–25.

CHAPTER 14.

JUDGMENT OF THE RIGHTEOUS

We now come to the third of the primary end-time events. Following the return of Christ and the physical resurrection of the faithful, God will pass judgment. But on what criteria will we be judged?

Will God's assessment boil down to "justified" or "damned" in a pass/fail sense? Or will he judge all our works individually, adjusting our eternal reward or penalty based on the degree of our faithfulness?

According to the Bible, both types of judgment will occur, presenting us with yet another paradox. And once again this paradox is based on the fact that God's nature includes both the law and grace. Due to his grace and the righteousness of Christ, he will find us justified. But to uphold his law, he will also grade our works.

Why do some verses state that we will not be judged, while other verses that state we will be judged? The law-and-grace paradox reconciles this contradiction. Note that the judgment follows the resurrection. We will receive eternal life without being judged since Christ is willing to cover us with his righteousness. But our works will be judged following the resurrection to determine our eternal rewards within the kingdom.

Scripture says we will be rewarded in proportion to our humility; the more thoroughly we reject our selfish desires and ambitions, the greater our eternal reward. The Sermon on the Mount (Matthew 5:3–12) speaks to this concept in the beatitudes where Christ summarizes the prophetic blessings of the Old Testament.[1]

To enter eternal life with God, we the accused need to be perfect. We need to keep the law to perfection, to show selfless love in literally every circumstance. God will not allow any amount of sin to tarnish the eternal kingdom. Nobody but Christ has accomplished a sinless life, so it is only under his covering and advocacy that we can humbly approach God and receive grace without being condemned by the law.

The Bible states we can enter eternity with God only through the sacrifice of Christ's life. He gave up his will, and through his perfect obedience he was justified by the law.[2] After sacrificing his life on the cross, Christ was then glorified in his resurrection, enabling him to mediate justice. He invites us to share in his inheritance and receive new glorified bodies of our own. God's plan for redemption included this "once and for all" sacrifice to save all people via the same means of grace and perfect fulfillment of the law.[3]

---

1. Also see James 2:5.
2. See Philippians 2:5–8.
3. See Romans 5:8; 6:10; Hebrews 10:10.

According to the biblical plan of redemption, we can only pass or fail. Either Christ stamps "paid in full" on our entry ticket, or we reject God's offer of grace. No other options are available for any person. Scripture mentions two distinct categories of people: those who are saved and those who are lost. We see no biblical examples of a person who is "borderline" saved.

*"Or do you not know that your body is a temple of the Holy Spirit within you, whom you have from God? **You are not your own**, for **you were bought with a price**. So glorify God in your body."*

—1 Corinthians 6:19–20

Anyone not sealed by the Spirit is still under the bondage of slavery to death, but Christ paid for us all and offers us a different destiny. Instead of perishing, we can live forever with him.

Through God's plan of salvation, he predestined us all to escape the curse of death. Unfortunately, not everyone accepts this change of destiny. God initiated his plan in Genesis 3:15 and carried it out all the way through the Bible. This plan was fully established through the new covenant, which Christ sealed with his own blood. From the start, God intended to base salvation on unconditional grace. He included a conditional plan through which Israel would receive a special blessing within the overarching salvation of humanity. Ultimately, Israel broke the terms of this conditional law-based covenant, so Christ fulfilled the law instead. If we reject the gospel, we will remain under the penalty of death that is our human destiny, based upon the curse of death that afflicts our nature.

God graciously delivered his message of salvation (Genesis 3:15) before implementing the curse of death (Genesis 3:19, repeated in Hebrews 9:27). Yet another paradox is that we are destined to die under the law, yet destined to receive eternal life through God's grace. One destiny is unconditional (we will all die) and one is conditional (if we do not reject the Spirit, we will be resurrected). Though we are mortal beings, we have received a conditional gift of immortality.

By default, our human destiny is to die and remain dead. We don't need to do anything to achieve this destiny. But God has established for us an alternate destiny of eternal life; it is conditional in that we must believe God's Word, receive God's Spirit, and act obediently in faith.

God's Word, his Spirit, and our faith are all gifts we receive from God. We do not produce the works that seal our new destiny. We must simply believe God and remain in him. Many people try to add to the gospel by prescribing some amount of works to achieve salvation, or they try to change the gospel by promoting inherent immortality. These are dangerous beliefs. Literal renderings of Scripture contradict both concepts.

We were under the power of the devil, destined to sin against God and die. Now we have been called out of darkness into the light (1 Peter 2:9). God called us; we did not call him. Numerous passages speak to the conflict between darkness and light. For example, immediately after Jesus mentions grace in John 3:16, he compares light and darkness, good and sinful works—and ties it all back to his grace.

*"And this is the judgment: the light has come into the world, and people loved the darkness rather than the light because their works were evil. For everyone who does wicked things hates the light and does not come to the light, lest his works should be exposed. But whoever does what is true comes to the light, so that it may be clearly seen **that his works have been carried out in God.**"*

—John 3:19–21

The wicked reject Christ ("the light") and stay in the darkness of sinful human nature. In John 3:16, Jesus states we need to "believe in him." If we trust in him, we will be able to stand with him in confidence. We are first introduced to God's light at the baptism of the Holy Spirit. Once we receive God's Word and believe in his truth, we will not stray far from his light, preferring to remain in him. A literal translation of John 3:21 states that our good works are "wrought", "done," or "performed" in God (not of our self).

The first epistle of John expands upon this a little further. The message of grace within the gospel always comes first, just as in John 3:16. Once the light is revealed, then we can keep God's law and remain in the light.

"This is the message we have heard from him and proclaim to you, that God is light [truth, life, righteousness], and in him is no darkness at all. If we say we have fellowship with him while we walk in darkness, we lie and do not practice the truth. But if we walk in the light, as he is in the light, we have fellowship with one another, and the blood of Jesus his Son cleanses us from all sin. If we say we have no sin, we deceive ourselves, and the truth is not in us. If we confess our sins, he is faithful and just to forgive us

our sins and to cleanse us from all unrighteousness. If we say we have not sinned, we make him a liar, and his word is not in us."

—1 John 1:5–10

If we reject God ("the light"), we stay in the darkness of sin and death. If we believe in the message of the gospel, God will reveal to us his truth and life. If we remain in God's light, then we will keep his law.

The key to understanding this passage and many like it is to understand conditional statements (for example, he will cleanse us *if* we confess). Conditions are based on the law, but we are no longer under the law once we first believe in God. We believe that he cleanses us by giving us his Spirit to replace our unclean heart; he does not directly clean the heart itself. Faith and immortality are both conditional gifts we receive as part of salvation. We look outward to God to receive faith and immortality; we are not intrinsically immortal, nor do we have the ability to summon faith from within our old nature.

Cleansing is a part of sanctification, the ongoing process God uses to give us righteousness over time. We need to understand that God is cleansing neither an immortal soul nor our old heart. Cleansing is different from the single act of justification that forgives past, present, and future sins and covers us with the righteousness of Christ. Justification is conditional upon faith; we must trust in Christ's once-for-all work while we deny our nature's ability to do works of any merit. Sanctification is similar to justification but is based on the ongoing work of God's Spirit.

Justification and sanctification are each connected to both

grace and law. Christ fulfilled the law to justify us, and we receive his justification as a gift of grace. The gift arrives before we can do good works or be made clean. Sanctification is the process by which we keep the law through the Holy Spirit working in our new heart, which we received by grace. Both justification and sanctification are gifts from God, as we cannot keep the law on our own. A way to understand sanctification and justification is through the use of verb tenses.

- **Past-tense verbs** (*we have been justified, marked, preserved*): Christ justified everyone throughout all time with his one-time sacrifice.[4] We were individually justified when we received the Holy Spirit. We began the sanctification process of being set apart from the world when we were first justified. We were marked, sealed, saved, kept, and preserved at that time.

- **Present-tense verbs** (*we believe, obey, are being sanctified*): We are continually sanctified and justified today through the work of the Holy Spirit. We are sealed today (justified) if we "hold on" to the gospel through belief. We are cleansed today (sanctified) so we can be used for God's purposes. We obey the law by loving others, giving generously, and doing other good works, taking care not to be conformed to the world.

- **Future** (*we will be resurrected, glorified*): The completion of justification and sanctification happens when we are resurrected to eternal life.

When Christ returns, we may hope to be included among

---

4. See Romans 5:8, 6:10; Hebrews 10:10.

those resurrected and judged. Don't let the traditional names for these events—the "judgment of the righteous" and the "resurrection of the just"—intimidate you. Although we are not righteous or just on our own merit, Christ justified us to inherit eternal life.

Remember, inheritance is not earned. Children do not "deserve" inheritance. They receive it on the basis of who they belong to. An inheritance is only conditional in the sense that a person can be disinherited if he rejects his parent's wishes. Just as children are born into an earthly inheritance, we become co-heirs with Christ when we are reborn in the Spirit.

Peter opens his first epistle by describing salvation as an inheritance. Later in chapter 5, he relates the second coming to the gift that we will receive at the resurrection. The "crown of glory that never fades" is eternal life.

*"Then **when the Chief Shepherd appears, you will receive the crown of glory that never fades away**. In the same way, you who are younger, be subject to the elders. And all of you, clothe yourselves with humility toward one another, because God **opposes the proud but gives grace to the humble**. And **God will exalt you in due time**, if you humble yourselves under his mighty hand by casting all your cares on him because he cares for you."*

—1 Peter 5:4–7, NET Bible

Peter states that we will receive the crown of eternal life at the second coming, which agrees with all other biblical teaching on the matter. Notice that God "will exalt" us "in due time," meaning that we do not have the full extent of our gifts today.

Remember that Christ did not receive his exaltation until after his resurrection. The Transfiguration event merely offered a glimpse or preview of the glorified, resurrected Christ. When Christ was baptized, a heavenly voice spoke and a dove descended upon him, but this was not his exaltation either. His exaltation had to wait until after he accepted the cup of wrath, fulfilled the law, and sealed the new covenant with his blood. Christ had to humble himself and submit in obedience. Only then could he be resurrected and exalted.

Notice Peter's reference to Proverbs 3:34 (also see James 4:6), which says that God resists the proud. The proud are those who reject God and trust in their own understanding. God gives grace to the humble—those who trust in him alone. God offers grace to the whole world, but only those who are humble like a child and believe in the gift of faith will receive grace.

When considering the Big Three end-time events, notice that Christ will bring rewards and justice with him upon his return (1 Peter 5:4). We will be paid back for what we have done on earth (Revelation 22:12).

Scripture is clear: Christ will settle all accounts when he returns to earth.[5] But what is this payment for if we did not contribute anything towards salvation? Indeed, Christ already paid for our salvation at the cross. So this new, final payment must be something different.

---

5. See Isaiah 35:4; 40:10; 59:17–20; and 62:11.

After we receive our new resurrected bodies, Christ will pay us an eternal reward. We will be redeemed first, then immediately rewarded. But what is this reward for? How can we be rewarded if Christ did all the work? We'll look at the answer shortly.

Many second-advent passages describe God "awarding" judgment. He is prophesied to distribute rewards, crowns, and other gifts after Christ's appearing:

- Isaiah 35:4; 40:10; 59:17–20; 62:11
- Daniel 7:22
- Matthew 16:27
- Luke 14:14
- 1 Corinthians 3:13–15; 4:5
- 1 Thessalonians 2:19
- 1 Timothy 6:19
- 2 Timothy 4:8
- Hebrews 9:27–28
- 1 Peter 5:4
- Revelation 22:12

Christ will share the inheritance with us when he returns.

"In him you also, when you heard the word of truth, the gospel of your salvation, and believed in him, were sealed with the promised

*Holy Spirit, who is the guarantee of our **inheritance until we acquire possession** of it, to the praise of his glory."*

—Ephesians 1:13–14

When we look at the preceding verses, the context of this passage is clear. God's plan will be carried out in the "fullness of time." God will unite the earthly and heavenly realms at the end of the age when the inheritance is granted. We are sealed as inheritors now. We will obtain possession at the end of this age.

*"In him we have redemption through his blood, the forgiveness of our trespasses, according to the riches of his grace, which he lavished upon us, in all wisdom and insight making known to us the mystery of his will, according to his purpose, which he set forth in Christ as **a plan** for the **fullness of time, to unite all things in him, things in heaven and things on earth**. In him **we have obtained an inheritance**, having been predestined according to the purpose of him who works all things according to the counsel of his will, so that we who were the first to hope in Christ might be to the praise of his glory."*

—Ephesians 1:7–11

This process is similar to how we use a will to determine the recipients of an inheritance after a death.[6] Christ claimed his inheritance already. The Holy Spirit who dwells inside us guarantees that we will be able to claim our portion in the fullness of time. Christ called the Holy Spirit the "Comforter" because he dwells with us while we wait to inherit the kingdom as promised.

---

6. See Hebrews 9:15–17.

Peter has more to say about our future inheritance.

*"Blessed be the God and Father of our Lord Jesus Christ! According to his great mercy, he has caused us to be born again to a living hope through the resurrection of Jesus Christ from the dead, to an **inheritance** that is imperishable, undefiled, and unfading, **kept in heaven** for you, who by God's power are being guarded through faith for a salvation ready to be **revealed in the last time**."*

—1 Peter 1:3–5

Notice that our inheritance is "kept in heaven." We have a claim to it now, but we don't have it in hand yet. Kept, sealed, preserved—these are saving terms. As jam kept in a jar in the cellar, we need to be preserved by the Spirit as we wait for the ultimate fulfillment of God's promise.

Judgment Day

We have a lot of preconceived notions about Judgment Day, the last of the Big Three end-time events. We are familiar with the concept of going before a judge to try to get a fine thrown out or reduced. Or in a positive sense, we think about judges awarding a prize in a sporting event or baking contest.

This chapter specifically focuses upon the judgment of the righteous, not the judgment of the unrighteous. Because the judgment follows the resurrection, the only people around for God to judge at this time are those who have already been granted eternal life. No punishment looms because Christ has presented his righteousness on our behalf. The only matter at hand is the extent to which we will be rewarded.

Scripture says the unrighteous will be judged separately.[7]

"And he has given him authority to execute judgment, because he is the Son of Man. Do not marvel at this, for an hour is coming when all who are in the tombs will hear his voice and come out, those who have done good to **the resurrection of life,** *and those who have done evil to the* **resurrection of judgment."**

—John 5:27–29

According to this teaching of Christ, there will be separate resurrection and judgment events for "those who have done good" and "those who have done evil."

Christ says we will hear his voice (other passages describe a shout at the second coming) and then be resurrected. Note that Christ warned of judgment for the unrighteous but did not mention judgment for the righteous; the righteous only receive the reward of eternal life for having passed their test of faith.

Paul also differentiates between types of resurrections. The "resurrection of the righteous" calls said people out from among the dead (Philippians 3:11), leaving the rest of the dead to remain until the "resurrection of the unrighteous." The righteous will be raised first.

"But this I confess to you, that according to the Way, which they call a sect, I worship the God of our fathers, believing everything laid down by the Law and written in the Prophets, having a hope

---

7. These judgments of the wicked will be discussed in Volume II.

in God, which these men themselves accept, that there will be a **resurrection of both the just and the unjust."**

—Acts 24:14–15

In the Old Testament, Daniel prophesied of two separate types of resurrection:

"At that time shall arise Michael, the great prince who has charge of your people. And there shall be a time of trouble, such as never has been since there was a nation till that time. But at that time your people shall be delivered, everyone whose name shall be found written in the book. And **many of those who sleep in the dust of the earth shall awake***, some to everlasting life, and some to shame and everlasting contempt. And those who are wise shall shine like the brightness of the sky above; and those who turn many to righteousness, like the stars forever and ever."*

—Daniel 12:1–3

Here Daniel doesn't explicitly separate those being resurrected into "just" and "unjust" categories, but taken in context with other prophetic passages, we can safely infer judgment is taking place. We should note that "many" people were raised, but not all. Only some are raised right away at the second advent.

Christ also described a separate resurrection of the just in this parable about charity.

"[Y]ou will be blessed, because they cannot repay you. For you will be **repaid at the resurrection of the just***."*

—Luke 14:14

The judgment of the just comes after Christ's second coming and our bodily resurrection. Rewards will be granted as we enter the kingdom of eternal life.

"I charge you in the presence of God and of Christ Jesus, who is **to judge the living and the dead**, and **by his appearing and his kingdom:** ...

"I have competed well; I have finished the race; I have kept the faith! Finally **the crown of righteousness** is reserved for me. The Lord, the righteous Judge, **will award it to me in that day**—and not to me only, but also to all who have set their affection **on his appearing**."

—2 Timothy 4:1, 7–8

"Just as people are destined to die once, and after that to face judgment, so Christ was sacrificed once to take away the sins of many; and **he will appear a second time**, not to bear sin, but **to bring salvation to those who are waiting for him**."

—Hebrews 9:27–28

Christ doesn't complete our salvation until the second advent. This is the salvation event we have all been waiting for. The Bible frequently groups two or three of the Big Three events together in the same passage. But we never see a sequence where a rapture or resurrection event leads into a long tribulation delay, with judgment to follow.

There is simply no biblical basis for separating the resurrection and judgment events, as proponents of a pre-tribulation rapture would try to do.

Passages on the tribulation period will be discussed in more detail in Volume II, but we'll take a brief look here.

Tribulation and Wrath

Will Christians and/or the Jewish people go through the tribulation period? We know we are not destined for the wrath of God, so a comparison of pre-wrath and post-tribulation raptures should be made. We know Noah went through tribulation but did not receive wrath. He was saved (kept) through it. This is the model we should refer to as we read apocalyptic prophecies.

Scripture only presents us with one more coming of Christ. He will not come a third time, nor appear privately to a select group. Indeed, even the Old Testament end-time prophecies align with what we read in Revelation—both in terms of the time of tribulation and the clustering of the Big Three events.

A pre-tribulation rapture is inspired by the Greek mythological model of souls or spirit-bodies ascending to the heavens. This concept is nowhere to be found in the Bible. Not one verse justifies a belief in a resurrected afterlife in the heavenly realm. Nor can we find a passage to suggest that the saints will hide in heaven to avoid the tribulation.

Wrath and tribulation are two different terms altogether. Although we must endure tribulation, the just are not destined to face God's wrath.[8]

It's difficult to imagine the world turning to the Bible

---

8. See 1 Thessalonians 1:10; 5:9.

during the tribulation—much less seeking out literal interpretations. They will be drowning in thousands of opinions as to why horrible events are happening. Should they read a biblical prophecy about an event clearly in progress, the devil will offer them a worldly explanation or "signs and wonders" of his own. Deceived, they will continue to reject God and his Word. This is what the Bible says will happen, and it lines up perfectly with what we know about human nature and our modern culture.

We already know people can't see the obvious. We're too distracted by our selfish pursuits and obsessions. God through his Word wants us to know what is imminent and to prepare ourselves accordingly. The beginning of the Great Tribulation may be a surprise to all, but according to the apocalyptic passages, there will be signs to warn us of what is coming. While the rest of the world argues over why such disastrous events are occurring, Christians should be able to calmly point to Scripture. But since we believers cannot seem to agree on a single gospel, how can we ever agree on how to interpret more complex prophecies?

God will continue to offer salvation to the whole world until the very end. "Wheat and tares" will live together. Hearts will continue to harden through the continual rejection of the gospel. Instead of considering the signs of the times, people will jeer, "Where is the promise of his coming?" (2 Peter 3:4). The second coming of Christ will always seem unlikely to the wicked, whether today or in the turbulent future.

"And none of the wicked shall understand, but those who are wise shall understand."

—Daniel 12:10b

Only those with the mind of Christ will understand end-time events. More on the judgment of the wicked later; now for some good news.

*"He made Him who knew no sin to be sin on our behalf, so that **we might become the righteousness** of God **in Him**."*

—2 Corinthians 5:21, NASB

We are born without any inherent righteousness, and we cannot become righteous in and of ourselves. We can only become righteous through Christ. He gives us 100 percent perfection.

*"**He who believes in Him is not judged** [or condemned]; he who does not believe has been judged already, because he has not believed in the name of the only begotten Son of God."*

—John 3:18

Remember that belief includes obedience; we can't simply say we believe in God while deliberately continuing in sin.

*"There is therefore now **no condemnation for those** who are **in Christ Jesus**."*

—Romans 8:1

God will determine our reward upon our resurrection. We will not be condemned at this judgment; no entrance exam stands in the way between us and the crown of eternal life.

*"Truly, truly, I say to you, **he who hears My word, and believes***

*Him who sent Me, has eternal life, and **does not come into judgment**, but has **passed out of death into life**."*

—John 5:24, NASB

Eternal Life and Second Death

We in our flesh are destined to die. This is very clear throughout Scripture. But will this be a physical death only, or will it include a spiritual death? If we believe we have an immortal soul, we must also believe in the specter of spiritual death to follow the death of our body. Physical death has no real consequences if we have an immortal soul. Unconditional immortality forces nonsensical interpretations onto passages like John 5. Immortal life in the heavenly realm draws from Greek mythology, not God's Word.

Hell may mean one thing if we're only expecting physical death, but something else entirely in the context of spiritual death. Hell in this context is marked by eternal death and fire—the "second death" presented in Revelation 20:14 and 21:8.[9]

We've already seen in John 5:25–29 how we receive a spiritual salvation today and a physical salvation at the resurrection. We will receive life if we hear God's Word and believe in him. Today we can be spiritually alive in Christ or spiritually dead in our flesh. In either case, physical death will follow. Then we will receive either a second physical life or a second physical death.

---

9. We will explore these passages, along with the "second death" generally, in more detail in Volume II.

The realms merge in the next age. There will be just one eternal realm: the kingdom of heaven on earth. Eternal death means being trapped outside the "gates."[10] We have already looked at numerous passages describing the resurrection to immortal life. But there is also a physical resurrection to judgment and eternal death.

The gifts we receive today as part of our spiritual salvation will preserve us until the time of the physical resurrection; here we will receive eternal life, be spared the punishment reserved for the people included in the judgment of the unrighteous. Instead of using the term "saved" in the past tense, we should use ongoing verbs such as "being kept, preserved, marked, or sealed" to clarify our state.

---

10. See Revelation 21:27; 22:14–15.

CHAPTER 15.

RECOMPENSE FOR FAITHFUL LABOR

*"For the Son of Man is going to come with his angels in the glory of his Father, and then he will **repay** each person according to what he has done."*

—Matthew 16:27

*"For we must all appear before the judgment seat of Christ, so that each one may be **paid back** according to what he has done while in the body, whether good or evil."*

—2 Corinthians 5:10

"Recompense" means to pay back. We are recompensated for the works we have done. Remember that eternal life is our inheritance, not our reward, and we did nothing to earn that gift of grace. However, Christ will offer us some other type of reward after we enter eternal life. We can also lose potential rewards.

*"[W]hatever good anyone does, this he will **receive back** from the Lord, whether he is a bondservant or is free."*

—Ephesians 6:8

Paul is speaking to a reward system that comes into effect after we pass the test of faith.

"[D]o you presume on the riches of his kindness and forbearance and patience, not knowing that God's kindness is meant to lead you to repentance? But because of your hard and impenitent heart you are storing up wrath for yourself on the day of wrath when God's righteous judgment will be revealed. **He will render to each one according to his works:** *to those who by patience in well-doing seek for glory and honor and immortality, he will give eternal life; but for those who are self-seeking and do not obey the truth, but obey unrighteousness, there will be wrath and fury."*

—Romans 2:4–8

First Corinthians provides more information about eternal rewards than any other book in the New Testament. Here we can see that God gets the credit and does the heavy lifting as he enables us to do good through the Holy Spirit. Some of this is implied based upon other passages. Our good works cannot happen without God's first work in us.

"I [Paul] planted, Apollos watered, but God gave the growth. So **neither he who plants nor he who waters is anything***, but* **only God who gives the growth.** *He who plants and he who waters are one, and* **each will receive his wages according to his labor.** *For we are God's fellow workers. You are God's field, God's building.*

*"***According to the grace of God given to me***, like a skilled master builder I laid a foundation, and someone else is building upon it. Let each one take care how he builds upon it. For no one can lay a foundation other than that which is laid, which is Jesus Christ. Now if anyone builds on the foundation with gold, silver, precious stones, wood, hay, straw—each one's work will become manifest,*

*for the Day will disclose it, because it will be revealed by fire, and the fire will test what sort of work each one has done. If the work that anyone has built on the foundation survives, **he will receive a reward**. If anyone's work is burned up, **he will suffer loss, though he himself will be saved**, but only as through fire."*

—1 Corinthians 3:6–15

Here is confirmation that we get rewarded for the labor we do through God's power.

Paul uses figurative language here to make a point, but there are literal meanings that he is trying to convey. He clearly describes the two-part judgment process God uses.

- First, we will either be saved or not. Just as a person cannot be half-pregnant, we cannot be nearly saved. The gift of salvation is granted to those who believe; they will be saved by grace through faith.
- Second, believers will get rewards for the work they completed. This work honored God's law but did not count towards salvation. Believers will either receive additional blessing, or they will "suffer loss."

The humblest servant who denied his "self" and did the greatest works through the Spirit will gain the largest reward. The person who was only minimally faithful to God's law will be as a beggar in the kingdom. All those made righteous by faith in God will enter the kingdom, yet some will be rewarded more richly than others. Of course, the believer who "suffers loss" will still have much to be grateful for:

"For a day in your courts is better than a thousand elsewhere. I

would rather be a doorkeeper in the house of my God than dwell in the tents of wickedness."

—Psalm 84:10

Based on this concept, the more obedient and humble we are today, the greater our treasure will be in the coming age. The faithful that enter the kingdom will be rewarded for their good deeds.

*"Command them to do good, to be rich in good deeds, and to be generous and willing to share. In this way they will **lay up treasure** for themselves as a firm foundation **for the coming age**, so that they may take hold of the life that is truly life."*

—1 Timothy 6:18–19

Christ called this "storing up treasure in heaven."

A passage from Matthew 19 begins with the disciples asking Christ about their rewards. Christ assures them repayment is coming. We may marvel at the thought that we will get rewarded by God for work done by his own power, but Christ has testified that this is what will happen.

Christ mentioned the two-fold judgment paradox through which eternal life is separate from rewards. This teaching from Christ covers a lot of other topics as well, summarizing many points to consider regarding judgment and the coming age.

"And Jesus said to his disciples, 'Truly, I say to you, only with difficulty will a rich person enter the kingdom of heaven. Again I tell you, it is easier for a camel to go through the eye of a needle

than for a rich person to enter the kingdom of God.' When the disciples heard this, they were greatly astonished, saying, 'Who then can be saved?'

"But Jesus looked at them and said, 'With man this is impossible, but with God all things are possible.' Then Peter said in reply, 'See, we have left everything and followed you. What then will we have?' Jesus said to them, 'Truly, I say to you, **in the new world [in the regeneration]***, when the Son of Man will sit on his glorious throne, you who have followed me will also sit on twelve thrones, judging the twelve tribes of Israel. And everyone who has left houses or brothers or sisters or father or mother or children or lands, for my name's sake,* **will receive a hundredfold** *and* **will inherit eternal life***. But many who are first will be last, and the last first.'"*

—Matthew 19:23–30

The phrase **in the regeneration** is based on the same Greek root word that occurs in Titus 3:5. Paul applies it there to the baptismal work of the Holy Spirit; an individual is being regenerated, born again. So here in Matthew, Jesus is saying that the earth itself will be "born again."[1]

"Jesus said to them, 'I tell you the truth: In the age when all things are renewed...'"

—Matthew 19:28, NET Bible

Christ told his disciples that the world will be regenerated. The disciple's rewards will be in this new earthly kingdom, as they were not rewarded in their lifetime. He also mentions inheritance into eternal life, which is a common

---

1. Also see Romans 8:18–24.

term tied to the land promise. Christ differentiates between the gift of eternal life and the hundredfold reward; one is based on grace, the other on law.

Eternal life is not automatically ours because we are not immortal. We will receive eternal life as a gift; it is part of the inheritance that is tied to God's promises to the descendants of Abraham (descendants of faith, not of blood).

Christ will sit on his "glorious throne" in the heavenly kingdom on earth; no longer will he be at the right hand of the Father in the heavenly realm. His new work on earth upon his return will be to destroy sin, death, and the devil. Once all evil is destroyed, his kingdom will be fully established. He will then hand over the kingdom as described in 1 Corinthians 15:24.

Christ could have told the disciples that their rewards would be paid out in heaven after they died, but he didn't. If the disciples were satisfied with a spiritual reign of Christ in the heavenly realm, they would have been satisfied after his resurrection. The work of salvation would have been complete at that point. However, based on numerous prophecies throughout the Old Testament, they knew a kingdom on earth was coming. Their attitude in Acts 1:6 and Matthew 19:25–27 shows that they hoped for the kingdom not yet established.

"...whom heaven must receive **until the time for restoring all the things** about which God spoke by the mouth of his holy prophets long ago."

—Acts 3:21

Passages about judgment often contain references to "new heavens and a new earth." Christ won't simply restore Israel's former kingdom (Acts 1:6), nor will he be satisfied to return the earth to the unspoiled state of Eden. No, the earth will be a better place than it has ever been. Restoring the earth is a major end-time event.

*"For behold, I create new heavens and a new earth, and the **former things shall not be remembered** or come into mind."*

—Isaiah 65:17

*"For as the new heavens and **the new earth that I make shall remain before me**, says the Lord, so shall your offspring and your name remain."*

—Isaiah 66:22

*"But according to his promise we are waiting for new heavens and **a new earth in which righteousness dwells**."*

—2 Peter 3:13

Christ's testimony, the passages above, and John's vision in Revelation 21:1 all foretell the renewal, regeneration, and restoration of earth. Christ intends to establish his kingdom on this new earth, not some unknown mystical realm. Righteousness will dwell on the earth. This fits the land promise and ties all end-time prophecies together.

We don't have to throw unfulfilled Old Testament prophecies into the figurative bucket of metaphors, dreaming up mystical realms and imagining a bodiless eternity. End-time passages make much more sense if we can move past our preconceived notion of a soul floating to heaven. Christ will dwell on the new earth, and we will dwell with him. We won't be playing harps on a cloud; all end-time passages are located on the "new" earth.

The new earth will be renewed, restored—God will cleanse it once his judgment is complete.

"Thus says the Lord God: On the day that I cleanse you from all your iniquities, I will cause the cities to be inhabited, and the waste places shall be rebuilt.... And they will say, 'This land that was desolate has become like the garden of Eden, and the waste and desolate and ruined cities are now fortified and inhabited.'"

—Ezekiel 36:33, 35

We may prefer to read passages about Eden—and the tree of life in particular—as metaphor. But whether the Edenic passages are literal accounts or metaphorical descriptions of what the world could have looked like without sin, the main point remains the same: God sustains life. His creation depends on him providing life. Notice that many passages describe God transforming us from death to life, giving us eternal life, or inviting us to live with him forever—but never does he grant us an inherent immortal soul. Instead, the mortal puts on immortal clothes and drinks life-giving water. The inspired writers stop short of saying we will become like God even after the resurrection. Even in our glorified state, our immortality will be a gift, not an inherent part of our nature.

"To the one who conquers I will grant to eat of the tree of life, which is in the paradise of God."

—Revelation 2:7b

"For the Lamb in the midst of the throne will be their shepherd, and he will guide them to springs of living water, and God will wipe away every tear from their eyes."

—Revelation 7:17

"Blessed are those who wash their robes, so that they may have the right to the tree of life and that they may enter the city by the gates."

—Revelation 22:14

"[I]f anyone takes away from the words of the book of this prophecy, God will take away his share in the tree of life and in the holy city, which are described in this book."

—Revelation 22:19[2]

We are not inherently immortal; death is our natural inheritance. Eternal life is Christ's inheritance he chooses to share with us. We were not given immortality at birth, nor will we receive such a gift at any point before the resurrection. The immortal soul myth concludes that not even God can destroy our being, so our soul must go to heaven or hell for eternity.

Christ himself contradicts this idea that unsaved souls will endure forever in a state of torment:

"And do not fear those who kill the body but cannot kill the soul. Rather fear him who can destroy both soul and body in hell."

---

2. Also see Ezekiel 47:12.

—Matthew 10:28

This statement is not a biblical aberration. Elsewhere in Scripture we read of the destruction of angels, also called gods or sons of god in some passages.[3] And we can find numerous passages about the death of souls.[4] Hypothetically, God has the power make a person endure so they might be punished for eternity, but this still wouldn't indicate an inherent immortality within a human being. Immortality is conditionally granted by God.

The complete gospel message reaches its conclusion through the Big Three end-time events: Christ's second coming, the resurrection of the just, and the judgment of the righteous. No other complete gospel is presented in the Bible. It is remarkable that we can be blind to what God's Word says, given how frequently the message is repeated. But cultural influence is a powerful thing. We are brainwashed into accepting culturally friendly interpretations instead of simply letting Scripture speak.

We should not judge well-meaning people who believe the hybrid gospel or promote its message. This book is meant to guide people into greater understanding of God's Word, not to cast judgment. God alone is the judge, and Christ will mediate on our behalf. We are judged based on what we have been given.

The devil is always working to water down the gospel, promote partial-truths, and distract us by any means at his disposal. I myself once held end-time beliefs based more

---

3. See Psalm 82:6–7.
4. See Ezekiel 18:4; Revelation 8:9.

on cultural mythology than biblical scholarship. As many others do, I presumed I had an immortal soul. But when God reveals his truth, it sets us free from preconceived notions and self-taught beliefs.

A literal reading of Scripture offers us the following truths about judgment:

- Salvation yields eternal life; without this gift, once we die we will remain "dead" for eternity.
- The just are resurrected then judged to determine the reward for their deeds, but there is no judgment standing between us and salvation—in this case, Christ's righteousness is judged on our behalf.
- Those who have faith are given a share of the inheritance: eternal life in the Promised Land.
- Eternal life is not granted until the resurrection, but we get a guarantee.
- God will not enact the final judgment until after Christ's second coming.
- We will be judged on earth after the resurrection, not in heaven after we die.
- Judgment presents a paradox in terms of timing: God judges our faith today (for our justification); he judges our deeds on the last day (to determine our eternal rewards). Our deeds are rewarded under the law; our sins are forgiven by grace.

So why we are rewarded for the works we perform when all the good we do is based upon the power of the Holy Spirit? How can we be rewarded for deeds that did not arise from our human nature? The answer is found in the grace-and-law paradox system. We will be rewarded or repaid for the good deeds we allow God to do through us, and we will receive the gift of eternal life despite our sinful deeds.

"Therefore, my beloved, as you have always obeyed, so now, not only as in my presence but much more in my absence, work out your own salvation with fear and trembling, **for it is God who works in you***, both* **to will and to work** *for his good pleasure."*

—Philippians 2:12–13

We get rewarded for this?

What an awesome God we serve! From a human perspective, it seems strange to be given something as a gift, then also be rewarded for using the gift. But such is the amazing goodness of God. Once we submit and obey out of a contrite heart, then we are rewarded by the God who is working in us and working out his will.

We get rewarded because of God's established concepts—many of which are foreign to us modern Christians. We prefer to adopt a grace-focused belief system that doesn't regard any of our direct works at any point in the entire judgment process. People who believe in an all-grace message for salvation generally think about eternal life as the only reward they need, avoiding passages that speak of rewards for works. This perspective has the commendable trappings of humility, but it is not founded in Scripture.

God, wanting as many to be saved as possible, elected to use us as his workers in his fields until the day of harvest—the day of Christ's return. We can find numerous passages that relate our kingdom work to sowing and laboring in the fields; many of these passages include discussions of payment and compensation for our labor.

"And when evening came, the owner of the vineyard said to his foreman, 'Call the laborers and pay them their wages, beginning with the last, up to the first.' And when those hired about the eleventh hour came, each of them received a denarius. Now when those hired first came, they thought they would receive more, but each of them also received a denarius. And on receiving it they grumbled at the master of the house, saying, 'These last worked only one hour, and you have made them equal to us who have borne the burden of the day and the scorching heat.' But he replied to one of them, 'Friend, I am doing you no wrong. Did you not agree with me for a denarius? Take what belongs to you and go. I choose to give to this last worker as I give to you. **Am I not allowed to do what I choose with what belongs to me?** *Or do you begrudge my generosity?' So the last will be first, and the first last."*

—Matthew 20:8–16

"And they came to Capernaum. And when he was in the house he asked them, 'What were you discussing on the way?' But they kept silent, for on the way they had argued with one another about who was the greatest. And he sat down and called the twelve. And he said to them, **'If anyone would be first, he must be last of all and servant of all.'** *And he took a child and put him in the midst of them, and taking him in his arms, he said to them, 'Whoever receives one such child in my name receives me, and whoever receives me, receives not me but him who sent me.'"*

—Mark 9:33–37

In order to gain the greatest reward, we must fully humble ourselves and put all our new nature's focus on serving others.

"Now to the one who works, his wages are not counted as a gift but as his due."

—Romans 4:4

Romans 4 explicitly differentiates between God's saving grace and the works we participate in as a result of our new nature. Here Paul is talking about Abraham's belief and uses verse 4 as a point of contrast; he is not trying to make a point about eternal rewards. However, it is useful to show in general terms that labor leads to compensation. This is completely customary and expected.

For some reason, God does not ask us to carry out his work for free, even though he freely offers eternal life. God provides the field and all the strength to carry out the work—and offers payment for our faithful effort.

"What then is Apollos? What is Paul? Servants through whom you believed, as the Lord assigned to each. I planted, Apollos watered, but God gave the growth. So neither he who plants nor he who waters is anything, but only God who gives the growth. He who plants and he who waters are one, and **each will receive his wages according to his labor.** *For we are God's fellow workers. You are God's field, God's building."*

—1 Corinthians 3:5–9

*"Jesus said to them, 'My food is to **do the will of him who sent me and to accomplish his work**. Do you not say, "There are yet four months, then comes the harvest"? Look, I tell you, lift up your eyes, and see that the fields are white for harvest. Already the one who reaps is receiving wages and gathering fruit for eternal life, so that sower and reaper may rejoice together. For here the saying holds true, "One sows and another reaps." I sent you to reap that for which you did not labor. Others have labored, and you have entered into their labor.'"*

—John 4:34–38

For further reading, the following passages echo the teaching that we will receive payment or a reward at the second advent. There is no question that Christ will grant us a reward beyond the gift of eternal life.

- Isaiah 40:10; 62:11
- Matthew 16:27; 19:29
- Luke 14:14
- 2 Timothy 4:7–8
- Revelation 22:12.

*"Be merciful, even as your Father is merciful. Judge not, and you will not be judged; condemn not, and you will not be condemned; forgive, and you will be forgiven; give, and it will be given to you. Good measure, pressed down, shaken together, running over, will be put into your lap. For with the measure you use **it will be measured back to you.**"*

—Luke 6:36–38

Since Scripture is absolutely clear that we cannot do good work under our own nature, and everything good we do is based upon God's gifted nature, we can surmise that God rewards us for how frequently we reject our very own nature and instead rely completely on him. We must reject the selfish desires of our old heart and humbly put others first. Then, as Jesus tells us, "the last shall be first." Those who put themselves last on earth are first in the kingdom of heaven.

We see in Luke 6:38 that our works are 'measured' back to us. This echoes the rewards in light mentioned in many other passages.

God's choice to reward our good deeds is based on Old Testament concepts of compensation. God pays for his workers to tend his fields.

"For the Scripture says, 'You shall not muzzle an ox when it treads out the grain,' and, 'The laborer deserves his wages.'"

—1 Timothy 5:18

Christ made and inherited the earth for his good pleasure, and he humbled himself on earth in order to have a relationship with us. Therefore we should recognize the special significance of the earth as God's chosen place of dwelling with his people. The earth has been specially designed as the ultimate site for God's kingdom. Through labor in our current age, and harvest at the end of our age, God will bring as many into the fold of the coming kingdom as possible. The feasts will follow the harvest when all the family of God has been gathered together.

The earth is related to God's promise of land. As we care for the land that will one day be our inheritance, we also figuratively work in God's fields, tending to the souls that have yet to sprout in faith. The time of harvest will come when Christ returns to reward the resurrected the faithful and establish his kingdom upon a rejuvenated earth.

The reward we will receive is payment for the work we have done in God's fields for his kingdom.

As mentioned in Matthew 6:19–21, 19:29, and in other passages, we notice that we do not receive our reward today but upon the full establishment of the kingdom of heaven. Revelation concludes with a fulfillment of the end-time payment themes that have been building over the entirety of Scripture:

"Behold, I am coming soon, bringing my recompense with me, to repay each one for what he has done."

—Revelation 22:12

Christ is coming again, and he is bringing his reward with him, along with the crown of eternal life. He has commanded his workers to call those whom he would choose into repentance. Christ began by calling prophets and apostles; now it is up to us to extend the call. How can the elect hear the gospel if the Word is not preached?

Does Christ elect to save all people, and only partially succeed? Or does he only elect those who ultimately receive him? Christians have argued over this point for centuries. How can we know who has the right interpretation?

Instead of debating our individual interpretive models, we must strive for unity in the Spirit. Our modern mindset would have us cling to our own perspectives and divide accordingly. But God calls us to gather together and seek his objective truth together. May we lay aside our self-centeredness and submit to the Spirit.

CHAPTER 16.

END-TIME UNITY

Institutional Christianity has divided over the years into many denominations and sects. At times over the course of history, these divisions have led to bloody conflict. We act with a little more civility than that these days, but our spiritual differences are still a problem. We are supposed to spread the gospel, yet we do not have a unified front.

In God's eyes, there are not many denominations of Churches, but one Church, unified by one Spirit, one baptism, one faith, and one Word. Why do we see so many splits within our body if there is only one message to proclaim? It is all about the interpretive method. This one seemingly small thing keeps us continually subdividing in to ever smaller and ever more numerous denominations and sects.

Any Church that claims inerrancy of the Bible in its mission statement misses the point if that Church engages in private interpretation. If we claim the Bible to be the true and the inspired Word of God, then make it fit into our community's shared worldview, we've got a problem. We need to trust the Spirit to illuminate the Word, exchanging our cultural biases for his objective truth.

Focusing on the Essential

Instead of diving into the reasons why Churches split or other symptoms of disunity, let's focus on solutions to bring more congregations into fellowship with the same gospel message. All Christians have the same job description: to spread the gospel. We have freedom to share the gospel in a manner that fits the gifts and personality of our given Church community, but every Church community must share the same gospel message. As a body, we must take care not to confuse or exasperate the world with an inconsistent message.

There are two important aspects relating to unity for every Church to consider.

1. **Core beliefs:** the objective cornerstones of the faith that cannot be compromised.

2. **Freedoms**: the particular interests and preferences within the local body that can be pursued and celebrated corporately—so long as the core beliefs are upheld.

We find many passages that discuss worship practices, ceremonies, food customs, and other topics that frankly don't mean a lot when compared to the heart of the gospel. People get bent out of shape when it comes to piety and tradition. We prioritize our personal preferences over the Church's core beliefs, or we misinterpret these core beliefs to match our cultural perspective. This has been happening for a long period of time.

God does not have many good things to say about established traditions. Here Christ strongly rebukes the religious leaders of his day:

"*So **for the sake of your tradition you have made void the word of God.** You hypocrites! Well did Isaiah prophesy of you, when he said:*

'This people honors me with their lips,

but their heart is far from me;

in vain do they worship me,

teaching as doctrines the commandments of men.'"

—Matthew 15:6b–9

To restore unity, we can start by putting "tradition" and "commandments of men" on the back burner by getting back to the biblical basics. Afterward, while remaining focused on the Spirit, we can engage in the ceremonies and laws that suit our personal preferences or cultural heritage.

We are not permitted to water down the gospel, such as we have done historically by blending Greek myths or secular values with Scripture. We cannot add to or take away from the gospel. To recover the biblical gospel message, we need to submit to the Holy Spirit within our local Churches, release our individualistic urges, and allow the Spirit to draw us closer to estranged members of the collective Body of Christ.

The Spirit first needs to come into our lives (and

congregations) to give us a new heart before we can keep the law in our heart of unity.

"Create in me a clean heart, O God, and renew a right spirit within me."

—Psalm 51:10

*"And **I will give them one heart**, and a new spirit I will put within them. I will remove the heart of stone from their flesh and give them a heart of flesh, that they may walk in my statutes and keep my rules and obey them. And they shall be my people, and I will be their God."*

—Ezekiel 11:19–20

*"But he who is joined to the Lord becomes **one spirit** with him."*

—1 Corinthians 6:17

*"And he came and preached peace to you who were far off and peace to those who were near. For through him we both have access in **one Spirit** to the Father. So then you are no longer strangers and aliens, but you are fellow citizens with the saints and members of the household of God, built on the foundation of the apostles and prophets, Christ Jesus himself being the cornerstone, in whom the whole structure, being joined together, grows into a holy temple in the Lord. In him you also are being built together into a dwelling place for God by the Spirit."*

—Ephesians 2:17–22

*"...that according to the riches of his glory he may grant you to be strengthened with power **through his Spirit** in your inner*

being [heart], so that **Christ may dwell in your hearts through faith**—that you, being rooted and grounded in love."

—Ephesians 3:16–17

After we have been baptized by the Holy Spirit through his Word, we will understand why we are to have unity with God and others. The same Spirit is in us all.

"So in Christ Jesus you are all children of God through faith, for all of you who were **baptized into Christ** have clothed yourselves with Christ. There is neither Jew nor Gentile, neither slave nor free, nor is there male and female, for you are **all one in Christ Jesus**."

—Galatians 3:26–28

Again we look to Christ's words; in one of his greatest prayers, he asks God to grant that we would believe in the same message, making us one with his new heart.

"My prayer is not for them alone. I pray also for those who will believe in me through their message, that all of them may be one, Father, just as you are in me and I am in you. May they also be in us so that the world may believe that you have sent me. I have given them the glory that you gave me, that they may be one as we are one—I in them and you in me—**so that they may be brought to complete unity**. Then the world will know that you sent me and have loved them even as you have loved me."

—John 17:20–23

The highlighted statements below speak to the law, which

we are to follow only after we obtain unity of Spirit from his grace.

*"I appeal to you, brothers and sisters, in the name of our Lord Jesus Christ, that **all of you agree with one another** in what you say and that there be no divisions among you, but that you **be perfectly united** in mind and thought....*

*"Just as a body, though one, has many parts, but all its many parts form one body, so it is with Christ. **For we were all baptized by one Spirit so as to form one body**—whether Jews or Gentiles, slave or free—and we were all given the one Spirit to drink."*

—1 Corinthians 1:10; 12:12–13

*"Beloved, if God so loved us, **we also ought to love one another**. No one has ever seen God; if we love one another, God abides in us and his love is perfected in us.*

*By this we know that we abide in him and he in us, because **he has given us of his Spirit**."*

—1 John 4:11–13

*"And those who belong to Christ Jesus have crucified the flesh with its passions and desires. If we live by the Spirit, **let us also keep in step with the Spirit**. Let us not become conceited, provoking one another, envying one another."*

—Galatians 5:24–26

*"So Christ himself gave the apostles, the prophets, the evangelists, the pastors and teachers, to equip his people for **works of service, so that the body of Christ may be built up until we all reach unity** in the faith and in the knowledge of the Son of God and*

*become mature, **attaining to the whole measure of the fullness of Christ.**"*

—Ephesians 4:11–13

*"Only **let your manner of life be worthy** of the gospel of Christ, so that whether I come and see you or am absent, I may hear of you that you are **standing firm in one spirit, with one mind striving** side by side for the faith of the gospel."*

—Philippians 1:27

*"Therefore if you have any encouragement from being united with Christ, if any comfort from his love, if any common sharing in the Spirit, if any tenderness and compassion, then make my joy complete by being like-minded, having **the same love, being one in spirit and of one mind. Do nothing out of selfish ambition or vain conceit.** Rather, in humility value others above yourselves, not looking to your own interests but each of you to the interests of the others. In your relationships with one another, **have the same mindset as Christ Jesus.**"*

—Philippians 2:1–5

All these verses talk about groups of people within the Church who have a right relationship with God and are united together through one Spirit. The Church will be ineffectual if it is full of individuals trying to find the meaning of life or salvation apart from the Body. It is very clear from a biblical perspective that God intends for us all to join in the true Church—the Body of Christ. This is where the gifts of salvation are distributed.

We are not to be islands. God demonstrates that by giving

us the rites of the Church. A person can only receive baptism or communion within Christian community.

One Plan of Salvation for All

One biblical theme of the gospel is that God continues to extend his ancient promise to Abraham that all people on earth will be blessed through his Descendant. By God's grace and by the work of his Son, he snatches (raptures) us from death's eternal grip, saving us from wrath and the judgment of the wicked. The new covenant and Abraham's promises are merged into a single plan of redemption that is administered through the Holy Spirit as he moves in the Church on earth. This fulfills the prophecies that God would pour out his Spirit on all flesh through the institutions given to the apostles to be passed down.

God established the Church and allows all the means of grace to be distributed through unity in one baptism, one faith, and one Spirit. Ephesians 4 sums it up.

*"I therefore, a prisoner for the Lord, urge you to **walk in a manner worthy of the calling** to which you have been called, with all humility and gentleness, with patience, bearing with one another in love, eager to **maintain the unity of the Spirit** in the bond of peace. There is **one body** and **one Spirit**—just as you were called to the **one hope** that belongs to your call—**one Lord, one faith, one baptism, one God** and Father of all, who is over all and through all and in all. But grace was given to each one of us according to the measure of Christ's gift."*

—Ephesians 4:1–7

All people are the same in the most important regard. We all share the same sinful nature and need a Savior to break our curse of death. And Christ is indeed willing to distribute grace through the Church in the forms of baptism, communion, and preaching of the Word. We also receive distinctive gifts paired specifically to our talents and personality as we pray and read the Word. So we need to interact with God both collectively and individually. However, the collective Body should be our primary focus. Here we can unite in the Spirit and combine our gifts to effectively and efficiently share the gospel message with our world.

"The cup of blessing that we bless, is it not a participation in the blood of Christ? The bread that we break, is it not a participation in the body of Christ? Because there is one bread, we who are many are one body, for we all partake of the one bread."

—1 Corinthians 10:16–17

We are members of the Body, not individual Christians who must deal with God and minister to the world in isolation. A personal relationship with Christ sounds nice, and it is nice to have, but God doesn't invite us to say, "I've got Jesus; I don't need the Church." Our relationship with God must be on his terms, not ours. We need to follow his prescribed methods and submit to divine revelation, resisting the temptation to develop private interpretations of God's Word.

There is only one Holy Spirit. The same Spirit in us was poured out on the saints of the Old Testament. The Old Testament prophesied that God would pour out his Spirit on all flesh (Joel 2:28), and Peter referred to that prophecy on the day of Pentecost. Pentecost was an extension of the new covenant that Christ began in the upper room with his small group of disciples. His disciples recorded Jesus' words; empowered by the Spirit, they would share the details of the new covenant with the whole world.

Through the Spirit, the apostles preached the good news to their local congregations and made disciples; these new believers then spread this gospel of the new covenant promise to the world. This model handed down to us is the example that we ought to follow.

The Word states we have unity in Christ alone. Paul states this many times through the inspiration of the Holy Spirit, including here:

"Therefore let no one pass judgment on you in questions of food and drink, or with regard to a festival or a new moon or a Sabbath. These are a shadow of the things to come, but **the substance belongs to Christ.**"

—Colossians 2:16–17

Paul expounded on this theme for the entire chapter of 1 Corinthians 8. It may be hard to maintain unity with fellow believers when we don't share their personal preferences and interpretations of how worship should be conducted. However, the Bible shows us that God allows great freedom in certain areas. The key for a local congregation is to adhere to core doctrine regarding our shared reliance on God's gifts of grace to us; then we may practice our freedoms as we worship God.

The Church has been debating minor issues for its entire

existence—we even see this in squabbles among the disciples when Jesus was personally on hand to speak truth. Paul offers this exhortation for peace.

"As for the one who is weak in faith, welcome him, but not to quarrel over opinions. One person believes he may eat anything, while the weak person eats only vegetables. Let not the one who eats despise the one who abstains, and let not the one who abstains pass judgment on the one who eats, for God has welcomed him. Who are you to pass judgment on the servant of another? It is before his own master that he stands or falls. And he will be upheld, for the Lord is able to make him stand.

"One person esteems one day as better than another, while another esteems all days alike. Each one should be fully convinced in his own mind. The one who observes the day, observes it in honor of the Lord. The one who eats, eats in honor of the Lord, since he gives thanks to God, while the one who abstains, abstains in honor of the Lord and gives thanks to God. For none of us lives to himself, and none of us dies to himself. For if we live, we live to the Lord, and if we die, we die to the Lord. So then, whether we live or whether we die, we are the Lord's....

"Therefore let us stop passing judgment on one another. Instead, make up your mind not to put any stumbling block or obstacle in the way of a brother or sister."

—Romans 14:1–8, 13

"May the God of endurance and encouragement grant you to live in such harmony with one another, in accord with Christ Jesus, that together you may with **one voice** *glorify the God and Father of our Lord Jesus Christ."*

—Romans 15:5-6

"[P]*ut on the new self, which is **being renewed in knowledge** after the image of its creator. Here there is not Greek and Jew, circumcised and uncircumcised, barbarian, Scythian, slave, free; but **Christ is all, and in all.**"*

—Colossians 3:10-11

Only by regeneration can we be united. Notice that "new" and "renewed are part of the same process over time. (In a similar manner, the regenerated or restored earth is called "new" in some passages.) Other passages describe us as a new creation. We will retain our identity, and the earth will still be the same earth to some extent, but the old nature will finally pass; all things will be made new.[1] The key concept for us is that renewal is a process of salvation. We are transformed over time.

Negotiating Conflict

Some clashes within the Church have been particularly intense:

· After Pentecost, new Gentile Christians entered the Church and chafed at some of the lingering distinctly Jewish traditions. They brought with them their own cultural heritage and biases. This clash of Hebrew and Greek perspectives is a frequent topic of concern in the book of Acts and in many epistles. The apostles helped the Church successfully navigate this tension without the Body splintering.

---

1. See Revelation 21:5.

- In the Great Schism of 1054, the Eastern Orthodox Church split off from the Roman Catholic Church.

- In the Protestant Reformation (beginning in 1517), reformers like Martin Luther and John Calvin inspired an exodus from the Roman Catholic Church.

We have access to some interesting writings from the Protestant period that discuss the reformers' struggle to develop their Church model; they had to decide what they wanted to keep and what they wanted to change. Which traditions were no longer helpful or relevant to the community?

The leaders of the early Church had to engage in similar conversations to determine how much of Judaism belonged in this new Body that God was forming. Not all teachings or traditions needed to go, but some were needlessly offensive to the growing number of non-Jewish believers.

The writings of the reformers may be able to help us yet again today, even though they are hundreds of years old. The issues facing the Church have not changed much over the centuries. In this case, Lutherans were debating whether to keep or abolish certain practices that remained from the Roman Catholic Church. Their community had grown up with these traditions, but were they necessary?

"Thus the worship and divine service of the Gospel is to receive from God gifts; on the contrary, the worship of the Law is to offer and present our gifts to God. We can, however, offer nothing to God unless we have first been reconciled and born again. This passage, too, brings the greatest consolation, as the chief worship

of the Gospel is to wish to receive remission of sins, grace, and righteousness."

—"The Defense of the Augsburg Confession," Article V[2]

"And nevertheless we teach that in these matters the use of liberty is to be so controlled that the inexperienced may not be offended, and, on account of the abuse of liberty, may not become more hostile to the true doctrine of the Gospel, or that without a reasonable cause nothing in customary rites be changed, but that, in order to cherish harmony, such old customs be observed as can be observed without sin or without great inconvenience. And in this very assembly... we have judged that such public harmony as could indeed be produced without offense to consciences ought to be preferred to all other advantages [other less important matters]."

—"The Defense of the Augsburg Confession," Article XV[3]

The Lutherans did not want to dilute the gospel by making it too friendly to the world or to human flesh, but neither did they want their ceremonies or traditions to offend the young in the faith. A visitor or someone new to the faith needed to be able to find the gospel in their midst.

This great advice from hundreds of years ago still applies today: don't water down the gospel, and don't make the gospel difficult to understand with overly exclusive culture or traditions. It is still that simple. Let's ask for unity.

---

2. "The Defense of the Augsburg Confession," Article V, paragraph 189. bookofconcord.org/defense_5_love.php#para189. Accessed May 30, 2019.
3. The Defense of the Augsburg Confession," Article XV, paragraphs 51–52. bookofconcord.org/defense_14_traditions.php#para51. Accessed May 30, 2019.

"How good and pleasant it is when God's people live together in unity!"

—Psalm 133:1

"For where two or three are gathered in my name, there am I among them."

—Matthew 18:20

"Let no one deceive himself. If anyone among you thinks that he is wise in this age, let him become a fool that he may become wise. For the wisdom of this world is folly with God. For it is written, 'He catches the wise in their craftiness,' and again, 'The Lord knows the thoughts of the wise, that they are futile.' So let no one boast in men. For all things are yours, whether Paul or Apollos or Cephas or the world or life or death or the present or the future—all are yours, and you are Christ's, and Christ is God's."

—1 Corinthians 3:18–23

APPENDIX 1 - OUTLINE OF INTERPRETIVE METHODOLOGY

This book utilizes an objective interpretive method.

Subjectivity (personal interpretation) is not capable of obtaining truth from the Bible.

Truth is objective and only comes through divine revelation.

Our freedoms, free will, and choices have nothing to do with finding truth.

The goal of this book is to identify divine truths with absolute meanings.

Whether a passage contains literal or figurative language, there must be a single, objectively true meaning. For example, "the heart" is a figurative term, but it refers to a specific objective concept of our innermost being.

There is a physical realm (seen) and a heavenly realm (unseen).

The two realms meet in the spirit realm. For example, we

on earth have a relationship with our heavenly Father because his Spirit dwells within us.

This leaves us with six total possibilities for interpretation of any passage:

1. Literal language speaking of the physical realm
2. Literal language speaking of the heavenly realm
3. Literal language speaking of dual-realm interaction (spirit realm)
4. Figurative language speaking of the physical realm
5. Figurative language speaking of the heavenly realm
6. Figurative language speaking of dual-realm interaction (spirit realm)

The realms interrelate in this fashion:

The Father is in the heavenly realm where the Son is now located.

The Son was in the earthly realm where we are located.

The Spirit "proceeds" from the Father and the Son in a dual-realm interaction (where heaven and earth meet).

Following his resurrection, the Son is at the "right hand" of the Father in the heavenly realm. He is the first dual-realm being, occasionally referred to in the Bible as the second Adam.

The earth and all believers will become part of this dual-realm merger after Christ's second coming.

Prophetic passages are filled with terms like transformation, regeneration, restoration, redemption, and renewal. These may relate to the earth or to our own bodies.

This book seeks to determine which passages are clearly literal, or if figurative language is present, what realm and concept are being spoken of to determine literal interpretation?

The following passages describe salvation timing based upon past or present tense spiritual salvation language, or utilize future tense salvation language describing the resurrection of the dead. Some passages describe both types salvation – spiritual salvation and salvation through bodily resurrection.

Present = focus on past/present spiritual salvation

Future = focus on salvation at the resurrection

Both = Present and Future salvation

Mostly = focus on one verb tense over another when both are stated

Job 19:25-27 – Future

Isaiah 26:19-21 – Future

Daniel 7:22 + 12:2 – Future

Matthew 24:30-31 – Future

Matthew 25:31-34 – Future

John 3:1-18 – **Present**

John 5:24-29 – **Mostly Future**

John 6:39-40 – **Both**

Romans 8:16-24 – **Mostly Future**

1 Corinthians 4:5 – **Future**

1 Corinthians 15:12-28 – **Future**

2 Corinthians 5:1-10 – **Future**

2 Corinthians 6:1-2 – **Present**

1 Thessalonians 4:13-17 – **Future**

1 Thessalonians 5:1-9 – **Future**

2 Thessalonians 2:1-12 – **Future**

2 Timothy 1:9-12 – **Mostly Present**

2 Timothy 4:8 – **Future**

Ephesians 2:4-9 – **Mostly Present**

Philippians 3:10-21 – **Future**

Colossians 3:1-4 – **Both**

Titus 2:11-13 – **Both**

Hebrews 9:27-28 – **Future**

1 Peter 1:3-9 – **Both**

1 Peter 5:4– **Future**

1 John 2:28-3:2– **Mostly Future**

Jude 20-24 – **Both**

APPENDIX 3 - GROUPINGS OF KEY PASSAGES

Christ inheriting the whole earth:

- Psalm 2:8
- Romans 4:13
- Galatians 3:16
- Colossians 1:16
- Hebrews 1:2; 2:10

The inheritance theme:

- Genesis 15:7; 17:5–8
- 1 Chronicles 29:14–18
- Psalm 2:8; 37:29; 105:6–11; 115:16
- Isaiah 45:18
- Ezekiel 47:13–23; 48:29
- Matthew 5:5; 19:27–29
- Romans 4:13–18; 8:16–17; 15:8–9

- Galatians 3:13–29
- Ephesians 2:11–22; 3:6
- Colossians 1:12–16
- Hebrews 1:2

Gentiles grafted into Israel:

- John 4:20–22; 10:16
- Romans 9:4–8, 24–26; 10:8–13, 17–20; 11:11–32; 15:8–12
- Galatians 3
- Ephesians 2:11–22, 3:6

The single second advent:

- Job 19:25
- Isaiah 26:21; 35:4; 40:10; 59:17–20; 62:11
- Daniel 7:22
- Matthew 16:27; 24:30–31; 25:31
- Luke 17:24–30; 21:25–28
- Acts 1:11
- 1 Corinthians 4:5; 15:23
- Philippians 3:20

- Colossians 3:4
- 1 Thessalonians 2:19; 3:13; 4:16–17; 5:1–4, 23
- 2 Thessalonians 1:7, 10; 2:8
- 1 Timothy 6:13–16
- 2 Timothy 4:1, 8
- Titus 2:13
- Hebrews 9:27–28
- 1 Peter 1:7; 5:4
- 1 John 2:28; 3:2
- Jude 1:14
- Revelation 1:7; 22:12

Resurrection:

- Job 19:26
- Psalm 16:10; 17:15; 49:15
- Isaiah 26:19
- Ezekiel 37:7–14
- Daniel 12:2–3
- Luke 14:14; 20:36
- John 5:28–29; 6:40; 11:24

- Acts 24:15
- 1 Corinthians 15:23, 52
- Philippians 3:21
- Colossians 3:4
- 1 Thessalonians 4:16
- 1 Peter 1:3–9; 5:4
- 1 John 3:2

Rewards being granted at the second advent:

- Isaiah 35:4; 40:10; 59:17–20; 62:11
- Daniel 7:22
- Matthew 16:27
- Luke 14:14
- 1 Corinthians 3:13–15; 4:5
- 1 Thessalonians 2:19
- 1 Timothy 6:19
- 2 Timothy 4:8
- Hebrews 9:27–28
- 1 Peter 5:4
- Revelation 22:12

Please visit www.kjsoze.com for more information or if you wish to contact the Publisher. Also, please leave a review online where you obtained a copy of this book from, or on Goodreads – www.goodreads.com/KJSoze.

BIBLIOGRAPHY

The Barna Group, "Americans Describe Their Views About Life After Death." October 21, 2003. www.barna.com/research/americans-describe-their-views-about-life-after-death. Accessed May 20, 2019.

The Barna Group, "The State of the Church 2016." September 15, 2016. www.barna.com/research/state-church-2016. Accessed May 20, 2019.

Berkhof, Louis. *Summary of Christian Doctrine*. 1938.

The Book of Concord: The Confessions of the Lutheran Church. 1580. www.bookofconcord.org.

"The Comma of Luke 23:43." Grace Communion International. www.gci.org/articles/the-comma-of-luke-2343. Accessed June 4, 2019.

Dictionary of Paul and His Letters. Ed. Daniel Reed, Gerald Hawthorne, Ralph Martin. InterVarsity Press, 1993.

Kennedy, Vans. *Researches Into the Nature and Affinity of Ancient and Hindu Mythology*. 1831.

Kittel, Gerhard. *Theological Dictionary of the N.T.*, Vol. VI. 1932. Abridged Version: Eerdmans, 1985.

Ladd, George Eldon. *A Theology of the New Testament*. Eerdmans, 1974.

Lange, J.P. and Schaff, P. *A Commentary on the Holy Scriptures: John.* Logos Bible Software. Bellingham, WA, 2008. Nelson, Ethel. "The Original Unknown God of China." June 1, 1998. Creation 20, no. 3 (June 1998), 50–53. www.answersingenesis.org/genesis/the-original-unknown-god-of-china/#a1. Accessed June 4, 2019.

"Post Tribulation Rapture Belief." Post Tribulation People. www.posttribpeople.com/Post-Tribulation-Belief.html. Accessed June 3, 2019.

Roller, John H. *The Doctrine of Immortality in the Early Church*. Kindle Version, 2012. ASIN: B008I802VI.

Tyndale, William. *An Answer to Sir Thomas More's Dialogue*. Parker, 1850.

Westermann, Claus. *Genesis 12-36: A Commentary*. Augsburg Publishing House, 1981.

"What is the End-Times Timeline?" Got Questions. www.gotquestions.org/end-times-timeline.html. Accessed June 3, 2019.

White, Chris. "The Pre-Wrath Rapture Explained." November 23. 2011. www.bibleprophecytalk.com/bpt-keeping-a-consistent-hermeneutic-with-the-rapture. Accessed June 3, 2019.

Withrow, W.H. *The Catacombs of Rome and Their Testimony Relative to Primitive Christianity,* pp 532–533. Nelson and Phillips, 1874.

www.ingramcontent.com/pod-product-compliance
Lightning Source LLC
Chambersburg PA
CBHW051349290426
44108CB00015B/1935